A NATION IN TRANSITION

Encyclopaedic History of India Series

A NATION IN TRANSITION

Dr. Mahesh Vikram Singh
Professor, Deptt. of History
Mahatma Gandhi Kashi Vidyapeeth
Varanasi (UP)

Dr. Brij Bhushan Shrivastava
Head of Deptt., Ancient History, Archeology & Culture
SMMTPG College, Ballia (UP)

CENTRUM PRESS
NEW DELHI-110002 (INDIA)

CENTRUM PRESS
H.O.: 4360/4, Ansari Road, Daryaganj,
New Delhi-110002 (India)
Tel: 23278000, 23261597, 23255577, 23286875
B.O.: No. 1015, Ist Main Road, BSK IIIrd Stage,
IIIrd Phase, IIIrd Block, Bangalore-560085 (INDIA)
Tel: 080-41723429
Email: centrumpress@gmail.com
Visit us at: www.centrumpress.com

A Nation in Transition

First Edition, 2011

ISBN 978-93-80921-51-8

PRINTED IN INDIA

Printed at Mehra Offset Press, Delhi

प्रो. विपिन चंद्रा
अध्यक्ष
Prof. Bipan Chandra
Chairman

नेशनल बुक ट्रस्ट, इंडिया
नेहरू भवन
5 इंस्टीट्यूशनल एरिया, फेज़-II, वसंत कुंज, नई दिल्ली-110 070
फोन/ Phone: 011-26121880 फैक्स/ Fax: 011-26121883

NATIONAL BOOK TRUST, INDIA
Nehru Bhawan
5 Institutional Area, Phase II, Vasant Kunj, New Delhi-110 070
ई-मेल / E-mail: chairman@nbtindia.org.in
वेबसाइट / Website: www.nbtindia.org.in

FOREWORD

The term 'history' is derived from the Greek word 'historia' that means knowledge acquired through investigation. Obviously, this knowledge can be correct if the method of investigation is objective and not vitiated by any kind of bias. In other words, if the study of human past is comprehensive and obtained through scientific inquiry, it can provide perspective on the present day problems and help one plan for the future.

A true historian has to identify the sources that can be most useful in a given context. Documents, coins, archaeology, anthropology, geography, travel accounts, oral traditions, mythology and so on can be useful but they can be used only after their veracity is tested and they are critically examined. They should be checked and counter-checked.

Over the centuries, one finds the study and writing of history vitiated by biases. There are numerous instances in which historical data have been distorted to support or oppose certain preconceived ideas and purposes. Strictly speaking such history is just like fiction to accord with preconceived notions and serve some ulterior purposes.

The study of the past has never been static. Conclusions go on changing because of the discovery of new materials and tools of investigation. To give a concrete example, the carbon 14 or radiocarbon dating test has revolutionized the study of civilizations and settlements, especially of prehistoric times, for which written documents, coins, etc. are seldom available. This method has enabled historians to determine more accurately than before the time period of a particular civilization or settlement. This method was discovered only 70 years ago by American scientists.

In our country, excavations brought to light the Indus Valley Civilization and its various features, hitherto unknown. Similarly, no complete text of Kautilya's Arthashastra was available before it was discovered by Shamasastry, the chief of the Mysore Government Oriental Library in the first decade of the last century. Likewise, people's knowledge of the history of the Buddhist period got extended after excavations at Sarnath and the ruins of the Asokan period at Patna. In the future, if the Harappan inscriptions are deciphered, our knowledge of the Indus Valley Civilization will increase enormously. All these instances underline the fact that our knowledge of history is never static and its frontiers go on extending.

In the light of what has been said above the encyclopedic history is going to be of great help to students interested in Indian history. It is comprehensive and as far as possible free from biases. It includes the latest materials, and objective conclusions.

Prof. Bipan Chandra
Professor Emeritus, JNU
Chairman, National Book Trust, India

Contents

Preface

The people of India have had a continuous civilization since 2500 B.C., when the inhabitants of the Indus River valley developed an urban culture based on commerce and sustained by agricultural trade. This civilization declined around 1500 B.C., probably due to ecological changes. During the second millennium B.C., pastoral, Aryan-speaking tribes migrated from the northwest into the subcontinent. As they settled in the middle Ganges River valley, they adapted to antecedent cultures.

The political map of ancient and medieval India was made up of myriad kingdoms with fluctuating boundaries. In the 4th and 5th centuries A.D., northern India was unified under the Gupta Dynasty. During this period, known as India's Golden Age, Hindu culture and political administration reached new heights. Islam spread across the Indian subcontinent over a period of 500 years. In the 10th and 11th centuries, Turks and Afghans invaded India and established sultanates in Delhi. In the early 16th century, descendants of Genghis Khan swept across the Khyber Pass and established the Mughal (Mogul) Dynasty, which lasted for 200 years. From the 11th to the 15th centuries, southern India was dominated by Hindu Chola and Vijayanagar Dynasties. During this time, the two systems—the prevailing Hindu and Muslim—mingled, leaving lasting cultural influences on each other.

The first British outpost in South Asia was established in 1619 at Surat on the northwestern coast. Later in the century, the East India Company opened permanent trading stations at Madras, Bombay, and Calcutta, each under the protection of native rulers. The British expanded their influence from these footholds until, by the 1850s, they controlled most of present-day India, Pakistan, and Bangladesh. In 1857, a rebellion in north India led by mutinous Indian soldiers caused the British Parliament to transfer all political power from the East India Company to the Crown. Great Britain began administering most of India directly while controlling the rest through treaties with local rulers.

In the late 1800s, the first steps were taken toward self-government in British India with the appointment of Indian councillors to advise the British viceroy and the establishment of provincial councils with Indian members; the British subsequently widened participation in legislative councils. Beginning in 1920, Indian leader Mohandas K. Gandhi transformed the Indian National Congress political party into a mass movement to campaign against British colonial rule.

—Authors

1

Princely States in British India

The early history of British expansion in India was characterised by the coexistence of two approaches towards the existing princely states. The first was a policy of annexation, where the British sought to forcibly absorb the Indian princely states into the provinces which constituted their Empire in India. The second was a policy of indirect rule, where the British assumed suzerainty and paramountcy over princely states, but conceded some degree of sovereignty to them. During the early part of the nineteenth century, the policy of the British tended towards annexation, but the Indian Rebellion of 1857 forced a change in this approach, by demonstrating both the difficulty of absorbing and subduing annexed states, and the usefulness of princely states as a source of support.

In 1858, the policy of annexation was formally renounced, and British relations with the princely states thereafter were based on indirect rule, whereby the British exercised paramountcy over all princely states with the British crown as ultimate suzerain, but at the same time respected and protected them as allies. The exact relations between the British and each princely state were regulated by individual treaties, and varied widely, with some states having significant autonomy, some being subject to significant control in internal affairs, and some being in effect the owners of a few acres of land with little autonomy.

During the 20th century, the British made several attempts to integrate the princely states more closely with British India, creating the Chamber of Princes in 1921 as a consultative and advisory body, transferring the responsibility for supervision of smaller states from the provinces to the centre in 1936, and creating direct relations between the Government of India and the larger princely states superseding political agents. The most ambitious was a scheme of federation in the Government of India Act 1935, which envisaged the princely states and British India being united under a federal government. This scheme came close to success, but was abandoned in 1939 as a result of the outbreak of the Second World War. As a result, in the 1940s, the relationship between the princely states and the crown remained regulated by the principle of paramountcy and the various treaties between the British crown and the states.

Neither paramountcy nor these arrangements could continue after Indian independence. The British took the view that because they had been established directly between the British crown and the princely states, they could not be transferred to independent India. At the same time, they imposed obligations on Britain that it was not prepared to continue to carry out, such as the obligation to maintain troops in India for the defence of the princely states. The British government therefore decided that paramountcy, together with all treaties between them and the princely states, would come to an end upon the transfer of power.

Reasons for Integration

The termination of paramountcy would have in principle meant that all rights that flowed from the states' relationship with the British crown would return to them, leaving them free to negotiate relationships with the new states of India and Pakistan "on a basis of complete freedom". Early British plans for the transfer of power, such as the offer produced by the Cripps Mission, recognised the possibility that some princely states might choose to stand out of independent India.

This was unacceptable to the Congress, which regarded the independence of princely states as a denial of the course of Indian history, and consequently regarded this scheme as a "Balkanisation" of India. The Congress had traditionally been less active in the princely states because of their limited resources which restricted their ability to organise there and their focus on the goal of independence from the British, and because Congress leaders, in particular Gandhi, were sympathetic to the more progressive princes as examples of the capacity of Indians to rule themselves. This changed in the 1930s as a result of the federation scheme contained in the Government of India Act 1935 and the rise of socialist Congress leaders such as Jayaprakash Narayan, and the Congress began to actively engage with popular political and labour activity in the princely states. By 1939, the Congress' official stance was that the states must enter independent India, on the same terms and with the same autonomy as the provinces of British India, and with their people granted responsible government. As a result, it insisted on the incorporation of the princely states into India in its negotiations with Mountbatten.

A few British leaders, particularly Lord Mountbatten, the last British viceroy in India, were also uncomfortable with breaking links between independent India and the princely states. The development of trade, commerce and communications during the 19th and 20th centuries had bound the princely states to British India through a complex network of interests. Agreements relating to railways, customs, irrigation, the use of ports, and other similar agreements would disappear, posing a serious threat to the economic life of the subcontinent.

Mountbatten was also persuaded by the argument of Indian leaders such as V. P. Menon that the integration of the princely states into independent India would to some extent assuage the wounds of partition. The result was that Mountbatten personally favoured and worked towards the accession of princely states to India following the transfer of power, as proposed by the Congress.

Accepting Integration

The Princes' Position

The rulers of the princely states were not uniformly enthusiastic about integrating their domains into independent India. Some, such as the kings of Cochin, Bikaner and Jawhar, were motivated to join India out of ideological and patriotic considerations, but others insisted that they had the right to join either India or Pakistan, to remain independent, or form a union of their own. Bhopal, Travancore and Hyderabad announced that they did not intend to join either dominion.

Hyderabad went as far as to appoint trade representatives in European countries and commencing negotiations with the

Portuguese to lease or buy Goa to give it access to the sea, and Travancore pointed to the strategic importance to western countries of its thorium reserves while asking for recognition. Some states proposed a subcontinent-wide confederation of princely states, as a third entity in addition to India and Pakistan. Bhopal attempted to build an alliance between the princely states and the Muslim League to counter the pressure being put on rulers by the Congress.

A number of factors contributed to the collapse of this initial resistance and to nearly all princely states agreeing to accede to India. An important factor was the lack of unity among the princes. The smaller states did not trust the larger states to protect their interests, and many Hindu rulers did not trust Muslim princes, in particular Hamidullah Khan, the Nawab of Bhopal and a leading proponent of independence, whom they viewed as an agent for Pakistan. Others, believing integration to be inevitable, sought to build bridges with the Congress, hoping thereby to gain a say in shaping the final settlement.

The resultant inability to present a united front or agree on a common position significantly reduced their bargaining power in negotiations with the Congress. The decision by the Muslim League to stay out of the Constituent Assembly was also fatal to the princes' plan to build an alliance with it to counter the Congress, and attempts to boycott the Constituent Assembly altogether failed on 28 April 1947, when the states of Baroda, Bikaner, Cochin, Gwalior, Jaipur, Jodhpur, Patiala and Rewa took their seats in the Assembly.

Many princes were also pressured by popular sentiment favouring integration with India, which meant their plans for independence had little support from their subjects. The King of Travancore, for example, definitively abandoned his plans for independence after the attempted assassination of his dewan, Sir C. P. Ramaswamy Aiyer. In a few states, the chief ministers or dewans played a significant role in convincing the princes to accede to India. The key factors that led the states to accept integration into India were, however, the efforts of Lord Mountbatten, the last Viceroy of British India, and Vallabhbhai Patel and V. P. Menon, who were respectively the political and administrative heads of the Indian Government's States Department, which was in charge of relations with the princely states.

Mountbatten's Role

Mountbatten believed that securing the states' accession to India was crucial to reaching a negotiated settlement with the Congress for the transfer of power. As a relative of the British King, he was trusted by most of the princes and was a personal friend of many, especially the Nawab of Bhopal, Hamidullah Khan. The princes also believed that he would be in a position to ensure the independent India adhered to any terms that might be agreed upon, because Jawaharlal Nehru and Patel had asked him to become the first Governor General of the Dominion of India.

Mountbatten used his influence with the princes to push them towards accession. He declared that the British Government would not grant dominion status to any of the princely states, nor would it accept them into the British Commonwealth, which meant that the states would sever all connections with the British crown unless they joined either India or Pakistan. He pointed out that the Indian subcontinent was one economic entity, and that the states would suffer most if the link were broken. He also pointed to the difficulties that princes would face maintaining order in the face of threats such as the rise of communal violence and communist movements.

Mountbatten stressed that he would act as the trustee of the princes' commitment, as he would be serving as India's head of state well into 1948. He engaged in a personal dialogue with reluctant princes, such as the Nawab of Bhopal, who he asked through a confidential letter to sign the Instrument of Accession making Bhopal part of India, which Mountbatten would keep locked up in his safe. It would be handed to the States Department on 15 August only if the Nawab did not change his mind before then, which he was free to do. The Nawab agreed, and did not renege over the deal.

At the time, several princes complained that they were being betrayed by Britain, who they regarded as an ally, and Sir Conrad Corfield resigned his position as head of the Political Department in protest at Mountbatten's policies. Mountbatten's policies were also criticised by the opposition Conservative Party. Winston Churchill compared the language used by the Indian government with that used by Adolf Hitler before the invasion of Austria. Modern historians such as Lumby and Moore, however, take the view that Mountbatten played a crucial role in ensuring that the princely states agreed to accede to India.

Pressure and Diplomacy

Vallabhbhai Patel as Minister for Home and States Affairs had the responsibility of welding the British Indian provinces and the princely states into a united India. By far the most significant factor that led to the princes' decision to accede to India was the policy of the Congress and, in particular, of the two key figures in the States Department, Sardar Vallabhbhai Patel and V. P. Menon. The Congress' stated position was that the princely states were not sovereign entities, and as such could not opt to be independent notwithstanding the end of paramountcy. The princely states, it declared, must therefore accede to either India or Pakistan. In July 1946, Nehru pointedly observed that no princely state could prevail militarily against the army of independent India. In January 1947, he said that independent India would not accept the Divine Right of Kings, and in May 1947, he declared that any princely state which refused to join the Constituent Assembly would be treated as an enemy state. Other Congress leaders, such as C. Rajagopalachari, argued that as paramountcy "came into being as a fact and not by agreement", it would necessarily pass to the government of independent India, as the successors of the British.

Patel and Menon, who were charged with the actual job of negotiating with the princes, took a more conciliatory approach than Nehru. The official policy statement of the Government of India made by Patel on 5 July 1947 made no threats. Instead, it emphasised the unity of India and the common interests of the princes and independent India, reassured them about the Congress' intentions, and invited them to join independent India "to make laws sitting together as friends than to make treaties as aliens". He reiterated that the States Department would not attempt to establish a relationship of domination over the princely states. Unlike the Political Department of the British Government, it would not be an instrument of paramountcy, but a medium whereby business could be conducted between the states and India as equals.

Instruments of Accession

Patel and Menon backed up their diplomatic efforts by producing treaties that were designed to be attractive to rulers of princely states. Two key documents were produced. The first was the Standstill Agreement, which confirmed that the agreements and administrative practices that existed as between the princely state in question and the British would be continued by India. The second was the Instrument of Accession, by which the ruler of the princely state in question agreed to the accession of his kingdom to independent India, and to granting India control over specified subject matters. The nature of the subject matters varied depending on the acceding state.

The states which had internal autonomy under the British signed an Instrument of Accession which only ceded three subjects to the government of India—defence, external affairs, and communications, each defined in accordance with List 1 to Schedule VII of the Government of India Act 1935. Rulers of states which were in effect estates or talukas, where substantial administrative powers were exercised by the Crown, signed a different Instrument of Accession, which vested all residuary powers and jurisdiction in the government of India. Rulers of states which had an intermediate status signed a third type of Instrument, which preserved the degree of power they had under the British.

The Instruments of Accession implemented a number of other safeguards. Clause 7 provided that the princes would not be bound to the Indian constitution as and when it was drafted. Clause 8 guaranteed their autonomy in all areas in which authority was not expressly ceded to the Government of India. This was supplemented by a number of promises. Rulers who agreed to accede would receive guarantees that their extra-territorial rights, such as immunity from prosecution in Indian courts and exemption from customs duty, would be protected, that they would be allowed to democratise slowly, that none of the eighteen major states would be forced to merge, and that they would remain eligible for British honours and decorations.

In discussions, Lord Mountbatten reinforced the statements of Patel and Menon by emphasising that the documents gave the princes all the "practical independence" they needed. Mountbatten, Patel and Menon also sought to give princes the impression that if they did not accept the terms put to them then, they would subsequently have to accede on substantially less favourable terms. The Standstill Agreement was also used as a negotiating tool, as the States Department categorically ruled out signing a Standstill

Agreement with princely states that did not sign an Instrument of Accession.

The Accession Process

The limited scope of the Instruments of Accession and the promise of a wide-ranging autonomy and the other guarantees they offered, gave sufficient comfort to many rulers, who saw this as the best deal they could strike given the lack of support from the British, and popular internal pressures. Between May 1947 and the transfer of power on 15 August 1947, the vast majority of states signed Instruments of Accession. A few, however, held out. Some simply delayed signing the Instrument of Accession. Piploda, a small state in central India, did not accede until March 1948. The biggest problems, however, arose with a few border states, such as Jodhpur, which tried to negotiate better deals with Pakistan, with Junagadh, which actually did accede to Pakistan, and with Hyderabad and Kashmir, which declared that they intended to remain independent.

Border States

The ruler of Jodhpur, Hanwant Singh, was antipathetic to the Congress, and did not see much future in India for him or the lifestyle he wished to lead, and entered into negotiations with Jinnah, who was the designated head of state for Pakistan, along with the ruler of Jaisalmer. Jinnah was keen to attract some of the larger border states, hoping thereby to attract other Rajput states to Pakistan and compensate for the loss of half of Bengal and Punjab. He offered to permit Jodhpur and Jaisalmer to accede to Pakistan on any terms they chose, giving their rulers blank sheets of paper and asking them to write down their terms, which he would sign.

Jaisalmer refused, arguing that it would be difficult for him to side with Muslims against Hindus in the event of communal problems. Hanwant Singh came close to signing. However, the atmosphere in Jodhpur was in general hostile to accession to Pakistan. Mountbatten also pointed out that the accession of a predominantly Hindu state to Pakistan would violate the principle of the two-nation theory on which Partition was based, and was likely to cause communal violence in the State. Hanwant Singh was persuaded by these arguments, and somewhat reluctantly agreed to accede to India.

Junagadh

Although the states were in theory free to choose whether they wished to accede to India or Pakistan, Mountbatten had pointed out that "geographic compulsions" meant that most of them must choose India. In effect, he took the position that only the states that shared a border with Pakistan could choose to accede to it.

The Nawab of Junagadh, a princely state located on the southwestern end of Gujarat and having no common border with Pakistan, chose to accede to Pakistan ignoring Mountbatten's views, arguing that it could be reached from Pakistan by sea. The rulers of two states that were subject to the suzerainty of Junagadh—Mangrol and Babariawad—reacted to this by declaring their independence from Junagadh and acceding to India. In response, the Nawab of Junagadh militarily occupied the states. The rulers of neighbouring states reacted angrily, sending their troops to the Junagadh frontier and appealed to the Government of India for assistance. A group of Junagadhi people, led by Samaldas Gandhi, formed a government-in-exile, the *Aarzi Hukumat* ("temporary government").

India believed that if Junagadh was permitted to go to Pakistan, the communal tension already simmering in Gujarat would worsen, and refused to accept the accession. The government pointed out that the state was 80% Hindu, and called for a plebiscite to decide the question of accession. Simultaneously, they cut off supplies of fuel and coal to Junagadh, severed air and postal links, sent troops to the frontier, and reoccupied the principalities of Mangrol and Babariawad that had acceded to India. Pakistan agreed to discuss a plebiscite, subject to the withdrawal of Indian troops, a condition India rejected. On 26 October, the Nawab and his family fled to Pakistan following clashes with Indian troops. On 7 November, Junagadh's court, facing collapse, invited the Government of India to take over the State's administration. The Government of India agreed. A plebiscite was conducted in February 1948, which went almost unanimously in favour of accession to India.

Kashmir

At the time of the transfer of power, Kashmir was ruled by Maharaja Hari Singh, a Hindu, although the state itself had a Muslim majority. Hari Singh was equally hesitant about acceding to either India or Pakistan, as either would have provoked adverse reactions in parts of his kingdom. He signed a Standstill Agreement with Pakistan and proposed one with India as well, but announced that Kashmir intended to remain independent. However, his rule was opposed by Sheikh Abdullah, the popular leader of Kashmir's largest political party, the National Conference, who demanded his abdication.

Pakistan, attempting to force the issue of Kashmir's accession, cut off supplies and transport links. The chaos in Punjab resulting from Partition had also severed transport links with India, meaning that Kashmir's only links with the two dominions was by air. Rumours about atrocities against the Muslim population of Poonch by the Maharajah's forces caused the outbreak of civil unrest.

Shortly thereafter, Pathan tribesmen from the North-West Frontier Province of Pakistan crossed the border and entered Kashmir. The invaders made rapid progress towards Srinagar. The Maharaja of Kashmir wrote to India, asking for military assistance, offering an Instrument of Accession, and setting up an interim government headed by Sheikh Abdullah. The accession was accepted, but Nehru declared that it would have to be confirmed by a plebiscite, although there was no legal requirement to seek such confirmation.

Indian troops secured Jammu, Srinagar and the valley itself during the First Kashmir War, but the intense fighting flagged with the onset of winter, which made much of the state impassable. Prime Minister Nehru, in a move that baffled political and military strategists, declared a ceasefire and sought U.N. arbitration, arguing that India would otherwise have to invade Pakistan itself, in view of its failure to stop the tribal incursions.

The plebiscite was never held, and on 26 January 1950, the Constitution of India came into force in Kashmir, but with special provisions made for it in the Constitution's Article 370. India did not, however, secure administrative control over all of Kashmir. The northern and western portions of Kashmir came under Pakistan's control in 1947, and are today referred to as 'Pakistan-Occupied Kashmir' by the Indian government. In the 1962 Sino-Indian War, China occupied Aksai Chin, the northeastern region bordering Laddakh, which it continues to control and administer.

Hyderabad

Hyderabad was a landlocked state that stretched over 82,000 square miles (over 212,000 square kilometres) in southeastern India. While 87% of its 17 million people were Hindus, its ruler Nizam Osman Ali Khan was a Muslim, and its politics were dominated by a Muslim elite. The Muslim nobility and the Ittehad-ul-Muslimeen, a powerful pro-Nizam Muslim party, insisted that Hyderabad must remain an independent state and stand on an equal footing to India and Pakistan. Accordingly, the Nizam in June 1947 issued a *firman* announcing that on the transfer of power, his state would be resuming independence.

The Government of India rejected the firman, terming it a "legalistic claim of doubtful validity". It argued that the strategic location of Hyderabad, which lay astride the main lines of communication between northern and southern India, meant it could easily be used by "foreign interests" to threaten India, and that in consequence, the issue involved India's peace and security. It also pointed out that the state's people, history and location made it unquestionably Indian, and that its own "common interests" therefore mandated its integration into India.

The Nizam was prepared to enter into a limited treaty with India, which gave Hyderabad safeguards not provided for in the standard Instrument of Accession, such as a provision guaranteeing Hyderabad's neutrality in the event of a conflict between India and Pakistan. India rejected this proposal, arguing that other states would demand similar concessions. A temporary Standstill Agreement was signed as a stopgap measure, even though Hyderabad had not yet agreed to accede to India. By December 1947, however, India was accusing Hyderabad of repeatedly violating the Agreement, while the Nizam alleged that India was blockading his state, a charge India denied.

The situation deteriorated further in 1948. The Razakars ("volunteers"), a militia affiliated to the Ittehad-ul-Muslimeen and set up under the influence of Muslim radical Qasim Razvi, assumed the role of supporting the Muslim ruling class against upsurges by the Hindu populace, and began intensifying its activities and was accused of attempting to intimidate villages. The Hyderabad State Congress Party, affiliated to the Indian National Congress, launched a political agitation.

Matters were made worse by Communist groups, which had originally supported the Congress but now switched sides and began attacking Congress groups. Attempts by Mountbatten to find a negotiated solution failed and, in August, the Nizam, claiming that he feared an imminent invasion, attempted to approach the UN Security Council and the International Court of Justice. Patel now insisted that if Hyderabad was allowed to continue its independence, the prestige of the Government would be tarnished and then neither Hindus nor Muslims would feel secure in its realm. On 13 September, the Indian Army was sent into Hyderabad in Operation Polo on the ground that the law and order situation there threatened the peace of South India.

The troops met little resistance and between 13 and 18 September took complete control of the state. The Nizam was retained as the head of state in the same manner as the other princes who acceded to India. He thereupon disavowed the complaints that had been made to the UN and, despite vehement protests from Pakistan and strong criticism from other countries, the Security Council did not deal further with the question, and Hyderabad was absorbed into India.

Completing Integration

The Instruments of Accession were limited, transferring control of only three matters to India, and would by themselves have produced a rather loose federation, with significant differences in administration and governance across the various states. Full political integration, in contrast, would require a process whereby the political actors in the various states were "persuaded to shift their loyalties, expectations, and political activities towards a new centre", namely, the Republic of India.

This was not an easy task. While some princely states such as Mysore had legislative systems of governance that were based on a broad franchise and not significantly different from those of British India, in others, political decision-making took place in small, limited aristocratic circles and governance was, as a result, at best paternalistic and at worst the result of courtly intrigue. Having secured the accession of the princely states, the Government of India between 1948 and 1950 turned to the task of welding the states and the former British provinces into one polity under a single republican constitution.

Fast-Track Integration

The first step in this process, carried out between 1947 and 1949, was to merge the smaller states that were not seen by the Government of India to be viable administrative units either into neighbouring provinces, or with other princely states to create a "princely union". This policy was contentious, since it involved the dissolution of the very states whose existence India had only recently guaranteed in the Instruments of Accession. Patel and Menon emphasised that without integration, the economies of states would collapse, and anarchy would arise if the princes were unable to provide democracy and govern properly.

They pointed out that many of the smaller states were very small and lacked resources to sustain their economies and support their growing populations. Many also imposed tax rules and other restrictions that impeded free trade, and which had to be dismantled in a united India. Given that merger involved the breach of guarantees personally given by Mountbatten, Patel and Nehru initially intended to wait until after his term as Governor-General. An Adivasi uprising in Orissa in late 1947, however, forced their hand. In December 1947, princes from the Eastern India Agency and Chhattisgarh Agency were summoned to an all-night meeting with Menon, in the course of which they were persuaded to sign Merger Agreements integrating their states into Orissa, the Central Provinces and Bihar with effect from 1 January 1948. Later that year, 66 states in Gujarat and the Deccan were merged into Bombay, including the large states of Kolhapur and Baroda. Other small states were merged into Madras, East Punjab, West Bengal, the United Provinces and Assam. Not all states that signed Merger Agreements were integrated into provinces, however. Thirty states of the former Punjab Hill States Agency which lay near the international border and had signed Merger Agreements were integrated into Himachal Pradesh, a distinct entity which was administered directly by the centre as a Chief Commissioner's Province, for reasons of security.

The Merger Agreements required rulers to cede "full and exclusive jurisdiction and powers for and in relation to governance" of their state to the Dominion of India. In return for their agreement to entirely cede their states, it gave princes a large number of guarantees. Princes would receive an annual payment from the Indian government in the form of a privy purse as compensation for the surrender of their powers and the dissolution of their states. While state property would be taken over, their private property would be protected, as would all personal privileges, dignities and titles. Succession was also guaranteed according to custom. In addition, the provincial administration was obliged to take on the staff of the princely states with guarantees of equal pay and treatment.

Although the Merger Agreements were principally intended for smaller, nonviable states, they were also applied to a few larger states. Kutch in western India, and Tripura and Manipur in North-East India, all of which lay along international borders, were also asked to sign Merger Agreements, despite being larger states, following which they became Chief Commissioners' Provinces.

Bhopal, whose ruler was proud of the efficiency of his administration and feared that it would lose its identity if merged with the Maratha states that were its neighbours, also became a directly administered Chief Commissioner's Province, as did Bilaspur, much of which was likely to be flooded on completion of the Bhakra dam.

Four-step Integration

Merger

The bulk of the larger states, and some groups of small states, were integrated through a different, four-step process. The first step in this process was to convince groups of large states to combine to form a "princely union" through the execution by their rulers of Covenants of Merger. Under the Covenants of Merger, all rulers lost their ruling powers, save one who became the Rajpramukh of the new union.

The other rulers were associated with two bodies—the council of rulers, whose members were the rulers of salute states, and a presidium, one or more of whose members were elected by the rulers of non-salute states, with the rest elected by the council. The Rajpramukh and a deputy Rajpramukh, or *Uprajpramukh*, were chosen by the council from among the members of the presidium. The Covenants made provision for the creation of a constituent assembly for the new union which would be charged with framing its constitution. In return for agreeing to the extinction of their states as discrete entities, the rulers were given a privy purse and guarantees similar to those provided under the Merger Agreements.

Through this process, Patel obtained the unification of 222 states in the Kathiawar peninsula of his native Gujarat into the princely union of Saurashtra in January 1948, with six more states joining the union the following year. Madhya Bharat emerged on 28 May 1948 from a union of Gwalior, Indore and eighteen smaller states. In Punjab, the Patiala and East Punjab States Union was formed on 15 July 1948 from Patiala, Kapurthala, Jind, Nabha, Faridkot, Malerkotla, Nalargarh, and Kalsia. The United State of Rajasthan was formed as the result of a series of mergers, the last of which was completed on 15 May 1949. Travancore and Cochin were merged in the middle of 1949 to form the princely union of Travancore-Cochin. The only princely states which signed neither Covenants of Merger nor Merger Agreements were Kashmir, Mysore and Hyderabad.

Democratisation

Merging the administrative machineries of each state and integrating them into one political and administrative entity was not easy, particularly as many of the merged states had a history of rivalry. In the former Central India Agency, whose princely states had initially been merged into a princely union called Vindhya Pradesh, the rivalry between two groups of states became so bad that the Government of India persuaded the rulers to sign a Merger Agreement abrogating the old Covenants of Merger, and took direct control of the state as a Chief Commissioner's State.

As such, the mergers did not meet the expectations of the Government of India or the States Department. In December 1947, Menon suggested requiring the rulers of states to take "practical steps towards the establishment of popular government". The States Department accepted his suggestion, and implemented it through a special covenant signed by the rajpramukhs of the merged princely unions, binding them to act as constitutional monarchs. This meant that their powers were *de facto* no different from those of the Governors of the former British provinces, thus giving the people of their territories the same measure of responsible government as the people of the rest of India.

The result of this process has been described as being, in effect, an assertion of paramountcy by the Government of India over the states in a more pervasive form. While this contradicted the British statement that paramountcy would lapse on the transfer of power, the Congress position had always been that independent India would inherit the position of being the paramount power.

Centralisation and Constitutionalisation

Democratisation still left open one important distinction between the former princely states and the former British provinces, namely, that since the princely states had signed limited Instruments of Accession covering only three subjects, they were insulated from government policies in other areas. The Congress viewed this as hampering its ability to frame policies that brought about social justice and national development. Consequently, they sought to secure to the central government the same degree of powers over the former princely states as it had over the former British provinces.

In May 1948, at the initiative of V. P. Menon, a meeting was held in Delhi between the Rajpramukhs of the princely unions and the States Department, at the end of which the Rajpramukhs signed new Instruments of Accession which gave the Government of India the power to pass laws in respect of all matters that fell within the seventh schedule of the Government of India Act 1935.

Subsequently, each of the princely unions, as well as Mysore and Hyderabad, agreed to adopt the Constitution of India drafted by the constituent assembly as the constitution of that state, thus ensuring that they were placed in exactly the same legal position vis-à-vis the central government as the former British provinces. The only exception was Kashmir, whose relationship with India continued to be governed by the original Instrument of Accession, and the constitution produced by the state's Constituent Assembly.

The Constitution of India classified the constituent units of India into three classes, which it termed Part A, B, and C states. The former British provinces, together with the princely states that had been merged into them, were the Part A states. The princely unions, plus Mysore and Hyderabad, were the Part B states. The former Chief Commissioners' Provinces and other centrally administered areas, except the Andaman and Nicobar Islands, were the Part C states. The only practical difference between the Part A states and the Part B states was that the constitutional heads of the Part B states were the Rajpramukhs appointed under the terms of the Covenants of Merger, rather than Governors appointed by the central government.

In addition, Constitution gave the central government a significant range of powers over the former princely states, providing amongst other things that "their governance shall be under the general control of, and comply with such particular directions, if any, as may from time to time be given by, the President". Apart from that, the form of government in both was identical.

Reorganisation

The distinction between Part A and Part B states was only intended to last for a brief, transitional period. In 1956, the States Reorganisation Act reorganised the former British provinces and princely states on the basis of language. Simultaneously, the Seventh Amendment to the Constitution removed the distinction between Part A and Part B states, both of which were now treated only as "states", with Part C states being renamed "union territories". The Rajpramukhs lost their authority, and were replaced as the constitutional heads of state by Governors, who were appointed by the central government. These changes finally brought the princely order to an end. In both legal and practical terms, the territories that formerly were part of the princely states were now fully integrated into India and did not differ in any way from those that were formerly part of British India. The personal privileges of the princes—the privy purse, the exemption from customs duty, and customary dignities—survived slightly longer, but were abolished in 1971.

Post-integration Issues

The Princes

Although the progressive integration of the princely states into India was largely peaceful, not all princes were happy with the outcome. Many had expected the Instruments of Accession to be permanent, and were unhappy about losing the autonomy and the guaranteed continued existence of their states they had expected to gain. Some felt uneasy about the disappearance of states that generations of their family had controlled, while others were unhappy about the disappearance of administrative structures they had worked hard to build up and which they believed to be efficient. The majority, however, despite the "strain and tension" of adapting to life as private citizens, were content to retire on the generous pension provided by the privy purse. Several took advantage of their eligibility to hold public offices under the central government. The Maharaja of Bhavnagar, Col. Krishna Kumarasingh Bhavasingh Gohil, for example, became the Governor of Madras State, and several others were appointed to diplomatic posts overseas.

Colonial Enclaves

The integration of the princely states raised the question of the future of the remaining colonial enclaves in India. At independence, the regions of Pondicherry, Karikal, Yanam, Mahe and Chandernagore were still colonies of France, and Daman and Diu, Dadra and Nagar Haveli and Goa remained colonies of Portugal. An agreement between France and India in 1948 provided for an election in France's remaining Indian possessions to choose their political future. A plebiscite held in Chandernagore on 19 June 1949 resulted in a vote of 7,463 to 114 in favour of being integrated with India. It was ceded to India on a *de facto* basis on 14 August 1949 and *de jure* on 2 May 1950.

In the other enclaves, however, the pro-French camp, led by Edouard Goubert, used the administrative machinery to suppress the pro-merger groups. Popular discontent rose, and in 1954 demonstrations in Yanam and Mahe resulted in pro-merger groups assuming power. A referendum in Pondicherry and Karaikal in October 1954 resulted in a vote in favour of merger, and on 1 November 1954, de facto control over all four enclaves was transferred to the Republic of India. A treaty of cession was signed in May 1956, and following ratification by the French National Assembly in May 1962, *de jure* control of the enclaves was also transferred.

Portugal, in contrast, resisted diplomatic solutions. It viewed its continued possession of its Indian enclaves as a matter of national pride and, in 1951, it amended its constitution to convert its possessions in India into Portuguese provinces. In July 1954, an uprising in Dadra and Nagar Haveli threw off Portuguese rule.

The Portuguese attempted to send forces from Daman to reoccupy the enclaves, but were prevented from doing so by Indian troops. Portugal initiated proceedings before the International Court of Justice to compel India to allow its troops access to the enclave, but the Court rejected its complaint in 1960, holding that India was within its rights in denying Portugal military access. In 1961, the Constitution of India was amended to incorporate Dadra and Nagar Haveli into India as a Union Territory.

Goa, Daman and Diu remained an outstanding issue. On 15 August 1955, five thousand nonviolent demonstrators marched against the Portuguese at the border, and were met with gunfire, killing 22.

In December 1960, the United Nations General Assembly rejected Portugal's contention that its overseas possessions were provinces, and formally listed them as "non-self-governing territories". Although Nehru continued to favour a negotiated solution, the Portuguese suppression of a revolt in Angola in 1961 radicalised Indian public opinion, and increased the pressure on the Government of India to take military action.

African leaders, too, put pressure on Nehru to take action in Goa, which they argued would save Africa from further horrors. On 18 December 1961, following the collapse of an American attempt to find a negotiated solution, the Indian Army entered Goa, Daman and Diu. The Portuguese took the matter to the Security Council but a resolution calling on India to withdraw its troops immediately was defeated by the USSR's veto. Portugal surrendered on 19 December. This take-over ended the last of the European colonies in India. Goa was incorporated into India as a centrally administered union territory and, in 1987, became a state.

Sikkim

The former princely state of Sikkim, located at a strategically important point on the border between India and China, was integrated into India in 1975 as its 22nd state.

Three princely states bordering India—Nepal, Bhutan and Sikkim—were not integrated into the Republic of India in the period between 1947 and 1950. Nepal had been recognised by the British and the Government of India as being *de jure* independent. Bhutan had in the British period been considered a protectorate outside the international frontier of India. The Government of India entered into a treaty with Bhutan in 1949 continuing this arrangement, and providing that Bhutan would abide by the advice of the Government of India in the conduct of its external affairs.

Historically, Sikkim was a British dependency, with a status similar to that of the other princely states, and was therefore considered to be within the frontiers of India in the colonial period. On independence, however, the Chogyal of Sikkim resisted full integration into India.

Given the region's strategic importance to India, the Government of India signed first a Standstill Agreement and then in 1950 a full treaty with the Chogyal of Sikkim which in effect made it a protectorate which was no longer part of India. India had responsibility for defence, external affairs and communications, and ultimate responsibility for law and order, but Sikkim was otherwise given full internal autonomy.

In the late 1960s and early 1970s, the Chogyal, supported by the minority Bhutia and Lepcha upper classes, attempted to negotiate greater powers, particularly over external affairs, in order to give Sikkim more of an international personality. These policies were opposed by Kazi Lhendup Dorji and the Sikkim State Congress, who represented the ethnic Nepali middle classes and took a more pro-Indian view. In April 1973, an anti-Chogyal agitation broke out; the agitators demanded the conduct of popular elections. The Sikkim police were unable to control the demonstrations, and Dorji asked India to exercise its responsibility for law and order and intervene.

India facilitated negotiations between the Chogyal and Dorji, and produced an agreement which envisaged the reduction of the Chogyal to the role of a constitutional monarch and the holding of elections based on a new ethnic power-sharing formula. The Chogyal's opponents won an overwhelming victory, and a new Constitution was drafted providing for Sikkim to be associated with the Republic of India. On 10 April 1975, the Sikkim Assembly passed a resolution calling for the state to be fully integrated into India. This resolution was endorsed by 97% of the vote in a referendum held on 14 April 1975, following which the Indian Government amended the constitution to admit Sikkim into India as its 22nd state.

Secessionism and Sub-nationalism

While the majority of princely states absorbed into India have been fully integrated, a few outstanding issues remain. The most prominent of these is in relation to Kashmir, where a violent secessionist insurgency has been raging since the late 1980s.

Some academics suggest that the insurgency in Kashmir is at least partly a result of the manner in which it was integrated into India. Kashmir, uniquely amongst princely states, was not required to sign either a Merger Agreement or a revised Instrument of Accession giving India control over a larger number of issues than the three originally provided for.

Instead, the power to make laws relating to Kashmir was granted to the Government of India by Article 5 of the Constitution of Jammu and Kashmir and was, under Article 370 of the Constitution of India, somewhat more restricted than in relation to other states.

Widmalm argues that during the 1980s, a number of Kashmiri youth began to feel that the Indian government was increasingly interfering in the politics of Jammu and Kashmir. The elections of 1987 caused them to lose faith in the political process and begin the violent insurgency which is still ongoing. Similarly, Ganguly suggests that the policies of the Indian government towards Kashmir meant that the state, unlike other parts of India, never developed the solid political institutions associated with a modern multi-ethnic democracy. As a result, the growing dissatisfaction with the *status quo* felt by an increasingly politically aware youth was expressed through non-political channels which Pakistan, seeking to weaken India's hold over Kashmir, transformed into an active insurgency.

Separatist movements also exist in two other former princely states located in North-East India, Tripura and Manipur. These separatist movements are generally treated by scholars as being part of the broader problem of insurgencies in Northeast India, rather being a result of specific problems in integrating the princely states into India, as the Kashmir problem is and, in particular, to reflect the failure of the Government of India to adequately address the aspirations of tribal groups in the Northeast, or to tackle the tensions arising from the immigration of people from other parts of India to the northeastern areas.

The integration of former princely states with other provinces to form new states has also given rise to some issues. The Telengana region, comprising the Telugu-speaking districts of the former Hyderabad State, were in many ways different from the Telugu-speaking areas of British India with which they were merged. In recognition of these differences, the States Reorganisation Commission originally recommended that Telengana be created as a separate state, rather than as part of a broader Telugu-speaking entity.

This recommendation was rejected by the Government of India, and Telengana was merged into Andhra Pradesh. The result was the emergence in the 1960s of a movement demanding a separate Telengana state. The demand has been accepted by the Union Government in December 2009. A similar movement, although less strong, exists in the Vidarbha region of Maharashtra, which consists of the former Nagpur state and the Berar region of the former Hyderabad state.

Critical Perspectives on the Process of Integration

As this article has discussed, the integration process repeatedly brought Indian and Pakistani leaders into conflict. During negotiations, Jinnah, representing the Muslim League, strongly supported the right of the princely states to remain independent, joining neither India nor Pakistan, an attitude which was diametrically opposed to the stance taken by Nehru and the Congress and which was reflected in Pakistan's support of Hyderabad's bid to stay independent. Post-partition, the Government of Pakistan accused India of hypocrisy on the ground that there was little difference between the accession of the ruler of Junagadh to Pakistan—which India refused to recognise—and the accession of the Maharajah of Kashmir to India, and for several years refused to recognise the legality of India's incorporation of

Junagadh, treating it as *de jure* Pakistani territory.

Different theories have been proposed to explain the designs of Indian and Pakistani leaders in this period. Rajmohan Gandhi postulates that an ideal deal working in the mind of Patel was that if Muhammad Ali Jinnah let India have Junagadh and Hyderabad, Patel would not object to Kashmir acceding to Pakistan. In his book *Patel: A Life*, Gandhi asserts that Jinnah sought to engage the questions of Junagadh and Hyderabad in the same battle. It is suggested that he wanted India to ask for a plebiscite in Junagadh and Hyderabad, knowing thus that the principle then would have to be applied to Kashmir, where the Muslim-majority would, he believed, vote for Pakistan.

A speech by Patel at the Bahauddin College in Junagadh following the latter's take-over, where he said that "we would agree to Kashmir if they agreed to Hyderabad", suggests that he may have been amenable to this idea. Although Patel's opinions were not India's policy, nor were they shared by Nehru, both leaders were angered at Jinnah's courting the princes of Jodhpur, Bhopal and Indore, leading them to take a harder stance on a possible deal with Pakistan.

Modern historians have also re-examined the role of the States Department and Lord Mountbatten during the accession process. Ian Copland argues that the Congress leaders did not intend the settlement contained in the Instruments of Accession to be permanent even when they were signed, and at all times privately contemplated a complete integration of the sort that ensued between 1948 and 1950.

He points out that the mergers and cession of powers to the Government of India between 1948 and 1950 contravened the terms of the Instruments of Accession, and were incompatible with the express assurances of internal autonomy and preservation of the princely states which Mountbatten had given the princes. Menon in his memoirs stated that the changes to the initial terms of accession were in every instance freely consented to by the princes with no element of coercion. Copland disagrees, on the basis that foreign diplomats at the time believed that the princes had been given no choice but to sign, and that a few princes expressed their unhappiness with the arrangements.

He also criticises Mountbatten's role, saying that while he stayed within the letter of the law, he was at least under a moral obligation to do something for the princes when it became apparent that the Government of India was going to alter the terms on which accession took place, and that he should never have lent his support to the bargain given that it could not be guaranteed after independence. Both Copland and Ramusack argue that, in the ultimate analysis, one of the reasons why the princes consented to the demise of their states was that they felt abandoned by the British, and saw themselves as having little other option.

Older historians such as Lumby, in contrast, take the view that the princely states could not have survived as independent entities after the transfer of power, and that their demise was inevitable. They therefore view successful integration of all princely states into India as a triumph for the Government of India and Lord Mountbatten, and as a tribute to the sagacity of the majority of princes, who jointly achieved in a few months what the Empire had attempted, unsuccessfully, to do for over a century—unite all of India under one rule.

2

Political Integration of India

At the time of Indian independence, India was divided into two sets of territories, the first being the territories of "British India", which were under the direct control of the India Office in London and the Governor-General of India, and the second being the "Princely states", the territories over which the Crown had suzerainty, but which were under the control of their hereditary rulers. In addition, there were several colonial enclaves controlled by France and Portugal. The political integration of these territories into India was a declared objective of the Indian National Congress, which the Government of India pursued over the next decade.

Through a combination of factors, Vallabhbhai Patel and V. P. Menon convinced the rulers of almost all of the hundreds of princely states to accede to India. Having secured their accession, they then proceeded to, in a step-by-step process, secure and extend the central government's authority over these states and transform their administrations until, by 1956, there was little difference between the territories that had formerly been part of British India and those that had been part of princely states. Simultaneously, the Government of India, through a combination of diplomatic and military means, acquired *de facto* and *de jure* control over the remaining colonial enclaves, which too were integrated into India. Although this process successfully integrated the vast majority of princely states into India, it was not as successful in relation to a few states, notably the former princely state of Kashmir, the accession of which to India was disputed by Pakistan, the state of Hyderabad, whose ruler was determined to remain independent, and the states of Tripura and Manipur, where active secessionist movements existed.

Princely States in British India

The early history of British expansion in India was characterised by the coexistence of two approaches towards the existing princely states. The first was a policy of annexation, where the British sought to forcibly absorb the Indian princely states into the provinces which constituted their Empire in India. The second was a policy of indirect rule, where the British assumed suzerainty and paramountcy over princely states, but conceded some degree of sovereignty to them. During the early part of the nineteenth century, the policy of the British tended towards annexation, but the Indian Rebellion of 1857 forced a change in this approach, by demonstrating both the difficulty of absorbing and subduing annexed states, and the usefulness of princely states as a source of support.

In 1858, the policy of annexation was formally renounced, and British relations with the princely states thereafter were based on indirect rule, whereby the British exercised paramountcy over all princely states with the British crown as ultimate suzerain, but at the same time respected and protected them as allies. The exact relations between the British and each princely state were regulated by individual treaties, and varied widely, with some states having significant autonomy, some being subject to significant control in internal affairs, and some being in effect the owners of a few acres of land with little autonomy.

During the 20th century, the British made several attempts to integrate the princely states more closely with British India, creating the Chamber of Princes in 1921 as a consultative and advisory body, transferring the responsibility for supervision of smaller states from the provinces to the centre in 1936, and creating direct relations between the Government of India and the larger princely states superseding political agents. The most ambitious was a scheme of federation in the Government of India Act 1935, which envisaged the princely states and British India being united under a federal government. This scheme came close to success, but was abandoned in 1939 as a result of the outbreak of the Second World War. As a result, in the 1940s, the relationship between the princely states and the crown remained regulated by the principle of paramountcy and the various treaties between the British crown and the states. Neither paramountcy nor these arrangements could continue after Indian independence. The British took the view that because they had been established directly between the British crown and the princely states, they could not be transferred to independent India. At the same time, they imposed obligations on Britain that it was not prepared to continue to carry out, such as the obligation to maintain troops in India for the defence of the princely states. The British government therefore decided that paramountcy, together with all treaties between them and the princely states, would come to an end upon the transfer of power.

Sikkim

Three princely states bordering India—Nepal, Bhutan and Sikkim—were not integrated into the Republic of India in the period between 1947 and 1950. Nepal had been recognised by the British and the Government of India as being *de jure* independent. Bhutan had in the British period been considered a protectorate outside the international frontier of India. The Government of India entered into a treaty with Bhutan in 1949 continuing this arrangement, and providing that Bhutan would abide by the advice of the Government of India in the conduct of its external affairs.

Historically, Sikkim was a British dependency, with a status similar to that of the other princely states, and was therefore considered to be within the frontiers of India in the colonial period. On independence, however, the Chogyal of Sikkim resisted full integration into India. Given the region's strategic importance to India, the Government of India signed first a Standstill Agreement and then in 1950 a full treaty with the Chogyal of Sikkim which in effect made it a protectorate which was no longer part of India. India had responsibility for defence, external affairs and communications, and ultimate responsibility for law and order, but Sikkim was otherwise given full internal autonomy.

In the late 1960s and early 1970s, the Chogyal, supported by the minority Bhutia and Lepcha upper classes, attempted to negotiate greater powers, particularly over external affairs, in order to give Sikkim more of an international personality. These policies were opposed by Kazi Lhendup Dorji and the Sikkim State Congress, who represented the ethnic Nepali middle classes and took a more pro-Indian view. In April 1973, an anti-Chogyal agitation broke out; the agitators demanded the conduct of popular elections. The Sikkim police were unable to control the demonstrations, and Dorji asked India to exercise its responsibility for law and order and intervene. India facilitated negotiations between the Chogyal and Dorji, and produced an agreement which envisaged the reduction of the Chogyal to the role of a constitutional monarch and the holding of elections based on a new ethnic power-sharing formula. The Chogyal's opponents won an overwhelming victory, and a new Constitution was drafted providing for Sikkim to be associated with the Republic of India. On 10 April 1975, the Sikkim Assembly passed a resolution calling for the state to be fully integrated into India. This resolution was endorsed by 97% of the vote in a referendum held on 14 April 1975, following which the Indian Government amended the constitution to admit Sikkim into India as its 22nd state.

Critical Perspectives on the Process of Integration

As this article has discussed, the integration process repeatedly brought Indian and Pakistani leaders into conflict. During negotiations, Jinnah, representing the Muslim League, strongly supported the right of the princely states to remain independent, joining neither India nor Pakistan, an attitude which was diametrically opposed to the stance taken by Nehru and the Congress and which was reflected in Pakistan's support of Hyderabad's bid to stay independent. Post-partition, the Government of Pakistan accused India of hypocrisy on the ground that there was little difference between the accession of the ruler of Junagadh to Pakistan—which India refused to recognise—and the accession of the Maharajah of Kashmir to India, and for several years refused to recognise the legality of India's incorporation of Junagadh, treating it as *de jure* Pakistani territory.

Different theories have been proposed to explain the designs of Indian and Pakistani leaders in this period. Rajmohan Gandhi postulates that an ideal deal working in the mind of Patel was that if Muhammad Ali Jinnah let India have Junagadh and Hyderabad, Patel would not object to Kashmir acceding to Pakistan. In his book *Patel: A Life*, Gandhi asserts that Jinnah sought to engage the questions of Junagadh and Hyderabad in the same battle. It is suggested that he wanted India to ask for a plebiscite in Junagadh and Hyderabad, knowing thus that the principle then would have to be applied to Kashmir, where the Muslim-majority would, he believed, vote for Pakistan. A speech by Patel at the Bahauddin College in Junagadh following the latter's take-over, where he said that "we would agree to Kashmir if they agreed to Hyderabad", suggests that he may have been amenable to this idea. Although Patel's opinions were not India's policy, nor were they shared by Nehru, both leaders were angered at Jinnah's courting the princes of Jodhpur, Bhopal and Indore, leading them to take a harder stance on a possible deal with Pakistan.

Modern historians have also re-examined the role of the States Department and Lord Mountbatten during the accession process. Ian Copland argues that the Congress leaders did not intend the settlement contained in the Instruments of Accession to be permanent even when they were signed, and at all times privately contemplated a complete integration of the sort that ensued between 1948 and 1950. He points out that the mergers and cession of powers to the Government of India between 1948 and 1950 contravened the terms of the Instruments of Accession, and were incompatible with the express assurances of internal autonomy and preservation of the princely states which Mountbatten had given the princes.

Menon in his memoirs stated that the changes to the initial terms of accession were in every instance freely consented to by the princes with no element of coercion. Copland disagrees, on the basis that foreign diplomats at the time believed that the princes had been given no choice but to sign, and that a few princes expressed their unhappiness with the arrangements. He also criticises Mountbatten's role, saying that while he stayed within the letter of the law, he was at least under a moral obligation to do something for the princes when it became apparent that the Government of India was going to alter the terms on which accession took place, and that he should never have lent his support to the bargain given that it could not be guaranteed after independence.

Both Copland and Ramusack argue that, in the ultimate analysis, one of the reasons why the princes consented to the demise of their states was that they felt abandoned by the British, and saw themselves as having little other option. Older historians such as Lumby, in contrast, take the view that the princely states could not have survived as independent entities after the transfer of power, and that their demise was inevitable. They therefore view successful integration of all princely states into India as a triumph for the Government of India and Lord Mountbatten, and as a tribute to the sagacity of the majority of princes, who jointly achieved in a few months what the Empire had attempted, unsuccessfully, to do for over a century—unite all of India under one rule.

Sardar Patel Biography

Born: October 31, 1875

Died: December 15, 1950

Achievements: Successfully led Kheda Satyagraha and Bardoli revolt against British government; elected Ahmedabad's municipal president in 1922, 1924 and 1927; elected Congress President in 1931; was independent India's first Deputy Prime Minister and Home Minister; played a key role in political integration of India; conferred Bharat Ratna in 1991.

Sardar Patel was popularly known as Iron Man of India. His full name was Vallabhbhai Patel. He played a leading role in the Indian freedom struggle and became the first Deputy Prime Minister and Home Minister of India. He is credited with achieving political integration of India.

Vallabhbhai Patel was born on October 31, 1875 in Nadiad, a small village in Gujarat. His father Jhaverbhai was a farmer and mother Laad Bai was a simple lady. Sardar Vallabhai's early education took place in Karamsad. Then he joined a school in Petlad. After two years he joined a high school in a town called Nadiad. He passed his high school examination in 1896. Sardar Vallabhbhai Patel was a brilliant student throughout his schooling.

Vallabhbhai wanted to become a barrister. To realize this ambition he had to go to England. But he did not have the financial means to even join a college India. In those days a candidate could study in private and sit for an examination in Law. Sardar Vallabh Bhai Patel borrowed books from a lawyer of his acquaintance and studied at home. Occasionally he attended courts of law and listened attentively to the arguments of lawyer. Vallabhbhai passed the Law examination with flying colours.

Sardar Vallabhbhai Patel started his Law practice in Godhra. Soon his practice flourished. He got married to Jhaberaba. In 1904, he got a baby daughter Maniben, and in 1905 his son Dahyabhai was born. Vallabhbhai sent his elder brother Vitthalbhai, who himself was a lawyer, to England for higher studies in Law. Patel was only thirty-three years old when his wife died. He did not wish to marry again. After his brother's return, Vallabhbhai went to England. He studied with single-minded devotion and stood first in the Barrister-at-Law Examination.

Sardar Patel returned to India in 1913 and started his practice in Ahmedabad. Soon he became popular. At the urging of his friends, Patel contested and won elections to become the sanitation commissioner of Ahmedabad in 1917. Sardar Patel was deeply impressed by Gandhiji's success in Champaran Satyagraha. In 1918, there was a drought in the Kheda division of Gujarat. Peasants asked for relief from the high rate of taxes but the British government refused. Gandhiji took up peasants cause but could not devote his full time in Kheda. He was looking for someone who could lead the struggle in his absence. At this point Sardar Patel volunteered to come forward and lead the struggle. He gave up his lucrative legal practice and entered public life.

Vallabhbhai successfully led peasants revolt in Kheda and the revolt ended in 1919 when the British government agreed to suspend collection of revenue and roll back the rates. Kheda Satyagraha turned Vallabhbhai Patel into a national hero. Vallabhbhai supported Gandhi's Non-Cooperation Movement, and as president of the Gujarat Congress, helped in organizing bonfires of British goods in Ahmedabad. He gave up his English clothes and started wearing Khadi. Sardar Vallabh Bhai Patel was elected Ahmedabad's municipal president in 1922, 1924 and 1927. During his terms, Ahmedabad was extended a major supply of electricity and underwent major education reforms. Drainage and sanitation systems were extended over all the city.

In 1928, Bardoli Taluka in Gujarat suffered from floods and famine. In this hour of distress the British government raised the revenue taxes by thirty percent. Sardar Patel took up cudgels on behalf of the farmers and appealed to the Governor to reduce the taxes. The Governor refused and the government even announced the date of the collection of the taxes. Sardar Patel organized the farmers and told them not to pay even a single pie of tax. The government tried to repress the revolt but ultimately bowed before Vallabhbhai Patel. It was during the struggle and after the victory in Bardoli that caused intense excitement across India, that Patel was increasingly addressed by his colleagues and followers as Sardar.

Disobedience Movement in 1930. After the signing of Gandhi-Irwin pact in 1931, Sardar Patel was released and he was elected Congress president for its 1931 session in Karachi. Upon the failure of the Round Table Conference in London, Gandhiji and Sardar Patel were arrested in January 1932 and imprisoned in the Yeravada Central Jail. During this term of imprisonment, Sardar Patel and Mahatma Gandhi grew close to one another, and the two developed a close bond of affection, trust, and frankness without reserve. Sardar Patel was finally released in July 1934.

In August 1942, the Congress launched the Quit India Movement. The government jailed all the important leaders of the Congress, including Vallabhai Patel. All the leaders were released after three years. After achieving independence on 15th of August 1947, Pandit Jawaharlal Nehru became the first Prime Minister of independent India and Sardar Patel became the Deputy Prime Minister. He was in charge of Home Affairs, Information and Broadcasting and the Ministry of States.

There were 565 princely states in India at that time. Some of the Maharajas and Nawabs who ruled over these were sensible and patriotic. But most of them were drunk with wealth and power. They were dreaming of becoming independent rulers once the British quit India. They argued that the government of free India should treat them as equals. Some of them went to the extent of planning to send their representatives to the United Nations Organization. Patel invoked the patriotism of India's monarchs, asking them to join in the freedom of their nation and act as responsible rulers who cared about the future of their people.

He persuaded the princes of 565 states of the impossibility of independence from the Indian republic, especially in the presence of growing opposition from their subjects. With great wisdom and political foresight, he consolidated the small kingdoms.

The public was with him. He tackled the Nizam of Hyderabad and the Nawab of Junagarh who initially did not want to join India. Sardar Patel's untiring efforts towards the unity of the country brought success. He united a scattered nation without much bloodshed. Due to the achievement of this massive task, Sardar Patel got the title of 'Iron Man'. Sardar Patel died of cardiac arrest on December 15, 1950. For his services to the nation Sardar Patel was conferred with Bharat Ratna in 1991.

Sardar Vallabhbhai Patel

Vallabhbhai Patel was a political and social leader of India who played a major role in the country's struggle for independence and guided its integration into a united, independent nation. He was called as "Iron Man Of India" In India and across the world, he was often addressed as Sardar, which means *Chief* in many languages of India.

Raised in the countryside of Gujarat in Gurjar community and largely self-educated, Vallabhbhai Patel was employed in successful practice as a lawyer when he was first inspired by the work and philosophy of Mahatma Gandhi. Patel subsequently organised the peasants of Kheda, Borsad, and Bardoli in Gujarat in nonviolent civil disobedience against oppressive policies imposed by the British Raj; in this role, he became one of the most influential leaders in Gujarat. He rose to the leadership of the Indian National Congress and was at the forefront of rebellions and political events, organising the party for elections in 1934 and 1937, and promoting the Quit India movement.

As the first Home Minister and Deputy Prime Minister of India, Patel organised relief for refugees in Punjab and Delhi, and led efforts to restore peace across the nation. Patel took charge of the task to forge a united India from the 565 semi-autonomous princely states and British-era colonial provinces. Using frank diplomacy backed with the option (and the use) of military action, Patel's leadership enabled the accession of almost every princely state. Hailed as the Iron Man of India, he is also remembered as the "Patron Saint" of India's civil servants for establishing modern all-India services. Patel was also one of the earliest proponents of property rights and free enterprise in India.

Early Life

Vallabhbhai Jhaverbhai Patel was born at his maternal uncle's house Desai Vago in Nadiad in Leva Patidar Gurjar community of Gujarat. His actual date of birth was never officially recorded—Patel entered 31 October as his date of birth on his matriculation examination papers. He was the fourth son of Jhaverbhai and his wife Ladba Patel. They lived in the village of Karamsad, in the Kheda district where Jhaverbhai owned a homestead. Somabhai, Narsibhai and Vithalbhai Patel (also a future political leader) were his elder brothers. He had a younger brother, Kashibhai and a sister, Dahiba. As a young boy, Patel helped his father in the fields and bimonthly kept a day-long fast, abstaining from food and water—a Hindu cultural observance that enabled him to develop physical toughness. When he was eighteen years old, Patel's marriage was arranged with Jhaverba, a young girl of twelve or thirteen years from a nearby village. According to custom, the young bride would continue to live with her parents until her husband started earning and could establish their household.

Patel travelled to attend schools in Nadiad, Petlad and Borsad, living self-sufficiently with other boys. He reputedly cultivated a stoic character—a popular anecdote recounts how he lanced his own painful boil without hesitation, even as the barber supposed to do it trembled. Patel passed his matriculation at the late age of 22; at this point, he was generally regarded by his elders as an unambitious man destined for a commonplace job. Patel himself harboured a plan—he would study to become a lawyer, work and save funds, travel to England and study to become a barrister. Patel spent years away from his family, studying on his own with books borrowed from other lawyers and passed examinations within two years.

Fetching Jhaverba from her parents' home, Patel set up his household in Godhra and enrolled at the bar. During the many years it took him to save money, Vallabhbhai—now a pleader—earned a reputation as a fierce and skilled lawyer. His wife bore him a daughter, Manibehn, in 1904 and later a son, Dahyabhai, in 1906. Patel also cared for a friend suffering from Bubonic plague when it swept across Gujarat. When Patel himself came down with the disease, he immediately sent his family to safety, left his home and moved into an isolated house in Nadiad (by other accounts, Patel spent this time in a dilapidated temple); there, he recovered slowly.

Vallabhbhai Patel, when a Young Lawyer.

Patel practised law in Godhra, Borsad and Anand while taking on the financial burdens of his homestead in Karamsad. When he had saved enough for England and applied for a pass and a ticket, they arrived in the name of "V. J. Patel," at Vithalbhai's home, who bore the same initials. Having harboured his own plans to study in England, Vithalbhai remonstrated to his younger brother that it would be disreputable for an older brother to follow his younger brother. In keeping with concerns for his family's honour, Patel allowed Vithalbhai to go in his place. He also financed his brother's stay and began saving again for his own goals.

In 1909, Patel's wife Jhaverba was hospitalised in Mumbai (then Bombay) to undergo a major surgical operation for cancer. Her health suddenly worsened and despite successful emergency surgery, she died in the hospital. Patel was given a note informing him of his wife's demise as he was cross-examining a witness in court. According to others who witnessed, Patel read the note, pocketed it and continued to intensely cross-examine the witness and won the case. He broke the news to others only after the proceedings had ended. Patel himself decided against marrying again. He raised his children with the help of his family and sent them to English-medium schools in Mumbai.

At the age of 36, he journeyed to England and enrolled at the Middle Temple Inn in London. Finishing a 36-month course in 30 months, Patel topped his class despite having no previous college background. Returning to India, Patel settled in the city of Ahmedabad and became one of the city's most successful barristers. Wearing European-style clothes and urbane mannerisms, he also became a skilled bridge player. Patel nurtured ambitions to expand his practise and accumulate great wealth and to provide his children with modern education. He had also made a pact with his brother Vithalbhai to support his entry into politics in the Bombay Presidency, while Patel himself would remain in Ahmedabad and provide for the family.

Fighting for Independence

At the urging of his friends, Patel won an election to become the sanitation commissioner of Ahmedabad in 1917. While often clashing with British officials on civic issues, he did not show any interest in politics. Upon hearing of Mohandas Gandhi, he joked to Mavlankar that Gandhi would "ask you if you know how to sift pebbles from wheat. And that is supposed to bring independence." But Patel was deeply impressed when Gandhi defied the British in Champaran for the sake of the area's oppressed farmers. Against the grain of Indian politicians of the time, Gandhi wore Indian-style clothes and emphasised the use of one's mother tongue or any Indian language as opposed to English—the lingua franca of India's intellectuals. Patel was particularly attracted to

Gandhi's inclination to action—apart from a resolution condemning the arrest of political leader Annie Besant, Gandhi proposed that volunteers march peacefully demanding to meet her.

Patel gave a speech in Borsad in September 1917, encouraging Indians nationwide to sign Gandhi's petition demanding *Swaraj*—independence—from the British. Meeting Gandhi a month later at the Gujarat Political Conference in Godhra, Patel became the secretary of the Gujarat Sabha—a public body which would become the Gujarati arm of the Indian National Congress—at Gandhi's encouragement. Patel now energetically fought against *veth*—the forced servitude of Indians to Europeans—and organised relief efforts in wake of plague and famine in Kheda. The Kheda peasants' plea for exemption from taxation had been turned down by British authorities. Gandhi endorsed waging a struggle there, but could not lead it himself due to his activities in Champaran. When Gandhi asked for a Gujarati activist to devote himself completely to the assignment and Patel volunteered, much to Gandhi's personal delight. Though his decision was made on the spot, Patel later said that his desire and commitment came after intensive personal contemplation, as he realised he would have to abandon his career and material ambitions.

Satyagraha in Gujarat

Supported by Congress volunteers Narhari Parikh, Mohanlal Pandya and Abbas Tyabji, Vallabhbhai Patel began a village-to-village tour in the Kheda district, documenting grievances and asking villagers for their support for a statewide revolt by refusing the payment of taxes. Patel emphasised potential hardships with the need for complete unity and non-violence despite any provocation. He received enthusiastic responses from virtually every village. When the revolt was launched and revenue refused, the government sent police and intimidation squads to seize property, including confiscating barn animals and whole farms.

Patel organised a network of volunteers to work with individual villages—helping them hide valuables and protect themselves during raids. Thousands of activists and farmers were arrested, but Patel was not. The revolt began evoking sympathy and admiration across India, including with pro-British Indian politicians. The government agreed to negotiate with Patel and decided to suspend the payment of revenue for the year, even scaling back the rate. Patel emerged as a hero to Gujaratis and admired across India. In 1920, he was elected president of the newly formed Gujarat Pradesh Congress Committee—he would serve as its president till 1945.

Patel supported Gandhi's Non-cooperation movement and toured the state to recruit more than 300,000 members and raise over Rs. 1.5 million in funds. Helping organise bonfires of British goods in Ahmedabad, Patel threw in all his English-style clothes. With his daughter Mani and son Dahya, he switched completely to wearing khadi. Patel also supported Gandhi's controversial suspension of resistance in wake of the Chauri Chaura incident. He worked extensively in the following years in Gujarat against alcoholism, untouchability and caste discrimination, as well as for the empowerment of women. In the Congress, he was a resolute supporter of Gandhi against his Swarajist critics.

Patel was elected Ahmedabad's municipal president in 1922, 1924 and 1927—during his terms, Ahmedabad was extended a major supply of electricity and the school system underwent major reforms. Drainage and sanitation systems were extended over all the city. He fought for the recognition and payment of teachers employed in schools established by nationalists (out of British control) and even took on sensitive Hindu-Muslim Issues. Sardar Patel personally led relief efforts in the aftermath of the intense torrential rainfall in 1927, which had caused major floods in the city and in the Kheda district and great destruction of life and property. He established refuge centres across the district, raised volunteers, arranged for supply of food, medicines and clothing, as well as emergency funds from the government and public.

When Gandhi was in prison, Sardar Patel was asked by Members of Congress to lead the satyagraha in Nagpur in 1923 against a law banning the raising of the Indian flag. He organised thousands of volunteers from all over the country in processions hoisting the flag. Patel negotiated a settlement that obtained the release of all prisoners and allowed nationalists to hoist the flag in public. Later that year, Patel and his allies uncovered evidence suggesting that the police were in league with local dacoits in the Borsad taluka even as the government prepared to levy a major tax for fighting dacoits in the area. More than 6,000 villagers assembled to hear Patel speak and supported the proposed agitation against the tax, which was deemed immoral and unnecessary.

He organised hundreds of Congressmen, sent instructions and received information from across the district. Every village in the *taluka* resisted payment of the tax, and through cohesion, also prevented the seizure of property and lands. After a protracted struggle, the government withdrew the tax. Historians believe that one of Patel's key achievements was the building of cohesion and trust amongst the different castes and communities, which were divided on socioeconomic lines.

In April 1928, Sardar Patel returned to the freedom struggle from his municipal duties in Ahmedabad when Bardoli suffered from a serious predicament of a famine and steep tax hike. The revenue hike was steeper than it had been in Kheda even though the famine covered a large portion of Gujarat. After cross-examining and talking to village representatives, emphasizing the potential hardship and need for non-violence and cohesion, Patel initiated the struggle—complete denial of taxes. Sardar Patel organised volunteers, camps and an information network across affected areas.

The revenue refusal was stronger than in Kheda and many sympathy satyagrahas were undertaken across Gujarat. Despite arrests, seizures of property and lands, the struggle intensified. The situation reached a head in August, when through sympathetic intermediaries, he negotiated a settlement repealing the tax hike, reinstating village officials who had resigned in protest and the return of seized property and lands. It was during the struggle and after the victory in Bardoli that Patel was increasingly addressed by his colleagues and followers as Sardar.

Leading the Congress

Maulana Azad, Sardar Patel (third from left, in the foreground), and other Congressmen at Wardha

As Gandhi embarked on the Dandi Salt March, Patel was arrested in the village of Ras and tried without witnesses, with no lawyer or pressman allowed to attend. Patel's arrest and Gandhi's subsequent arrest caused the Salt Satyagraha to greatly intensify in Gujarat—districts across Gujarat launched an anti-tax rebellion until and unless Patel and Gandhi were released. Once released, Patel served as interim Congress president, but was re-arrested while leading a procession in Mumbai. After the signing of the Gandhi-Irwin Pact, Patel was elected Congress president for its

1931 session in Karachi—here the Congress ratified the pact, committed itself to the defence of fundamental rights and human freedoms, and a vision of a secular nation, minimum wage and the abolition of untouchability and serfdom.

Patel used his position as Congress president in organising the return of confiscated lands to farmers in Gujarat. Upon the failure of the Round Table Conference in London, Gandhi and Patel were arrested in January 1932 when the struggle re-opened, and imprisoned in the Yeravda Central Jail. During this term of imprisonment, Patel and Gandhi grew close to each other, and the two developed a close bond of affection, trust, and frankness. Their mutual relationship could be described as that of an elder brother (Gandhi) and his younger brother (Patel). Despite having arguments with Gandhi, Patel respected his instincts and leadership. During imprisonment, the two would discuss national and social issues, read Hindu epics and crack jokes.

Gandhi also taught Patel Sanskrit language. Gandhi's secretary Mahadev Desai kept detailed records of conversations between Gandhi and Patel. When Gandhi embarked on a fast-unto-death protesting the separate electorates allocated for untouchables, Patel looked after Gandhi closely and himself refrained from partaking of food. Patel was later moved to a jail in Nasik, and refused a British offer for a brief release to attend the cremation of his brother Vithalbhai, who had died in 1934. He was finally released in July of the same year.

Patel's position at the highest level in the Congress was largely connected with his role from 1934 onwards (when the Congress abandoned its boycott of elections) in the party organization. Based at an apartment in Mumbai, he became the Congress's main fund-raiser and chairman of its Central Parliamentary Board, playing the leading role in selecting and financing candidates for the 1934 elections to the Central Legislative Assembly in New Delhi and also for the Provincial elections of 1936. As well as collecting funds and selecting candidates, he would also determine the Congress stance on issues and opponents.

Not contesting a seat for himself, Patel nevertheless guided Congressmen elected in the provinces and at the national level. In 1935, Patel underwent surgery for hemorrhoids, yet guided efforts against plague in Bardoli and again when a drought struck

Gujarat in 1939. Patel would guide the Congress ministries that had won power across India with the aim of preserving party discipline—Patel feared that the British would use opportunities to create conflicts among elected Congressmen, and he did not want the party to be distracted from the goal of complete independence. But Patel would clash with Nehru, opposing declarations of the adoption of socialism at the 1936 Congress session, which he believed was a diversion from the main goal of achieving independence.

In 1938, Patel organized rank and file opposition to the attempts of then-Congress president Subhash Bose to move away from Gandhi's principles of nonviolent resistance. Patel considered Bose to want more power over the party. He led senior Congress leaders in a protest, which resulted in Bose's resignation. But criticism arose from Bose's supporters, socialists and other Congressmen that Patel himself was acting in an authoritarian manner in his defence of Gandhi's authority.

Quit India

When World War II broke out, Patel supported Nehru's decision to withdraw the Congress from central and provincial legislatures, contrary to Gandhi's advice, as well as an initiative by senior leader Chakravarthi Rajagopalachari to offer Congress's full support to Britain if it promised Indian independence at the end of the war and install a democratic government right away. Gandhi had refused to support Britain on the grounds of his moral opposition to war, while Subhash Chandra Bose was in militant opposition to the British. The British rejected Rajagopalachari's initiative, and Patel embraced Gandhi's leadership again. He participated in Gandhi's call for individual disobedience, and was arrested in 1940 and imprisoned for nine months. He also opposed the proposals of the Cripps' mission in 1942. Patel lost more than twenty pounds during his period in jail.

While Nehru, Rajagopalachari and Maulana Azad initially criticized Gandhi's proposal for an all-out campaign of civil disobedience to force the British to *Quit India*, Patel was its most fervent supporter. Arguing that the British would retreat from India as they had from Singapore and Burma, Patel stressed that the campaign start without any delay. Though feeling that the British would not quit immediately, Patel favoured an all-out rebellion which would galvanize Indian people, who had been divided in their response to the war, In Patel's view, an all-out rebellion would force the British to concede that continuation of colonial rule had no support in India, and thus speed power transfer to Indians. Believing strongly in the need for revolt, Patel stated his intention to resign from the Congress if the revolt was not approved.

Gandhi strongly pressured the All India Congress Committee to approve of an all-out campaign of civil disobedience, and the AICC approved the campaign on 7 August 1942. Though Patel's health had suffered during his stint in jail, Patel gave emotional speeches to large crowds across India asking people to refuse paying taxes and participate in civil disobedience, mass protests and a shutdown of all civil services. He raised funds and prepared a second-tier of command as a precaution against the arrest of national leaders. Patel made a climactic speech to more than 100,000 people gathered at Gowalia Tank in Bombay (Mumbai) on 7 August:

"The Governor of Burma boasts in London that they left Burma only after reducing everything to dust. So you promise the same thing to India?... You refer in your radio broadcasts and newspapers to the government established in Burma by Japan as a puppet government? What sort of government do you have in Delhi now?...When France fell before the Nazi onslaught, in the midst of total war, Mr. Churchill offered union with England to the French. That was indeed a stroke of inspired statesmanship. But when it comes to India? Oh no! Constitutional changes in the midst of a war? Absolutely unthinkable...The object this time is to free India before the Japanese can come and be ready to fight them if they come. They will round up the leaders, round up all. Then it will be the duty of every Indian to put forth his utmost effort—within non-violence. No source is to be left untapped; no weapon untried. This is going to be the opportunity of a lifetime."

Historians believe that Patel's speech was instrumental in electrifying nationalists, who had been skeptical of the proposed rebellion. Patel's organising work in this period is credited by historians for ensuring the success of the rebellion across India. Patel was arrested on 9 August and was imprisoned with the entire Congress Working Committee from 1942 to 1945 at the fort in Ahmednagar. Here he spun cloth, played bridge, read a large number of books, took long walks, practised gardening. He also provided emotional support to his colleagues while awaiting news and developments of the outside. Patel was deeply pained at the news of the deaths of Mahadev Desai and Kasturba Gandhi later in the year.

But Patel wrote in a letter to his daughter that he and his colleagues were experiencing "fullest peace" for having done "their duty." Even though other political parties had opposed the struggle and the British had employed ruthless means of suppression, the Quit India movement was "by far the most serious rebellion since that of 1857," as the viceroy cabled to Winston Churchill. More than one hundred thousand people were arrested and thousands killed in police firings. Strikes, protests and other revolutionary activities had broken out across India. When Patel was released on 15 June 1945 he realised that the British were preparing proposals to transfer power to Indian hands.

Independence, Integration and Role of Gandhi

In the 1946 election for the Congress presidency, Patel stepped down in favour of Nehru at the request of Gandhi. The election's importance stemmed from the fact that the elected President would lead free India's first Government. Gandhi asked all 16 states representatives and Congress to elect the right person and Sardar Patel's name was proposed by 13 states representatives out of 16, but Patel respected Gandhi's request to not be the first prime minister. As a Home Minister, Patel merged all parts of India under federal control but Jammu and Kashmir was left out because of Nehru. After the election of Nehru as the party's president, Patel began directing the Congress campaign for the general elections of the Constituent Assembly of India. In the elections, the Congress won a large majority of the elected seats, dominating the Hindu electorate. But the Muslim League led by Muhammad Ali Jinnah won a large majority of Muslim electorate seats. The League had resolved in 1940 to demand Pakistan—an independent state for Muslims—and was a fierce critic of the Congress. The Congress formed governments in all provinces save Sindh, Punjab and Bengal, where it entered into coalitions with other parties.

Cabinet Mission and Partition

When the British mission proposed two plans for transfer of power, there was considerable opposition within the Congress to both. The plan of 16 May 1946 proposed a loose federation with extensive provincial autonomy, and the "grouping" of provinces based on religious-majority. The plan of 16 June 1946 proposed the partition of India on religious lines, with over 600 princely states free to choose between independence or accession to either dominion. The League approved both plans, while the Congress flatly rejected the 16 June proposal. Gandhi criticised the 16 May proposal as being inherently divisive, but Patel, realizing that rejecting the proposal would mean that only the League would be invited to form a government, lobbied the Congress Working Committee hard to give its assent to the 16 May proposal.

Patel engaged the British envoys Sir Stafford Cripps and Lord Pethick-Lawrence and obtained an assurance that the "grouping" clause would not be given practical force, Patel converted Nehru, Rajendra Prasad and Rajagopalachari to accept the plan. When the League retracted its approval of the 16 May plan, the viceroy Lord Wavell invited the Congress to form the government. Under Nehru, who was styled the "Vice President of the Viceroy's Executive Council," Patel took charge of the departments of home affairs and information and broadcasting. He moved into a government house on 1, Aurangzeb Road in Delhi—this would be his home till his death in 1950.

Vallabhbhai Patel was one of the first Congress leaders to accept the partition of India as a solution to the rising Muslim separatist movement led by Muhammad Ali Jinnah. He had been outraged by Jinnah's Direct Action campaign, which had provoked communal violence across India and by the viceroy's vetoes of his home department's plans to stop the violence on the grounds of constitutionality. Patel severely criticised the viceroy's induction of League ministers into the government, and the revalidation of the grouping scheme by the British without Congress approval.

Although further outraged at the League's boycott of the assembly and non-acceptance of the plan of 16 May despite entering government, he was also aware that Jinnah did enjoy popular support amongst Muslims, and that an open conflict between him and the nationalists could degenerate into a Hindu-Muslim civil war of disastrous consequences. The continuation of a divided and weak central government would in Patel's mind, result in the wider fragmentation of India by encouraging more than 600 princely states towards independence. Between the months of December 1946 and January 1947, Patel worked with civil servant

V. P. Menon on the latter's suggestion for a separate dominion of Pakistan created out of Muslim-majority provinces. Communal violence in Bengal and Punjab in January and March 1947 further convinced Patel of the soundness of partition.

Patel, a fierce critic of Jinnah's demand that the Hindu-majority areas of Punjab and Bengal be included in a Muslim state, obtained the partition of those provinces, thus blocking any possibility of their inclusion in Pakistan. Patel's decisiveness on the partition of Punjab and Bengal had won him many supporters and admirers amongst the Indian public, which had tired of the League's tactics, but he was criticised by Gandhi, Nehru, secular Muslims and socialists for a perceived eagerness to do so. When Lord Louis Mountbatten formally proposed the plan on 3 June 1947, Patel gave his approval and lobbied Nehru and other Congress leaders to accept the proposal. Knowing Gandhi's deep anguish regarding proposals of partition, Patel engaged him in frank discussion in private meetings over the perceived practical unworkability of any Congress-League coalition, the rising violence and the threat of civil war. At the All India Congress Committee meeting called to vote on the proposal, Patel said:

"I fully appreciate the fears of our brothers from [the Muslim-majority areas]. Nobody likes the division of India and my heart is heavy. But the choice is between one division and many divisions. We must face facts. We cannot give way to emotionalism and sentimentality. The Working Committee has not acted out of fear. But I am afraid of one thing, that all our toil and hard work of these many years might go waste or prove unfruitful. My nine months in office has completely disillusioned me regarding the supposed merits of the Cabinet Mission Plan. Except for a few honourable exceptions, Muslim officials from the top down to the chaprasis (peons or servants) are working for the League. The communal veto given to the League in the Mission Plan would have blocked India's progress at every stage. Whether we like it or not, de facto Pakistan already exists in the Punjab and Bengal. Under the circumstances I would prefer a de jure Pakistan, which may make the League more responsible. Freedom is coming. We have 75 to 80 percent of India, which we can make strong with our own genius. The League can develop the rest of the country."

Following Gandhi's and Congress' approval of the plan, Patel represented India on the Partition Council, where he oversaw the division of public assets, and selected the Indian council of ministers with Nehru. However, neither he nor any other Indian leader had foreseen the intense violence and population transfer that would take place with partition. Patel would take the lead in organising relief and emergency supplies, establishing refugee camps and visiting the border areas with Pakistani leaders to encourage peace. Despite these efforts, the death toll is estimated at between five hundred thousand to a million people.

The estimated number of refugees in both countries exceeds 15 million. Understanding that Delhi and Punjab policemen, accused of organising attacks on Muslims, were personally affected by the tragedies of partition, Patel called out the Indian Army with South Indian regiments to restore order, imposing strict curfews and shoot-at-sight orders. Visiting the Nizamuddin Auliya Dargah area in Delhi, where thousands of Delhi Muslims feared attacks, he prayed at the shrine, visited the people and reinforced the presence of police. He suppressed from the press reports of atrocities in Pakistan against Hindus and Sikhs to prevent retaliatory violence. Establishing the Delhi Emergency Committee to restore order and organising relief efforts for refugees in the capital, Patel publicly warned officials against partiality and neglect.

When reports reached Patel that large groups of Sikhs were preparing to attack Muslim convoys heading for Pakistan, Patel hurried to Amritsar and met Sikh and Hindu leaders. Arguing that attacking helpless people was cowardly and dishonourable, Patel emphasised that Sikh actions would result in further attacks against Hindus and Sikhs in Pakistan. He assured the community leaders that if they worked to establish peace and order and guarantee the safety of Muslims, the Indian government would react forcefully to any failures of Pakistan to do the same. Additionally, Patel addressed a massive crowd of approximately 200,000 refugees who had surrounded his car after the meetings:

"Here, in this same city, the blood of Hindus, Sikhs and Muslims mingled in the bloodbath of Jallianwala Bagh. I am grieved to think that things have come to such a pass that no Muslim can go about in Amritsar and no Hindu or Sikh can even think of living in Lahore. The butchery of innocent and defenceless men, women and children does not behove brave men... I am quite certain that India's interest lies in getting all her men and women across the border and sending out all Muslims from East Punjab.

I have come to you with a specific appeal. Pledge the safety of Muslim refugees crossing the city.

Any obstacles or hindrances will only worsen the plight of our refugees who are already performing prodigious feats of endurance. If we have to fight, we must fight clean. Such a fight must await an appropriate time and conditions and you must be watchful in choosing your ground. To fight against the refugees is no fight at all. No laws of humanity or war among honourable men permit the murder of people who have sought shelter and protection. Let there be truce for three months in which both sides can exchange their refugees. This sort of truce is permitted even by laws of war. Let us take the initiative in breaking this vicious circle of attacks and counter-attacks. Hold your hands for a week and see what happens. Make way for the refugees with your own force of volunteers and let them deliver the refugees safely at our frontier. "

Following his dialogue with community leaders and his speech, no further attacks occurred against Muslim refugees, and a wider peace and order was re-established soon over the entire area. However, Patel was criticised by Nehru, secular Muslims and taxed by Gandhi over his alleged wish to see Muslims from other parts of India depart. While Patel vehemently denied such allegations, the acrimony with Maulana Azad and other secular Muslim leaders increased when Patel refused to dismiss Delhi's Sikh police commissioner, who was accused of discrimination.

Hindu and Sikh leaders also accused Patel and other leaders of not taking Pakistan sufficiently to task over the attacks on their communities there, and Muslim leaders further criticised him for allegedly neglecting the needs of Muslims leaving for Pakistan, and concentrating resources for incoming Hindu and Sikh refugees. Patel clashed with Nehru and Azad over the allocation of houses in Delhi vacated by Muslims leaving for Pakistan—Nehru and Azad desired to allocate them for displaced Muslims, while Patel argued that no government professing secularism must make such exclusions.

However, Patel was publicly defended by Gandhi and received widespread admiration and support for speaking frankly on communal issues and acting decisively and resourcefully to quell disorder and violence.

Political Integration of India

This event formed the cornerstone of Patel's popularity in post-independence era and even today, he is remembered as the man who united India. He is, in this regard, compared to Otto von Bismarck of Germany, who did the same thing in 1860s. Under the 3 June plan, more than 600 princely states were given the option of joining either India or Pakistan, or choosing independence. Indian nationalists and large segments of the public feared that if these states did not accede, most of the people and territory would be fragmented. The Congress as well as senior British officials considered Patel the best man for the task of achieving unification of the princely states with the Indian dominion.

Gandhi had said to Patel *"the problem of the States is so difficult that you alone can solve it"*. He was considered a statesman of integrity with the practical acumen and resolve to accomplish a monumental task. Patel asked V. P. Menon, a senior civil servant with whom he had worked over the partition of India, to become his right-hand as chief secretary of the States Ministry. On 6 May 1947, Patel began lobbying the princes, attempting to make them receptive towards dialogue with the future Government and trying to forestall potential conflicts. Patel used social meetings and unofficial surroundings to engage most monarchs, inviting them to lunch and tea at his home in Delhi.

At these meetings, Patel stated that there was no inherent conflict between the Congress and the princely order. Nonetheless, he stressed that the princes would need to accede to India in good faith by 15 August 1947. Patel invoked the patriotism of India's monarchs, asking them to join in the freedom of their nation and act as responsible rulers who cared about the future of their people. He persuaded the princes of 565 states of the impossibility of independence from the Indian republic, especially in the presence of growing opposition from their subjects. He proposed favourable terms for the merger, including creation of *privy purses* for the descendants of the rulers. While encouraging the rulers to act with patriotism, Patel did not rule out force, setting a deadline of 15 August 1947 for them to sign the instrument of accession document. All but three of the states willingly merged into the Indian union—only Jammu and Kashmir, Junagadh, and Hyderabad did not fall into his basket.

Junagadh was especially important to Patel, since it was in his home state of Gujarat. The Nawab had under pressure from Sir Shah Nawaz Bhutto acceded to Pakistan. It was however, quite far from Pakistan and 80% of its population was Hindu. Patel combined diplomacy with force, demanding that Pakistan annul the accession, and that the Nawab accede to India. He sent the Army to occupy three principalities of Junagadh to show his resolve. Following widespread protests and the formation of a civil government, or *Aarzi Hukumat*, both Bhutto and the Nawab fled to Karachi, and under Patel's orders, Indian Army and police units marched into the state. A plebiscite later organised produced a 99.5% vote for merger with India. In a speech at the Bahauddin College in Junagadh following the latter's take-over, Patel emphasised his feeling of urgency on Hyderabad, which he felt was more vital to India than Kashmir:

"If Hyderabad does not see the writing on the wall, it goes the way Junagadh has gone. Pakistan attempted to set off Kashmir against Junagadh. When we raised the question of settlement in a democratic way, they (Pakistan) at once told us that they would consider it if we applied that policy to Kashmir. Our reply was that we would agree to Kashmir if they agreed to Hyderabad. "

Hyderabad was the largest of the princely states, and included parts of present-day Andhra Pradesh, Karnataka, and Maharashtra states. Its ruler, the Nizam Osman Ali Khan was a Muslim, although over 80% of its people were Hindu. The Nizam sought independence or accession with Pakistan. Muslim forces loyal to Nizam, called the Razakars, under Qasim Razvi pressed the Nizam to hold out against India, while organising attacks on people on Indian soil. Even though a Standstill Agreement was signed due to the desperate efforts of Lord Mountbatten to avoid a war, the Nizam rejected deals and changed his positions. In September 1948, Patel emphasised in Cabinet meetings that India should talk no more, and reconciled Nehru and the Governor-General, Chakravarti Rajgopalachari to military action. Following preparations, Patel ordered the Indian Army to integrate Hyderabad (in his capacity as Acting Prime Minister) when Nehru was touring Europe. The action was termed Operation Polo, in which thousands of Razakar forces had been killed, but Hyderabad was comfortably secured into the Indian Union. The main aim of Mountbatten and Nehru in avoiding a forced annexation was to prevent an outbreak of Hindu-Muslim violence. Patel insisted that if Hyderabad was allowed to continue with its antics, the prestige of the Government would fall and then neither Hindus nor Muslims would feel secure in its realm. After defeating Nizam, Patel retained him as the ceremonial chief of state, and held talks with him.

Hyderabad Integration into India

Hyderabad State under Nizams

Nizams never wanted to join India rather insisted that Hyderabad should be a Third dominion. August 7 1947, observed as Join India day in Hyderabad by many leaders people of Hyderabad natually wanted the state to be integrated in India. As the Independence day for India was approaching the Nizam issued a Farman declaring his independence on 13 August 1947. Government of Hyderabad banned hoisting the National flag on August 15, 1947, many leaders wanted to carry on Join India movement in Hyderabad on the lines of Satyagraha, younger members wanted to carry on their movement on the line of quit India movement, this in very short time became a mass movement against the autocracy of Nizam. To face this challenge Nizam took many suppression actions against the people. Nizam sent a delegation to Hyderabad which made many negotiations with Mountbatten and finally agreed to enter into a Standstill agreement for 1 year and it was made in 29 November 1947 under which Indian Government would take control of Defence and External affairs of the State.

Kasim Razvi president of Ittahadul Muslimeen an Organisation established in 1927 opposed Join India Movement and announced the same in a public speech on 19 June 1947. His army was called Razakars. He was supported by Nizam as his acts were like improving the future of Nizam political power to stabilise the state of Hyderabad. After signing the Standstill agreement Razvi wanted Mir Laik Ali to be appointed as the Prime Minister for Hyderabad.

Standstill agreement was violated by Nizam. He made Indian currency not a Legal tender in his state and banned the export of gold. He appointed trade agents in London and Karachi. He made loan advances of 200 million to Pakistan. El Edroos, the commander-in-chief of Hyderabad Army visited Czechoslovakia and France to purchase military aircrafts and an attempt to purchase Goa from Portugal was made. Arms and ammuniations were smuggled into the state. K.M.Munshi was appointed as Agent-General in Hyderabad by Indian Government as per Standstill agreement. Nizam opposed this but Munshi reached Hyderabad and occupied his residence Deccan House at bolaram near Secunderabad.

After the Standstill agreement the Razakars attacks were maximised and even they attacked Bombay-Madras train. Razvi in his speeches announced the re-establishment of Islam empire in India and also made a statement that Nizam army would annex the terriroties around it. Shoebullah Khan, the young editor of Urdu journal 'Imroze' condemned the attrocities of Razvi and Razakars and he was murdered. Mir Laik Ali made a secret visit to Pakistan and met the leaders where he was advised to make an appeal to UNO. On this note Mir Laik Ali. After returning to Hyderabad he sent one delegation to UNO on 10 September headed by Moin Nawaz Jung.

Police Action on Hyderabad

In light of all the foregoing incidences Indian Government launched its Police Action on Hyderabad on 13 September 1948. The Indian Army under the command of J.N.choudhary entered Hyderabad State from five directions. This military action was named as 'Operation Polo' which was completed in five days with the surrendering of Nizam forces under El Edroos. Mir Laik Ali and Kasim Razvi were arrested, Later they escaped to Pakistan. J.N.choudhary was made Military governor of Hyderabad.

Operation Polo

The liberation of Hyderabad in September 1948 by "Hyderabad Police Action" (code-named "Operation Polo") was the operation by the Indian armed forces that ended the rule of the Nizam of Hyderabad and led to the integration of the princely state of Hyderabad into the Indian Union.

The operation was necessitated as the princely State of Hyderabad under Nizam Osman Ali Khan, Asif Jah VII, decided to not join either India or Pakistan after the partition of India. The Nisam's defiance was backed by Qasim Razvi's armed militias, known as *Razakars* and had the moral support of Pakistan,. When all attempts to persuade the Nizam to act friendly towards India failed, and wary of a hostile independent state right in the middle of India, Deputy Prime Minister Sardar Patel decided to annex the state of Hyderabad. He sent the Indian army and the Hyderabad State Forces were defeated within five days.

At that time, Hyderabad state had some 17 polo grounds, the largest number in India. Hence the name "Operation Polo".

Background

The State of Hyderabad, located over most of the Deccan Plateau in southern India, was established in 1724 by Nizam-ul-Mulk Asif Jha after the collapse of the Mughal Indian Empire. As was the case in several Indian royal states, the Nizam was a Muslim, while a majority of the subject population was Hindu. In 1798, Hyderabad became the first Indian royal state to accede to British protection under the policy of Subsidiary Alliances instituted by Arthur Wellesley. When the British finally departed from the Indian subcontinent in 1947, they offered the various princely states in the sub-continent the option of assimilating into either India or Pakistan, or staying on as an independent state.

The State of Hyderabad under the leadership of its 7th Nizam, Mir Osman Ali, was the largest and most prosperous of all princely states in India. It covered 82,698 square miles (214,190 km) of fairly homogenous territory and comprised a population of roughly 16.34 million people (as per the 1941 census) of which a majority (85%) was Hindu. Hyderabad State had its own army, as well as its own airline, telecommunication system, railway network, postal system, currency and radio broadcasting service, with a GDP larger than that of Belgium.

It was in this context that the Nizam, then the richest man in the world, desired to retain independence for his state. The Indians however, were wary of having an independent-and possibly hostile in the heart of its territory, and were determined to assimilate Hyderabad into the Indian Union, in the same manner as the other five hundred and sixty five royal states that had already acceded.

Events Preceding Hostilities

Political and Diplomatic Negotiations

The Nizam of Hyderabad initially approached the British government with a request to take on the status of an independent constitutional monarchy under the British Commonwealth of Nations. This request was however rejected.

When Indian Home Minister Sardar Vallabhai Patel requested the Hyderabad Government to sign the instrument of accession, the Nizam refused and instead declared Hyderabad as an independent nation on 15 August 1947, the same day that India became independent. Alarmed at the idea of an independent Hyderabad in the heart of Indian territory, Sardar Patel approached the governor general of India, Lord Mountbatten who advised him to resolve the issue without the use of force.

Accordingly, the Indian government offered Hyderabad a 'Standstill Agreement' which made an assurance that the status quo would be maintained and no military action would be taken. Unlike in the case of other royal states, instead of an explicit guarantee of eventual accession to India, only a guarantee stating that Hyderabad would not join Pakistan was given. Negotiations were opened through K.M. Munshi, India's envoy and agent general to Hyderabad, and the Nizam's envoys, Laik Ali and Sir Walter Monckton. Lord Mountbatten, who presided over the negotiations, offered several possible deals to the Hyderabad government which were rejected. The Hyderabadi envoys accused India of setting up armed barricades on all land routes and of attempting to economically isolate their nation. The Indians retaliated by accusing the Hyderabad government of importing arms from Pakistan. Hyderabad had given Rupees 200 million to Pakistan, and had stationed a bomber squadron there.

In June 1948, Mountbatten prepared the 'Heads of Agreement' deal which offered Hyderabad the status of an autonomous dominion nation under India. The deal called for the restriction of the regular Hyderabadi armed forces along with a disbanding of its voluntary forces. While it allowed the Nizam to continue as the executive head of the state, it called for a plebiscite along with general democratic elections to set up a constituent assembly. The Hyderabad government would continue to administer its territory as before, leaving only foreign affairs to be handled by the Indian government.

Although the plan was approved and signed by the Indians, it was rejected by the Nizam who demanded only complete independence or the status of a dominion under the British Commonwealth.

The Nizam also made unsuccessful attempts to seek the arbitration of the President Harry S. Truman of the United States of America and intervention of the United Nations.

Civil Unrest in Hyderabad

The 1941 census had estimated the population of Hyderabad to be 16.34 million, over 85% of who were Hindus and with Muslims accounting for about 12%. It was also a multilingual state consisting of peoples speaking Telugu (48.2%), Marathi (26.4%), Kannada (12.3%) and Urdu (10.3%). In spite of the overwhelming Hindu majority, Hindus were severely under-represented in government, police and the military. Of 1765 officers in the State Army, 1268 were Muslims, 421 were Hindus, and 121 others were Christians, Parsis and Sikhs. Of the officials drawing a salary between Rs.600-1200 per month, 59 were Muslims, 5 were Hindus and 38 were of other religions. The Nizam and his nobles, who were mostly Muslims, owned 40% of the total land in the State.

Even as India and Hyderabad negotiated, most of the sub-continent had been thrown into chaos as a result of communal Hindu-Muslim riots pending the imminent partition of India. Fearing a Hindu civil uprising in his own kingdom, the Nizam allowed Qasim Razvi, a close advisor, and leader of the radical Majlis-e-Ittehadul Muslimeen (MIM) Party, to set up an voluntary militia of Muslims called the 'Razakars'. The Razakars-who numbered up to 200,000 at the height of the conflict-swore to uphold Islamic domination in Hyderabad and the Deccan plateau in the face of growing public opinion amongst the majority Hindu population favouring the accession of Hyderabad into the Indian Union. As the manpower and arsenal of the Razakars grew, there was an escalation of violence between the Razakars and Hindu communities. In all, more than 150 villages (of which 70 were in Indian territory outside Hyderabad State) were pushed into violence. In Telengana, large groups of peasants, aided by the Communist Party of India revolted against local Muslim landlords, and also came into direct confrontation with the Razakars. Meanwhile, parties like the Hyderabad State Congress were involved in nonviolent protests against the Nizam's rule.

On December 4, 1947, Narayan Rao Pawar, a member of a Hindu nationalist organisation called the Arya Samaj made a failed attempt to assassinate the Nizam outside his palace.

Hyderabadi Military Preparations

The Nizam of Hyderabad had a large army with a tradition of hiring mercenary forces. These included Arabs, Rohillas, North Indian Muslims and Pathans. The State Army consisted of three armoured regiments, a horse cavalry regiment, 11 infantry battalions and artillery. These were supplemented by irregular units with horse cavalry, four infantry battalions (termed as the Saraf-e-khas, paigah, Arab and Refugee) and a garrison battalion-all forming a total of 22,000 men. This army was commanded by Major General El Edroos, an Arab. 55 per cent of the Hyderabadi army was composed of Muslims, with 1,268 Muslims in a total of 1,765 officers as of 1941.

In addition to these, there were about 200,000 irregular militia called the Razakars under the command of civilian leader Qasim Razvi. A quarter of these were armed with modern small firearms, while the rest were predominantly armed with muzzle-loaders and swords.

It is reported that the Nizam received arms supplies from Pakistan and from the Portuguese administration based in Goa. In addition, additional arms supplies were received via airdrops from an Australian arms trader Sidney Cotton.

Breakdown of Negotiations

As the Indian government received information that Hyderabad was arming itself and was preparing to ally with Pakistan in any future war with India, Sardar Patel described the idea of an independent Hyderabad as an ulcer in the heart of India-which had to removed surgically. In response, Hyderabad's prime minister Laik Ali stated "India thinks that if Pakistan attacks her, Hyderabad will stab her in the back. I am not so sure we would not." Sardar Patel responded later by stating "If you threaten us with violence, swords will be met with swords".

In Hyderabad, militia leader Qasim Razwi told a crowd of Razakars, "Death with the sword in hand, is always preferable to extinction by a mere stroke of the pen.". Razwi was later described by Indian government officials as "The Nizam's Frankenstein Monster". In response to reports that India was planning to invade Hyderabad Razwi stated, "If India attacks us I can and will create a turmoil throughout India. We will perish but India will perish also." The magazine "Time" pointed out that if India invaded

Hyderabad, the Razakars would massacre Hindus, which would lead to retaliatory massacres of Muslims across India.

Skirmish at Kodar

On September 6 an Indian police post near Chillakallu village came under heavy fire from Razakar units. The Indian Army command sent a squadron of The Poona Horse led by Abhey Singh and a company of 2/5 Gurkha Rifles to investigate who were also fired upon by the Razakars. The tanks of the Poona Horse then chased the Razakars to Kodar, in Hyderabad territory. Here they were opposed by the armoured cars of 1 Hyderabad Lancers. In a brief action the Poona Horse destroyed one armoured car and forced the surrender of the state garrison at Kodar.

Indian Military Preparations

On receiving directions from the government to seize and annex Hyderabad, the Indian army came up with the Goddard Plan (laid out by Lt. Gen E.N. Goddard, the C-in-C of the Southern Command). The plan envisaged two main thrusts-from Vijayawada in the East and Solapur in the West-while smaller units pinned down the Hyderabadi army along the border. Overall command was placed in the hands of Lt. Gen. Rajendrasinghji, DSO. The attack from Solapur was led by Major General J.N. Chaudhari and was composed of four task forces:

1. Strike Force comprising a mix of fast moving infantry, cavalry and light artillery,
2. Smash Force consisting of predominantly armoured units and artillery,
3. Kill Force composed of infantry and engineering units
4. Vir Force which comprised infantry, anti-tank and engineering units.

The attack from Vijaywada was led by Major General A.A. Rudra and comprised the 2/5 Gurkha Rifles, one squadron of the 17th (Poona) Horse, and a troop from the 19th Field Battery along with engineering and ancillary units. In addition, four infantry battalions were to neutralize and protect lines of communication. Two squadrons of Hawker Tempest aircraft were prepared for air support from the Pune base. The date for the attack was fixed as 13 September, even though General Sir Roy Bucher, the Indian chief of staff, had objected on grounds that Hyderabad would be an additional front for the Indian army after Kashmir.

Commencement of Hostilities

Day 1, September 13

The first battle was fought at Naldurg Fort on the Solapur Secundarabad Highway between a defending force of the 1st Hyderabad Infantry and the attacking force of the 7th Brigade. Using speed and surprise, the 7th Brigade managed to secure a vital bridge on the Bori river intact, following which an assault was made on the Hyderabadi positions at Naldurg by the 2nd Sikh Infantry. The bridge and road secured, an armoured column of the 1st Armoured Brigade-part of the Smash force-moved into the town of Jalkot, 8 km from Naldurg, at 0900 hours, paving the way for the Strike Force units under Lt. Col Ram Singh Commandant of 9 DOGRA (a motorised battalion) to pass through.

This armoured column reached the town of Umarge, 61 km inside Hyderabad by 1515 hours, where it quickly overpowered resistance from Razakar units defending the town. Meanwhile, another column consisting of a squadron of 3rd Cavalry, a troop from 18th King Edward's Own Cavalry, a troop from 9 Para Field Regiment, 10 Field Company Engineers, 3/2 Punjab Regiment, 2/1 Gurkha Rifles, 1 Mewar Infantry, and ancillary units attacked the town of Tuljapur, about 34 km northwest of Naldurg.

They reached Tuljapur at dawn, where they encountered resistance from a unit of the 1st Hyderabad Infantry and about 200 Razakars who fought for two hours before surrendering. Further advance towards the town of Lohara was stalled as the river had swollen. The first day on the Western front ended with the Indians inflicting heavy casualties on the Hyderabadis and capturing large tracts of territory. Amongst the captured defenders was a British mercenary who had been tasked with blowing up the bridge near Naldurg.

In the East, forces led by Lt. Gen A.A. Rudra met with fierce resistance from two armoured units of Humber armoured cars and Staghound armoured cars, but managed to reach the town of Kodar by 0830 hours. Pressing on, the force reached Mungala by the afternoon.

There were further incidents in Hospet-where the 1st Mysore assaulted and secured a sugar factory from units of Razakars and Pathans-and at Tungabhadra-where the 5/5 Gurkha attacked and secured a vital bridge from the Hyderabadi army.

Day 2, September 14

The force that had camped at Umarge proceeded to the town of Rajasur, 48 km east. As aerial reconnaissance had shown well entrenched ambush positions set up along the way, the air strikes from squadrons of Tempests were called in. These air strikes effectively cleared the route and allowed the land forces to reach and secure Rajasur by the afternoon.

The Assault force from the East was meanwhile slowed down by an anti-tank ditch and later came under heavy fire from hillside positions of the 1st Lancers and 5th Infantry 6 km from Surriapet. The positions were assaulted by the 2/5 Gurkha-veterans of the Burma Campaign-and was neutralised with the Hyderabadis taking severe casualties.

At the same time, the 3/11 Gurkha Rifles and a squadron of 8th Cavalry attacked Osmanabad and took the town after heavy street combat with the Razakars who determinedly resisted the Indians

A force under the command of Maj. Gen. D.S. Brar was tasked with capturing the city of Aurangabad. The city was attacked by six columns of infantry and cavalry, resulting in the civil administration emerging in the afternoon and offering a surrender to the Indians.

There were further incidents in Jalna where 3 Sikh, a company of 2 Jodhpur infantry and some tanks from 18 Cavalry faced stubborn resistance from Hyderabadi forces.

Day 3, September 15

Leaving a company of 3/11 Gurkhas to occupy the town of Jalna, the remainder of the force moved to Latur, and later to Mominabad where they faced action against the 3 Golconda Lancers who gave token resistance before surrendering.

At the town of Surriapet, air strikes cleared most of the Hyderabadi defences, although some Razakar units still gave resistance to the 2/5 Gurkhas who occupied the town. The retreating Hyderabadi forces destroyed the bridge at Musi to delay the Indians but failed to offer covering fire, allowing the bridge to be quickly repaired. Another incident occurred at Narkatpalli where a Razakar unit was decimated by the Indians.

Day 4, September 16

The task force under Lt. Col. Ram Singh moved towards Zahirabad at dawn, but was slowed down by a minefield, which had to be cleared. On reaching the junction of the Bidar road with the Solapur-Hyderabad City Highway, the forces encountered gunfire from ambush positions. However, leaving some of the units to handle the ambush, the bulk of the force moved on to reach 15 kilometres beyond Zahirabad by nightfall in spite of sporadic resistance along the way. Most of the resistance was from Razakar units who ambushed the Indians as they passed through urban areas. The Razakars were able to use the terrain to their advantage until the Indians brought in their 75 mm guns.

Day 5, September 17

In the early hours of September 17, the Indian army entered Bidar. Meanwhile, forces led by the 1st Armoured regiment were at the town of Chityal about 60 km from the capital city, while another column took over the town of Hingoli. By the morning of the 5th day of hostilities, it had become clear that the Hyderabad army and the Razakars had been routed on all fronts and with extremely heavy casualties. The Nizam's defeat was now imminent.

Capitulation and Surrender

Consultations with Indian Envoy

On September 16, faced with imminent defeat, the Nizam summoned the Prime Minister Mir Laik Ali and requested his resignation by the morning of the following day. The resignation was delivered along with the resignations of the entire cabinet.

On the noon of September 17, a messenger brought a personal note from the Nizam to India's Agent General to Hyderabad, K.M. Munshi summoning him to the Nizam's office at 1600 hours. At the meeting, the Nizam stated "The vultures have resigned. I don't know what to do". Munshi advised the Nizam to secure the safety of the citizens of Hyderabad by issuing appropriate orders to the Commander of the Hyderabad State Army, Major General El Edroos. This was immediately done.

Radio Broadcast of Surrender Offer

Munshi also suggested that the Nizam might make a broadcast welcoming the Police Action and withdrawing his complaint to the Security Council. Munshi explained and offered to help draft the speech.

It was the Nizam's first visit to the radio station. No red carpet was spread for him; no formalities were observed. No music, no anthem was played before or after the broadcast. The speech was in English. Nobody bothered to translate it into Urdu. After the broadcast the Nizam drove back to King Kothi Palace to brood.

The Surrender Ceremony

The surrender ceremony was fixed at 4 p.m. General Chaudhuri spoke gravely:

"I have been ordered by Lt. General Maharaj Rajendrasinhji, General Officer Commanding-in-Chief, Southern Command to take the surrender of your army".

"You have it".

"You understand that this surrender is unconditional".

"Yes, I understand".

Chaudhuri smiled and shook hands with Edroos. Then he opened his cigarette case and offered him a cigarette. Edroos proffered a lighter. Chaudhuri's team joined them. The party drove to the residence of India's Agent General. A jubilant crowd cheered the victorious general there. He waved in return and then sat down to discuss the details with Munshi, Edroos and others.

The Aftermath

"Operation Polo" resulted in moderate casualties for Indian forces, with significantly higher losses for Hyderbadi forces. Indian losses were 32 killed and 97 wounded. Among the Indian units, the Punjab Regiment had by far suffered the greatest number of casualties, with 20 of its soldiers killed in action. The losses suffered by Hyderbad state forces and Irregular forces combined were 1,863 killed, 122 wounded, and 3,558 captured. In the following weeks the state erupted in widespread communal violence. 50,000 people may have died in the reprisals that followed the invasion. Most of the violence occurred in the state's rural districts, sparking large scale migration both to the capital at Hyderabad, and to Pakistan.

The Nizam received the ceremonial post of Rajpramukh in 1950, but resigned from this office when the states were reorganized in 1956 on linguistic basis and large parts of Hyderabad state went to Bombay State. Many officials and members of the royal family fled and re-settled in Pakistan where they now live.

Hyderabad State

Hyderabad state pronunciation (help·info) was the largest princely state in the erstwhile British Indian Empire. It was located in the south-central region of the Indian subcontinent, and was ruled, from 1724 until 1948, by a hereditary Nizam. The Berar region of the state was merged with the Central Provinces of British India in 1903, to form the Central Provinces and Berar.

In 1947, at the time of the partition of India and the formation of the Union of India and the Dominion of Pakistan, the then Nizam, Osman Ali Khan, decided not to join either new nation. However, the following year, the Government of India incorporated Hyderabad into the Indian Union, using military force, in what was known as Operation Polo, led by Sardar Vallabhbhai Patel.

The Mughal Empire began to weaken during the reign of Aurangzeb's grandson, Muhammad Shah. A Mughal official, Asif Jah, treacherously defeated a rival Mughal governor to seize control of the empire's southern provinces, declaring himself Nizam-al-Mulk of Hyderabad in 1724. The Mughal emperor, under renewed attack from the Marathas, was unable to prevent it.

The Nizams patronized Islamic art, culture and literature and developed railway network in Hyderabad. Islamic Sharia law was the guiding principle of the Nizams' official machinery.

During the British Raj

The seniormost (21-gun) salute state during the period of British India, Hyderabad was an 82,000 square mile (212,000 km^2) region in the Deccan ruled by the Asif Jahi dynasty, who had the title of Nizam and was bestowed the title of His Exalted Highness by the British. The Nizam set up numerous institutions in the name of the dynasty. He set up schools, colleges, madrasas and a university that imparted education in Urdu. Inspired by the elite and prestigious Indian Civil Service he founded the Hyderabad Civil Service. The pace with which he amassed wealth made him to be the world's richest men in the 1930s, (*Time* cover story Feb. 22, 1937). Carrying a gift, called Nazrana, in accordance with one's net worth while meeting Nizam was a *de facto* necessity.

Industries in Pre-Independence Hyderabad

Various industries emerged in pre-independence Hyderabad, the major industries that were established in various parts of Hyderabad state are.

Industries in pre-Independence Hyderabad

Company	Year
Singareni Collieries	1921
Nizam Sugar Factory	1937
Allwyn Metal Works	1942
Praga Tools	1943
Sirsilk	1946
Hyderabad Asbestos	1947

After the British Raj (1947-48)

When India gained independence in 1947, the British left the choice of independence or unification up to the local rulers of the princely states. Razakars (some Muslim nobles under Nizam), wished to remain independent or consider joining Pakistan. In the case of Hyderabad however, this could not be applied as it was right in the middle of the new state of India.

Being Muslim-governed state, the Nizam wanted to join Pakistan but he was overruled by the viceroy Lord Mountbatten. As a result, the Indian Government carried out the so called "Hyderabad Police Action" against the Nizam. Code-named "Operation Polo" by the Indian military, this action by the Indian armed forces ended the rule of the Nizams of Hyderabad by the forceful incorporation of the princely state of Hyderabad into the Indian Union.

Operation Polo-Liberation Of Hyderabad.

At the time of Indiaa€™s independence, Hyderabad was the largest Indian princely state in terms of population and GNP. Its territory of 82,698 sq miles was more than that of England and Scotland put together. The 1941 census had estimated its population to be 16.34 million, over 85% of who were Hindus and with Muslims accounting for about 12%. It was also a multilingual state consisting of peoples speaking Telugu (48.2%), Marathi (26.4%), Kannada (12.3%) and Urdu (10.3%).

Its diversity and broad heritage could be seen in the historical monuments at Ajanta, Ellora and Daulatabad in Marathawada, Bijapur, Bidar, Gulbarga, Anegondi and Kampili in Karnataka, and Warangal and Nagarjunakonda in Telangana. Hyderabad state had a domestic product greater than that of Belgium. Its ruler, the Nizam was the richest man in the world at that time. He had over eleven thousand servants and famously used the 185-carat Jacob Diamond as a paperweight.

Hyderabad, not only had its own Army, but also had its own Railways, Airline, Postal Service, Radio Broadcasting network and currency. The Nizam and his court ruled over it with the British Resident keeping a close and watchful eye over everything. The British Army also had a permanent garrison, just in case the a€œfaithful ally of the King Emperor was found lacking in faith. The Nizam was the first to sign the Subsidiary Alliance with the British and had remained steadfastly loyal to the empire. Even during the Mutiny of 1857, he managed to keep his state free from uprisings.

As can be imagined it was a Muslim dominated state. Typically in 1911, 70% of the police, 55% of the army and 26% of the public administration were Muslims. In 1941 a report on the Civil Service revealed that of the 1765 officers, 1268 were Muslims, 421 were Hindus, and 121 others, presumably British, Christians, Parsis and Sikhs. Of the officials drawing a pay between Rs.600—1200 pm, 59 were Muslims, 38 were others, and a mere 5 were Hindus. The Nizam and his nobles, who were mostly Muslims, owned 40% of the total land in the kingdom.

In 1947 the infant Republic of India offered a simple choice to the erstwhile princely states that thronged the length and breadth of the nation. They were free to join the Union or declare independence themselves. A brief glance at the Indian map today is enough to show that the latter was not a popular choice among the rajahs and nizams. Today not a single princely state remains independent. They, all five hundred and sixty-five of them, were merged into the Republic under the masterful and rather persuasive supervision of Sardar Vallabhai Patel, the man of iron of India.

Some of these states did not go down without a fight however. Travancore, Jodhpur and Indore signed up after protracted political wrangling. Conflict situation arose in both Junagadh and Kashmir. The latter continues to have repercussions in modern Indian politics. But the most violent of all the accession operations was the one that occurred between the 12th and 18th of September, 1948. The invasion of the State of Hyderabad by the Indian Army which lasted less than a week was codenamed 'Operation Polo'.

The Nizam encouraged the Razakars, a fanatical relegious band under Kasim Rizwi who terrorized the Hindus of the state through organised massacres, rape, loot and arson while also conducting raids across the border. The Nizam had dreams of hoisting the Asafia flag on red fort.

In Hyderabad, the popular agitation against Nizam was gaining strength with the Congress, RSS and other organisations actively participating in both armed and unarmed struggle against the Razakars and Nizam's atrocities. In Hyderabad proper, the entire Telugu press and a section of Urdu press was also vocal against the razakars and majlis ittaihadul musalmeen. Shoaibullah khan was one of those patriotic Urdu press men who fearlessly wrote against the Nizam and razakars. He was brutally murdered as a consequence of his boldness.

The Nizam had advanced Rs 20 crore as help to Pakistan and stationed a bomber plane there. In fact, the then British Chief of Indian Army, Sir Rob Lockhart, had told Nehru that Pakistan would invade India and Hyderabad too had built up a strong military forces under his pal Gen. El Droos so that it could resist Indian forces for many months. Nizam also made unsuccessful attempts at making President Truman and UNO to back his scheme of independence with the support of Pakistan.

But nothing would stop the iron will of the indomitable Sardar Vallabhbhai Patel who was then the Home Minister of India. Despite heavy opposition from his own cabinet colleagues and even Pandit Nehru at times, he decided that Hyderabad had to be liberated at whatever cost to ensure safety of the innocent millions being massacred in Hyderabad. He considered an independent Hyderabad state as an ulcer in the heart of India which had to be removed, even surgically. He is said to have told the Hyderabad Prime minister who threatened India with dire consequences if Hyderabad was attacked-'don' threaten us with violence, swords will be met with swords'.

As long as Lord Mountbatten was in India he did not allow armed intervention in Hyderabad. But once he left, and the Nizam wanted an agreement with India, Sardar Vallabhbhai Patel told publicly, 'agreement has gone to England' Twice he had to postpone the date fixed for the operation. He finally fixed September 13th 1948 as the date of launching operation. And he stuck to the date even as he faced strong resistance even from his colleagues in the Govt. as Jinnah had expired the previous evening.

On the morning of September 13, 1948 five infantry battalions and an armoured regiment of the battle hardened Indian Army under the command of Maj Gen J N Chaudhry entered the princely state of Hyderabad, over a year after Independence and after the patience of the new Indian Union was tested beyond endurance. The mighty army of the Nizam surrendered by 18th September, 1948. Indian army suffered hardly a dozen casualties while over 2000 nizam troops and razaakars were killed and more were captured. Hyderabad was liberated and Gen .J.N. Chowdhury was appointed military governor of Hyderabad.

That was Operation Polo, or the Police Action as it is popularly called. It liberated Hyderabad from the tyrannical rule of the Nizam and merged it with the mainland India.

I dread to think that I would have been born in the state of Hyderabad and not India. And it is because of the will of one man, the great Sardar and the might of Indian Army and Air force that today I proudly say I am an Indian and a true Hyderabadi.

The entire matter was handled so efficiently by him and the operation itself was finished by the army so swiftly that world hardly had time to react. By the time Pakistan and other allies woke up, the issue was presented as a fait accompli. No serious discussion ever took place in any international forum about the accession of either Hyderabad or Junagadh as has been the case with Kashmir.

Patel treated the Nizam, whose Razakar lashkars were dreaming of conquering Red Fort, reasonably generously. He was kept as Rajpramukh of the State till the reorganisation of States in 1956. Ironically, this courtesy was not extended to Maharaja Hari Singh who had not fought India like the Nizam, but had merged the State willingly. He was forced to abdicate in June, 1949, and leave the State permanently and reside in Bombay at Sheikh Abdullah's pressure, despite promises of fair treatment to him prior to accession. Many attribute this to the Pandit Nehru-

Abdulla axis which prevented Maharaja Hari Singh from acceding to India, though he was willing.

Indian Integration of Junagadh

Junagadh was a former princely state of India, located in what is now Gujarat, outside but under the suzerainty of British India.

In the independence and partition of India and Pakistan of 1947, the 565 princely states were given a choice of whether to join India or Pakistan or to remain independent.

The Muslim Nawab of Junagadh, Muhammad Mahabat Khanji III, whose ancestors had ruled Junagadh and small principalities for some two hundred years, decided that Junagadh should become part of Pakistan, much to the displeasure of the people of the state, an overwhelming majority of whom were Hindus.

The Nawab acceded to the Dominion of Pakistan on 15 August 1947. Pakistan accepted this on 13 September. When Pakistan confirmed the acceptance of the accession in September, the Government of India was outraged that Muhammad Ali Jinnah could accept the accession of Junagadh despite his argument that Hindus and Muslims could not live as one nation. Sardar Vallabhbhai Patel believed that if Junagadh was permitted to go to Pakistan, it would exacerbate the communal tension already simmering in Gujarat.

The princely state was surrounded on all three sides by India, with an outlet to the Arabian Sea. The unsettled conditions in Junagadh had led to a cessation of all trade with India and the food position became precarious. The region was in crisis and the Nawab was forced to flee to Karachi with his family fearing for his life and established a provisional government with his followers.

Patel offered Pakistan time to void the accession and to hold a plebiscite in Junagadh. Samaldas Gandhi formed a government-in-exile, the *Aarzi Hukumat* (in Urdu:*Aarzi*: Temporary, *Hukumat*: Government) of the people of Junagadh. Eventually, Patel ordered the forcible annexation of Junagadh's three principalities. Junagadh's state government, facing financial collapse and lacking forces with which to resist Indian force, invited the Government of India to take control. A plebiscite was conducted in December, in which approximately 99% of the people chose India over Pakistan.

Background

After the announcement by the last Viceroy of India, Lord Mountbatten, on 3 June 1947, of the intention to partition British India, the British parliament passed the Indian Independence Act 1947 on 11 July 1947, as a result, the native states were left with these choices: to remain independent or to accede to either of the two new dominions, the Union of India or the Dominion of Pakistan.

The Indian Government made efforts to persuade Nawab Sahab of Junagadh to accede to India, but he remained firm. The Indian minister V. P. Menon came to request an accession to India, threatening consequences in case of denial. The Nawab however decided to accede to Pakistan, and an announcement to this effect was made in the gazette of Junagadh (*Dastrural Amal Sarkar Junagadh*) on 15 August 1947 as follows:

Published by Authority

Friday 15th August, 1997

Extra Ordinary

The following communique has been published by Junagadh State.

The Government of Junagadh has during the last few weeks been faced with the problem of making its choice between accession to the Dominion of India and accession to the Dominion of Pakistan. It has had to take into very careful consideration every aspect of this problem. Its main preoccupation has been to adopt a course that would in the long run make the largest contribution towards the permanent welfare and prosperity of the people of Junagadh and help to preserve the integrity of the State and to safeguard its independence and autonomy over the largest possible field. After anxious consideration and careful balancing of all factors the Government of the State has decided to accede to Pakistan and hereby announces its decision to that effect. The State is confident that its decision will be welcomed by all loyal subjects of the State who have its real welfare and prosperity at heart.

Now that the Dominions of India and Pakistan have been admitted to the fellowship of independence sovereign State on an equal footing, it is to be hoped that vast avenue of the progress will be thrown open to the people, of the both Dominions in every walk of life and that the peoples of both Dominions will combine to derive the fullest benefit from the opportunities which will now be made available to them in peace and cooperation with each other. The Government of Junagadh will continue to make every endeavour to secure for all classes of the people of Junagadh without distinction in fullest measure the blessing of security, peace and prosperity and is confident that in the furtherance of this object, it will receive the fullest cooperation from all classes and sections of the subjects of His Highness the Nawab Saheb Bahadur.

Instrument of Accession

Immediately after making the announcement in *Dastrural Amal Sarkar Junagadh,* the Jungadh government communicated to Pakistan its wish to accede, and a delegation headed by Ismail was sent to Karachi with the Instrument of Accession signed by the Nawab. The Constitutional Assembly of Pakistan considered the proposal in detail and approved it. The Quaid-e-Azam, Muhammad Ali Jinnah, as Governor General of Pakistan, counter-signed the Instrument of Accession on 15 September 1947.

The Instrument of Accession dated 15 September 1947 reads as follows:

Instrument of Accession Dated 15th September, 1947 Between Junagadh & Pakistan

WHEREAS the Indian Independence Act, 1947 provides that as from the fifteenth day of August, 1947, there shall be set up an independent Dominion known as Pakistan and that the Government of India Act, 1935, shall, with such omissions, additions, adaptations and modifications as the Governor General may order, specify, be applicable to the dominion of Pakistan.

AND WHEREAS the Government of India Act, 1935, as so adopted by the Governor General provides that an Indian State may accede to the Dominion of Pakistan by an Instrument of Accession executed by the Ruler thereof, NOW THEREFORE

I, Mohobat Khan Ruler of Junagadh State, in exercise of my sovereignty in and over my said State do hereby execute this my instrument of Accession, and

1. I hereby declare that I accede to Dominion of Pakistan with the intent that the Governor General of Pakistan, the

Dominion Legislature, the Supreme Court and any other Dominion shall by virtue of this my instrument of Accession, but subject always to the terms thereof, and for the purposes only of the Dominion, exercise in relation to the State of Jungadh (hereinafter referred to as "this State") such functions as may be vested in them by or under the Government of India Act, 1935, as in force in the Dominion of Pakistan on the 15th day of August, 1947 (which Act as so in force is hereinafter referred as "the Act").

2. I, hereby assume the obligation of ensuring that due effect is given to the provisions of the Act within this state so far as they are applicable therein by virtue of t his my instrument of Accession.
3. I accept the matters specified in the Schedule hereto as the matters with respect to which the Dominion Legislature may make laws for this State.
4. I hereby declare that I accede to the Dominion of Pakistan on the assurance that if an agreement is made between the Governor General and the Ruler of this State whereby any functions in relation to the administration in this state of any law of the Dominion Legislature shall be exercised by the Ruler of this State, then any such agreement shall be construed and have effect accordingly.
5. Nothing in the Instrument shall empower the Dominion Legislature to make any law for this State authorizing the compulsory acquisition of land for any purpose, but I hereby undertake that should the Dominion for the purpose of a Dominion law which applies in this State deem it necessary to acquire and land, I will at their request acquire the land at their expense or if the land belongs to me transfer it to them on such terms as may be agreed, or, in default of agreement determined by an arbitrator to be appointed by the Chief Justice of Pakistan.
6. The terms of this my instrument of Accession shall not be varied by any amendment of the Act or of the Indian Independence Act, 1947, unless such amendment is accepted by me by an Instrument supplementary to this Instrument.

7. Nothing in this Instrument shall be deemed to commit me in any way to acceptance of any future Constitution of Pakistan or to fetter my discretion to enter into arrangements with the Government of Pakistan under any such future Constitution.
8. Nothing in this Instrument effects the continuance of my sovereignty in and over this state, or, save as provided by or sovereignty in and over this state, or, save as provided by or under this Instrument, the exercise of any powers, authority and rights now enjoyed by me as Ruler of this State of the validity of any law at present in force in this State.
9. I hereby declare that I execute this Instrument on behalf of this State and that any reference in this Instrument to me or to the Ruler of the State is to be construed as including a reference to my heirs and successors.

Given under my hand this Fourteenth day of September, Nineteen Hundred and forty-seven.

[Signed] Mahabat Khan, Ruler of Junagadh

This was countersigned:

I do hereby accept this Instrument of Accession, Date this Fifteenth day of September, Nineteen Hundred and forty-seven.

[Signed] M. A. Jinnah

Governor General of Pakistan

This was notified in the *Gazette of Pakistan* and *Dasturul Amal*, the Gazette of Junagadh, on that date.

The Instrument of Accession provided for the right of Pakistan legislature to legislate in the areas of Defence and Communication, as well as others.

Although the territory of Junagadh was geographically not adjoining the existing Pakistan, it had a link by sea through the Verawal Port of Junagadh.

Menon's Reaction

V. P. Menon, the Secretary of the States department of the Government of India, travelled to Junagadh on 17 September 1947, and met Sir Shah Nawaz Bhutto, the dewan (or Chief Minister) of Junagadh. Menon said he had brought a message from the

Indian Government and wished to deliver it to the Nawab in person. Bhutto said he could not arrange a meeting with the Nawab as he was not feeling well. Menon expressed displeasure, but conveyed the message of the Indian Government to Bhutto, insisting that Junagadh should withdraw its accession to Pakistan. Bhutto told Menon that the accession was now complete and that according to international law only the Government of Pakistan was responsible.

Menon went to Bombay and met Saamar Das Gandhi, a journalist of Rajkot who was related to Mohandas Gandhi, and others, and unfolded the scheme of "Arziee Hukumat" (Provisional Government).

On 24 September 1947, Mohandas K. Gandhi condemned the action of the Junagadh government in a prayer meeting held at Delhi.

Provisional Government (Aarzee Hukumat)

On 25 September 1947, a meeting was held in the Madhav Garden of Mumbai, announcing the formation of "Arzee Hukumat" or a provisional government of Junagarh. Saamar Das Gandhi was nominated as the President of the Provisional Government and some of his colleagues were declared as ministers with various portfolios and took oath of their offices. Saamar Das Gandhi was a nephew of Mahatma Gandhi and was not a resident of Junagadh State. The ministers of the provisional government proceeded to Rajkot and occupied Junagadh House on 27 September.

In the meanwhile, there were exchanges between the governments of India and Pakistan. Pakistan told the Indian Government that the accession was in accordance with the Scheme of Independence announced by the outgoing British and that Junagadh was now part of Pakistan. While this exchange of correspondence was going on, Indian forces encircled Junagadh and stopped the movement of goods, transport and postal articles.

As a part of the preparation for occupation of the Junagadh, a "Kathiawar Defence Force" was formed by the Government of India with Brigadier Guru Dayal Singh as Commanding Officer and headquarters in Rajkot. Three warships were anchored at the port of Porbandar. A squadron of eight Tempest aircraft was stationed at Rajkot and additional companies of Armed Forces were deployed at Rajkot. The Indian aircraft started to fly over

Junagadh at low heights. Scattered attacks on villages and towns of Junagadh by the forces of the provisional government caused some damage to life and property of Muslims. In view of worsening situation, the Nawab and his family left Junagadh and arrived in Karachi on 25 October 1947.

On 27 October 1947, Bhutto, as Chief Minister of Junagadh, wrote a letter to Jinnah explaining the critical situation of which the State government. As the situation worsened, he wrote again on 28 October 1947 to Ikramullah, Secretary of the Pakistan Ministry of Foreign Affairs, seeking help and directions. There was no response from the Government of Pakistan.

When all hopes for assistance from Pakistan were lost, Bhutto wrote by telegram on 1 November 1947 to Nawab Saheb at Karachi, explaining the situation and the danger to life and property, considering an armed attack was imminent. In a return telegram, the Nawab authorised Bhutto to act in the best interests of the Muslim population of Junagadh.

A meeting of the Junagadh State Council was called on 5 November to discuss the critical situation. The Council authorised Bhutto to take appropriate action. He sent Captain Harvey Johnson, a senior member of the Council of Ministers, to Rajkot to meet Indian officials. Instead of meeting Indian officials, Johnson met those of the provisional government and brought back threats of consequences if Junagadh did not surrender to the provisional government.

Another meeting of the Junagadh State Council was convened on 7 November, and some prominent citizens of Junagadh state were also invited. The meeting continued till 3 o'clock in the morning and decided that instead of surrendering to the "Provisional Government", the Indian Government should be requested to take over the administration of Junagadh to protect the lives of its citizens, which were being threatened by Provisional Government forces.

On 8 November, Bhutto sent a letter to Nilam Butch, Provincial Head of the Indian Government in Rajkot, requesting him to help to restore law and order in Junagadh to prevent bloodshed. Harvey Johnson took the message to Rajkot. The head of the Indian administration telephoned V. P. Menon in Delhi and read out the letter. Menon immediately rushed to see Jawaharlal Nehru and explained the situation. After consultation with other ministers and V. B. Patel, the home minister, a formal order was drafted and a notification issued announcing the take-over of Junagadh at the request of its Chief Minister. The notification promised a referendum in due course.

Bhutto left Junagadh for Karachi on the night of 8 November 1947. On 9 November, the Indian Air Force flew several sorties at low level over Junagadh.

Entry of Indian Forces

Soon columns of Indian tanks and other vehicles carrying Indian soldiers entered Junagadh state. At 6 P. M. on 9 November, Captain Harvey Johnson and Chief Secretary Gheewala, a civil servant of Junagadh state, formally handed over the charge of the State to the Indian Government.

On the same day, Nehru sent a telegram to Liaquat Ali Khan about the Indian take-over of Junagadh. Khan sent a return telegram to Nehru stating that Junagadh was Pakistani territory, and nobody except the Pakistan government was authorised to invite anybody to Junagadh. He also accused the Indian Government of naked aggression on Pakistan's territory and of violating international law. The Government of Pakistan strongly opposed the Indian occupation. Nehru wrote

In view of special circumstances pointed out by Junagadh Dewan that is the Prime Minister of Junagadh – our Regional Commissioner at Rajkot has taken temporarily charge of Junagadh administration. This has been done to avoid disorder and resulting chaos. We have, however, no desire to continue this arrangement and wish to find a speedy solution in accordance with the wishes of the people of Junagadh. We have pointed out to you previously that final decision should be made by means of referendum or plebiscite. We would be glad to discuss this question and allied matters affecting Junagadh with representatives of your Government at the earliest possible moment convenient to you. We propose to invite Nawab of Junagadh to send his representatives to this conference.

The Government of Pakistan protested, saying that the accession of the state to Pakistan was already accepted. In reply to the above telegram, the Prime Minister of Pakistan sent the following:

Your telegram informing that your Government had taken charge of Junagadh was received by me on November 10, 1947. Your action in taking over State Administration and sending Indian troops to state without any authority from Pakistan Government and indeed without our knowledge, is a clear violation of Pakistan territory and breach of International law. Indian Government's activities on accession of Junagadh to Pakistan have all been directed to force the State to renounce accession and all kinds of weapons have been used by you to achieve this end. We consider your action in taking charge of Junagadh Administration and sending Indian troops to occupy Junagadh to be a direct act of hostility against Pakistan Dominion. We demand that you should immediately withdraw your forces, and relinquish charge of administration to the rightful ruler and stop people of Union of India from invading Junagadh and committing acts of violence.

This was the followed by a Press Statement made by the Prime Minister of Pakistan. It was communicated to Prime Minister of India on November 16, 1947 and read as follows:

Inspite of the gravest provocation, we have refrained from any action which should result in armed conflict. We could with full justification and legal right could have sent our forces to Junagadh but at no time since the accession of state, was a single soldier sent by us to Junagadh and our advice throughout to the State Authorities was to exercise the greatest restraint. Manavadar, another State which had acceded to Pakistan and Mangrol and Babariawad have also been occupied by Indian troops.

Immediately after the take-over of the state, all rebel Muslim officials of the state were put behind the bars. They included Ismail Abrehani, a senior minister in the Junagadh government, who had taken the instrument of Accession to the Quaid-e-Azam for his signature. Abrehani refused to leave Junagadh, even when he was offered in jail the option of going to Pakistan, saying that despite its occupation Junagadh was part of Pakistan according to international law and he preferred to remain. He stayed and later died in Junagadh.

Plebiscite

A plebiscite was held on 20 February 1948, in which all but 91 out of 190,870 who voted (from an electorate of 201,457) voted to join India.

Later Arrangements

Junagadh became part of the Indian state of Saurashtra until November 1, 1956, when Saurashtra became part of Bombay state. Bombay state was split into the linguistic states of Gujarat and Maharashtra in 1960, and Junagadh is now one of the modern districts of Saurasthra in Gujarat.

Samaldas Gandhi

Samaldas Gandhi was an Indian freedom fighter who headed the *Aarzi Hukumat* or *Temporary Government* of the erstwhile princely state of Junagadh.

Early Life

Samaldas was a relative and close follower of Mahatma Gandhi, the leader of the Indian independence movement.

Integration of Junagadh into India

When the Nawab of Junagadh acceded his state to Pakistan in 1947, Samaldas headed a government-in-exile created by citizens of Junagadh to reflect the wishes of its majority population who wished the state to become part of India instead.

When Indian forces entered Junagadh and its principalities, Mangrol and Manavadar, at the invitation of the Nawab's dewan, Sir Shah Nawaz Bhutto, Samaldas was invited to accept the reins of the state but deferred to the Government of India.

Commemoration

Samaldas Gandhi is widely remembered in Junagadh and the state of Gujarat today as a hero and patriot. There are several schools, public foundations and hospitals named after him.

Shah Nawaz Bhutto

Sir Shah Nawaz Bhutto, CIE, OBE, OBI (1888-1957) was a politician of a Rajput clan hailing from Larkana in Sindh province of British India, which is now part of Pakistan.

Early Life

Bhutto, the son of Ghulam Murtaza Bhutto, was born into a Rajput family that had accepted Islam. The father was impressed with western values, so he decided to send his son, Shah Nawaz, to the United Kingdom for his higher education.

Career

On his return to South Asia, then under British colonial rule, Shah Nawaz Bhutto joined the service of the Nawab of Junagadh, who was much impressed by his education and talents, and he ultimately rose to become the Dewan, or prime minister, of Junagadh.

In 1934, with G. M. Sayed, Bhutto founded the Sindh Peoples Party.

The British appointed him a Commander of the Order of the Indian Empire and an Officer of the Order of the British Empire.

At the time of the partition of British India in 1947, the princely states were left by the British to decide whether to accede to one of the newly independent states of India or Pakistan or to remain outside them.

Bhutto, as Dewan of Junagadh, claimed to have persuaded the Nawab to decide in favour of his state's accession to India, but the Nawab decided in favour of Pakistan, although this decision was soon defeated by Indian intervention. However there is no documentary proof of Bhutto's advice. Some commentators suggest that he gave the opposite advice to the Nawab.

After Junagadh was focibly made to become part of India, Bhutto moved with his family to Larkana District in Sindh, where land given to him for his services had made him one of the wealthiest and most influential landowners in Sindh.

Bhutto was a good friend of Governor General (later President) Iskander Mirza, who was a regular guest for the annual hunt in Larkana, staying at the Bhutto family home, Al-Murtaza. In the winter of 1955-1956, Mirza brought General Ayub Khan with him to Larkana for the hunt.

Family

Bhutto was a first cousin of Wahid Baksh Bhutto, who in 1924 was made a sardar and in 1926 was elected to the Imperial Legislative Assembly from Sindh, a constituency of the Bombay Presidency, becoming the first member of the Bhuttho family to be elected to public office.

Bhutto was married to Khursheed Begum, formerly Lakhi Bai, who was of a modest Hindu family. She converted from Hinduism to Islam before her marriage. Her brothers remained Hindu and eventually migrated to India.

Their children included Zulfikar Ali Bhutto, the first elected Prime Minister of Pakistan, and a daughter called Mumtaz, who married Brigadier Muhammad Mustafa Khan Bahadur of the Sidi clan.

Their first child, Sikandar, died from pneumonia at the age of seven in 1914, and their second child, Imdad Ali, died of cirrhosis at the age of thirty-nine in 1953. Their son Zulfikar Ali was born in his parents' residence near Larkana, and was their third child.

3

National Integration of India

The euphoria of independence was short-lived as partition brought disastrous consequences for India in the wake of communal conflict. Partition unleashed untold misery and loss of lives and property as millions of Hindu and Muslim refugees fled either Pakistan or India. Both nations were also caught up in a number of conflicts involving the allocation of assets, demarcation of boundaries, equitable sharing of water resources, and control over Kashmir. At the same time, Indian leaders were faced with the stupendous task of national integration and economic development.

When the British relinquished their claims to paramountcy, the 562 independent princely states were given the option to join either of the two nations. A few princely states readily joined Pakistan, but the rest—except Hyderabad (the largest of the princely states with 132,000 square kilometers and a population of more than 14 million), Jammu and Kashmir (with 3 million inhabitants), and Junagadh (with a population of 545,000)—merged with India. India successfully annexed Hyderabad and Junagadh after "police actions" and promises of privileges to the rulers.

The Hindu maharajah of predominantly Muslim Jammu and Kashmir remained uncommitted until armed tribesmen and regular troops from Pakistan infiltrated his domain, inducing him to sign the Instrument of Accession to India on October 27, 1947. Pakistan refused to accept the legality of the accession, and, as a result, war broke out. Kashmir remains a source of friction between the neighbours. The assassination of Mahatma Gandhi on January 30, 1948, in New Delhi, by a Hindu extremist opposed to Gandhi's openness to Muslims ended the tenuous celebration of independence and deepened the hatred and mutual suspicion in

Hindu-Muslim relations. Economic backwardness was one of the serious challenges that India faced at independence. Under three successive five-year plans, inaugurated between 1951 and 1964 under Nehru's leadership, India produced increasing amounts of food. Although food production did not allow self-sufficiency until fiscal year 1984, India has emerged as the nation with the seventh largest gross national product in the world.

Linguistic regionalism eventually reached a crisis stage and undermined the Congress' attempts at nation building. Whereas in the early 1920s, the Congress had deemed that the use of regional vernaculars in education and administration would facilitate the governance of the country, partition made the leaders, especially Nehru, realize how quickly such provincial or subnational interests would dismantle India's fragile unity.

However, in the face of widespread agitation for linguistic separation of states, beginning with the Telangana Movement in 1953, in 1956 Nehru reluctantly accepted the recommendations of the States Reorganisation Commission, and the number of states grew by reorganization along linguistic lines. The states became the loci for democratization of political processes at district levels, for expression of regional culture and popular demands against a national culture and unity, for economic development at strategic localities in the rural areas, and for proliferation of opposition parties that ended the possibility of a pan-Indian two-party system. LOC data

Political Integration of India

The political integration of India established a united nation for the first time in centuries from a plethora of princely states, colonial provinces and possessions. Despite partition, a new India united peoples of various geographic, economic, ethnic, linguistic and religious backgrounds. The process began in 1947, with the unification of 565 princely states through a critical series of political campaigns, sensitive diplomacy and military conflicts. India was transformed after independence through political upheaval and ethnic discontent, and continues to evolve as a federal republic natural to its diversity. The process is defined by sensitive religious conflicts between Hindus and Muslims, diverse ethnic populations, as well as by geo-political rivalry and military conflicts with Pakistan and China.

When the Indian independence movement succeeded in ending the British Raj on August 15, 1947, India's leaders faced the prospect of inheriting a nation fragmented between medieval-era kingdoms and provinces organised by colonial powers. Sardar Vallabhbhai Patel, one of India's most respected freedom fighters, as the new Minister of Home Affairs was the man responsible for employing political negotiations backed with the option (and the use) of military force to ensure the primacy of the Central government and of the Constitution then being drafted.

India's constitution pronounced it a *Union of States*, exemplifying a federal system with a strong central government. Over the course of the two decades following Independence the Governement of India reclaimed the possessions of the French Empire and Portugal. But the trend changed as popular movements arose for the recognition of regional languages, and attention for the special issues of diverse regions. A backlash ensued against *centralization* — the lack of attention and respect for regional issues resulted in cultural alienation and violent separatism. The Central government attempted to balance the use of force on separatist extremists with the creation of new States in order to reduce the pressures on the Indian State. The map has been redrawn, as the nature of the federation transforms. Today, the Republic of India is a Union of 28 states and 7 territories.

British India

British colonization of the Indian subcontinent began in the early 18th century. By the mid-19th century, most of the subcontinent was under British rule. With the arrival of Lord Mountbatten (the former Lord Louis Mountbatten later created Viscount Mountbatten of Burma, then promoted to Earl) as the Viceroy of India in early 1947, the British government under Prime Minister Clement Attlee made a clear indication that the independence of India was imminent. India's top political parties, the Indian National Congress and the All India Muslim League were both negotiating the impending transfer of power as well as the make-up of the new Indian government. To this end, elections were held for the Constituent Assembly of India. In June 1947, the Congress and the League agreed to the planned partition of British India into two independent British Commonwealth dominions: India and Pakistan. Burma had been separated from British India in 1937 and it became independent along with Ceylon (never a part of British India) in 1948.

Without the princely states, the Dominion of India would comprise the provinces of Bombay Presidency, Madras Presidency, the United Provinces of Agra and Oudh, the Central Provinces and Berar, Assam, Orissa, Bihar, and the chief commissioners' provinces of Coorg, Ajmer-Merwara, Panth-Piploda, and Delhi. The North West Frontier Province, Sindh, and the chief commissioners' province of Baluchistan would go to Pakistan. The provinces of Bengal and Punjab had been partitioned in 1946, with India retaining West Bengal and East Punjab, the Hindu-majority portions of the larger provinces. West Punjab and East Bengal were heavily Muslim, and went to Pakistan. The Andaman and Nicobar Islands and the Lakshadweep Islands would be turned over to the control of India.

The States

There were between 570 and 600 princely states which enjoyed special recognition by and relationship with the British Raj. The British government announced in the Indian Independence Act 1947 that with the transfer of power on August 15, 1947, all of these states would be freed of their obligations to the British Empire, and thus would be free to join either India or Pakistan, or to choose to become independent. The kingdom of Nepal was an independent treaty ally, and became a fully sovereign nation. The kingdom of Bhutan would dissolve its protectorate relationship similarly, but via treaty in 1949, India would become the guarantor of its security. The kingdom of Sikkim became a protectorate of India. Apart from a few which were geographically unalienable from Pakistan, approximately 565 princely states were clearly linked to India, the largest nation.

The largest of them included Hyderabad and Kashmir, while 222 states existed in the Kathiawar peninsula alone. The states comprised more than half of the territory of India and a large proportion of its population. It was believed that without a single federal structure India would be susceptible to political, military and social conflicts. The British had taken control of India piecemeal and over the course of a century; most of the states had signed different treaties at different times with the British East India Company and the British Crown, giving the British Raj varying degrees of control over foreign, interstate relations and defence. Indian monarchs accepted the suzerainty of Britain in India, paid tribute and allowed British authorities to collect taxes and appropriate finances, and in many cases, manage the affairs of governance via the Raj's Political Department. The princes were represented in the Imperial Legislative Council and the Chamber of Princes, and under law enjoyed relationships described as that of allies, not subordinates. Thus the princes maintained a channel of influence with the British Raj.

Process of Accession

The states of Gwalior, Bikaner, Patiala and Baroda were the first to join India on April 28, 1947. Others were wary, distrusting a democratic government led by revolutionaries of uncertain, and possibly radical views, and fearful of losing their influence as rulers. Travancore and Hyderabad announced their desire for independence while the Nawab of Bhopal, Hamidullah Khan, expressed his desire to either negotiate with Pakistan or seek independence.

The Nawab was a powerful influence on a number of princes, as he was the former chancellor of the *Chamber of Princes.* In addition, Jodhpur, Indore and Jaisalmer conducted a dialogue with Muhammad Ali Jinnah, the slated Governor-General of Pakistan, to discuss terms for a possible accession to it. While this surprised many in both India and Pakistan, neither party could ultimately ignore the fact that these kingdoms were Hindu-majority, which rendered their membership in overwhelmingly Muslim Pakistan untenable.

Sardar Vallabhbhai Patel was the Minister for Home and States Affairs, and was given the explicit responsibility of welding a united and strategically secure India in time for the transfer of power. Patel was considered the best man for the task by the Congress Party, as well as Lord Mountbatten and senior British officials. Mahatma Gandhi had, in fact, said to Patel *"the problem of the States is so difficult that you alone can solve it"*. He was recognised by the Princes and parliamentarians alike to be a man of integrity; and, in addition, he was believed to have the practical acumen and resolve to accomplish a monumental task. Patel asked V. P. Menon, a senior civil servant with whom he had worked over the partition of India, to become the Secretary in charge of the Home and States

Ministry, as it then was. Patel's admirers would later call him the *Iron Man of India* for his decisive actions at this time.

Instrument of Accession

Sardar Patel and V.P. Menon devised a formula to propose to the monarchs. The Instrument of Accession was the official treaty to be signed between the Government of India or the Government of Pakistan and the accession candidates. According to the basic tenets of the treaty, the Government of India would control only foreign affairs, defence and communications, leaving all internal issues to be administered by the states. On July 5, 1947, the official policy of the Government of India was released, and stated:

"We ask no more of the States than accession on these three subjects in which the common interests of the country are involved. In other matters we would scrupulously respect their autonomous existence. This country... is the proud heritage of the people who inhabit it. It is an accident that some live in the States and some in British India... None can segregate us into segments... I suggest that it is better therefore for us to make laws sitting together as friends than to make treaties as aliens. I invite my friends the rulers of States and their people to the councils of the Constituent Assembly in this spirit of friendliness... Congressmen are no enemies of the princely order."

Considering that the princes had to sign away the sovereignty of states where their families had reigned for centuries, and that they believed that India's security would be jeopardised if even one state refused to sign on, Patel and Menon were of the opinion that this was the best deal that could be put to the princes. While negotiating with the states, Patel and Menon also guaranteed that monarchs who signed on willingly would be retained as constitutional heads of state, although they would be 'encouraged' to hand their power over to an elected government. Once the Instrument of Accession was signed, the state would be represented in the Constituent Assembly of India, thus becoming an active participant in framing the new Constitution.

Patel's Diplomacy

On May 6, 1947, Patel began lobbying the princes, attempting to make them receptive towards dialogue with the future Government and trying to forestall potential conflicts. Patel used social meetings and unofficial surroundings to engage most monarchs, inviting them to lunch and tea at his home in Delhi. At these meetings, Patel would claim that there was no inherent conflict between the Congress and the princely order. Nonetheless, he stressed that Congress expected the princes to accede to India in good faith before the deadline, August 15, 1947. Patel also listened to the monarchs' opinions, seeking to address their two chief concerns:

The princes feared that the Congress would be hostile to the princely order, attacking their property and, indeed, their civil liberties. They were moved to this concern by the fact that a large proportion of Congress was of socialist inclination. Patel, no socialist himself, promised personally that the Congress, would not politically attack the Indian princes nor deprive them of any more political power or property than was 'necessary' for the stability and unity of India.

Patel assured the monarchs of the states that after acceding to India, they would be allowed to retain their property and estates. Further, they would be fully eligible to run for public office.

For the loss of income (from revenue), the monarchs would be compensated with a privy purse.

The princes were also worried that the guarantees offered by Patel while the British were still in charge would be scrapped after August 15. Patel thus had to promise to include the guarantees of privy purses and limited central powers in the as yet unframed Constitution.

Patel invoked the patriotism of India's monarchs, asking them to join in the freedom of their nation and act as responsible rulers who cared about the future of their people. V. P. Menon was frequently dispatched to hold talks with the ministers and monarchs. Menon would work each day with Patel, calling him twice, including a final status report in the night. Menon was Patel's closest advisor and aide on the diplomacy and tactics, and handling of potential conflicts, as well as his link with British officials. Patel also enlisted Lord Mountbatten, who was trusted by most of the princes and was a personal friend of many, especially the Nawab of Bhopal, Hamidullah Khan. Mountbatten was also a credible figure because Jawaharlal Nehru and Patel had asked him to become the first Governor General of the Dominion of India. In a July, 1947 gathering of rulers, Mountbatten laid out his argument:

"...The subcontinent of India acted as an economic entity. That link is now to be broken. If nothing can be put in its place, only chaos can result and that chaos, I submit, will hurt the states first. The States are theoretically free to link their future with whichever Dominion they may care. But may I point out that there are certain geographical compulsions which cannot be evaded?"

Mountbatten stressed that he would act as the trustee of the princes' commitment, as he would be serving as India's head of state well into 1948. Mountbatten engaged in a personal dialogue with the Nawab of Bhopal. He asked through a confidential letter to him, that he sign the instrument of accession, which Mountbatten would keep locked up in his safe. It would be handed to the States Department on August 15 only if the Nawab did not change his mind before then, which he was free to do. The Nawab agreed, and did not renege over the deal.

Accession of the States

From June to August 15, 1947, 562 of the 565 India-linked states signed the instrument of accession. Despite dramatic political exchanges, Travancore, Jodhpur and Indore signed on time. Patel was also willing to take on other Indian leaders for the sake of accomplishing the job. The *privy purse* pledge was offensive to many socialists, and Prime Minister Nehru had complained of Patel by-passing the Cabinet to make the pledge to the Princes. Patel described the pledge as an essential guarantee of the Government's intentions, and it was duly incorporated into the Constitution. (In 1971, Prime Minister Indira Gandhi's Congress Party would repeal the clause through a constitutional amendment.) Patel defended their right to retain property and contest elections for public office, and today, especially in states like Rajasthan and Madhya Pradesh, descendants of the formerly royal families play an important role in politics.

However, in the strenuous process of integration three major conflicts arose that posed a major threat to the Union:

Junagadh

Junagadh was a state on the southwestern end of Gujarat, with the principalities of Manavadar, Mangrol and Babriawad. The Arabian Sea stood between it and Pakistan, and over 80% of its population was Hindu. Possibly on the advice of his *Dewan,* Sir Shah Nawaz Bhutto, who was prominent in the Muslim League, the Nawab of Junagadh Mahabhat Khan acceded to Pakistan. The accession was announced on August 15, 1947, when Pakistan had come into being. When Pakistan confirmed the acceptance of the accession in September, the Government of India was outraged that Muhammad Ali Jinnah would accept the accession of Junagadh despite his argument that Hindus and Muslims could not live as one nation. Patel believed that if Junagadh was permitted to go to Pakistan, it would exacerbate the communal tension already simmering in Gujarat.

Patel gave Pakistan time to void the accession and hold a plebiscite in Junagadh. Samaldas Gandhi formed a democratic government-in-exile, the *Arzi Hukumat* (in Urdu: *Arzi*: People's Request, *Hukumat*: Government) of the people of Junagadh. Eventually, Patel ordered the forcible annexation of Junagadh's three principalities. Junagadh's court, facing financial collapse and no possibility of resisting Indian forces, first invited the *Arzi Hukumat,* and later the Government of India to accept the reins. A plebiscite was conducted in December, in which approximately 99% of the people chose India over Pakistan.

Kashmir

Maharaja Hari Singh, a Hindu, was equally hesitant about acceding to either India — he felt his mostly Muslim subjects would not like joining a Hindu-majority nation — or Pakistan — an eventuality which he would personally prefer to avoid. He personally believed that Kashmir could exercise its right to stay independent; a belief in which he was backed by Sheikh Abdullah, the leader of Kashmir's largest political party, the National Conference. However, Pakistan coveted the Himalayan kingdom, while Indian leaders including Gandhi and Nehru hoped that the kingdom would join India. Hari Singh signed a *Standstill Agreement* (preserving status quo) with Pakistan, but did not make his decision by August 15.

Pakistan, concerned about the lack of movement on the front, attempted to force the issue by permitting the incursions of tribals from the North-West Frontier, followed in September 1947 by regular forces. India offered military assistance to the Kashmiri Government, which was totally without an organised military; such assistance, however, was conditional on the Maharaja signing the Instrument of Accession, which he then did. By this time the raiders were close to the capital of Srinagar. Indian troops secured Jammu, Srinagar and the valley itself during the First Kashmir War, but the intense fighting flagged with the onset of winter, which made much of the state impassable.

Prime Minister Nehru, recognising the degree of international attention brought to bear on the dispute, declared a ceasefire and sought U.N. arbitration with the promise of a plebiscite. Patel had argued against both, describing Kashmir as a bilateral dispute and its accession as justified by international law. Patel had feared that the U.N.'s involvement would stall the process and allow Pakistan to reinforce its presence in Kashmir; in addition, it was far from clear, which way a plebiscite would go. In 1957, Kashmir was officially integrated into the Union, but with special provisions made for it in the Constitution's Article 370. The northwestern portion that remained under control of the Pakistan army is today Pakistan-administered Kashmir. In 1962, China occupied Aksai Chin, the northeastern region bordering Laddakh.

Hyderabad

Hyderabad was a state that stretched over 82,000 square miles (over 212,000 square kilometres) in the centre of India and with a population of 16 million, 85% of whom were Hindus. Its ruler was Nizam Osman Ali Khan, and had always enjoyed a special relationship with the British Raj. When the British ruled out dominion status, the Nizam set his mind upon independence, under the influence of Muslim radical Qasim Razvi. Without Hyderabad, a large gap would exist in the centre of the united nation envisioned by Indian nationalists and the Indian public. Patel believed that Hyderabad was looking to Pakistan for support, and could pose a constant threat to India's security in the future.

Patel argued that Hyderabad was essential for India's unity, but he agreed with Lord Mountbatten that force should not be used immediately. A *Standstill Agreement* was signed — an agreement made with no other princely state without an explicit assurance of eventual accession. However, Patel required Hyderabad promise it would not join Pakistan. Mountbatten and

India's agent K.M. Munshi engaged the Nizam's envoys into negotiations. However, no deal was reached that both sides found acceptable, and the Nizam alleged that India had created a blockade. India, on the other hand, charged that Hyderabad was receiving arms from Pakistan, and that the Nizam was allowing Razvi's Razakar militants to intimidate Hindus and attack villages in India.

Lord Mountbatten crafted a proposal called the *Heads of Agreement*, which called for the disbandment of the Razakars and restriction of the Hyderabad army, for the Nizam to hold a plebiscite and elections for a constituent assembly, and for eventual accession. While India would control Hyderabad's foreign affairs, the deal allowed Hyderabad to set up a parallel government and delay accession. Hyderabad's envoys assured Mountbatten that the Nizam would sign the agreement, and he lobbied Patel hard to sign for India. Patel signed the deal but retained his belief that the Nizam would not accept it. The Nizam, taking Razvi's advice dismissed the plan.

In September 1948, Patel made it clear in Cabinet meetings that he intended to use force against the Nizam. He obtained the agreement of the new Governor-General Chakravarthi Rajagopalachari and Prime Minister Nehru after some contentious debate, and under Operation Polo, sent the Army to invade Hyderabad. Between September 13 and 18th, Indian troops fought Hyderabadi troops and Razakars and defeated them. Patel retained the Nizam as the head of state as a conciliatory gesture. The main aim of Mountbatten and Nehru in attempting to achieve integration through diplomacy had been to avoid an outbreak of Hindu-Muslim violence. Patel insisted that if Hyderabad was allowed to continue its independence, the prestige of the Government would be tarnished and then neither Hindus nor Muslims would feel secure in its realm. The successful annexation of Hyderabad was praised by many Indian Muslim leaders, and there were no episodes of civil violence.

Conflicting Agendas

Different theories have been proposed to explain the designs of Indian and Pakistani leaders in this period. Rajmohan Gandhi postulates that an ideal deal working in the mind of Patel was that if Muhammad Ali Jinnah let India have Junagadh and Hyderabad,

Patel would not object to Kashmir acceding to Pakistan. In his book *Patel: A Life*, Gandhi asserts that Jinnah sought to engage the questions of Junagadh and Hyderabad in the same battle. It is suggested that he wanted India to ask for a plebiscite in Junagadh and Hyderabad, knowing thus that the principle then would have to be applied to Kashmir, where the Muslim-majority would, he believed, vote for Pakistan. In a speech at the Bahauddin College in Junagadh following the latter's take-over, Patel said:

"If Hyderabad does not see the writing on the wall, it goes the way Junagadh has gone. Pakistan attempted to set off Kashmir against Junagadh. When we raised the question of settlement in a democratic way, they (Pakistan) at once told us that they would consider it if we applied that policy to Kashmir. Our reply was that we would agree to Kashmir if they agreed to Hyderabad."

Patel's opinions were not India's policy, nor were they shared by Nehru, but both leaders were angered at Jinnah's courting the princes of Jodhpur, Bhopal and Indore. In her book *The Sole Spokesman*, Ayesha Jalal argues that Jinnah had never actually wanted partition, but once created, he wanted Pakistan to become a secular state that was inclusive to its Hindu minority and strategically secure from a geographically-larger India, thus encouraging Hindu states to join. When Jinnah remained adamant about Junagadh, and when the invasion of Kashmir began in September 1947, Patel exerted himself over the defence and integration of Kashmir into India. India and Pakistan clashed over Kashmir in 1965 and 1971, as well as over the sovereignty of the Rann of Kutch in August, 1965.

Integrating the Union

Many of the 565 states that had joined the Union were very small and lacked resources to sustain their economies and support their growing populations. Many published their own currency, imposed restrictions and their own tax rules that impeded free trade. Although *Prajamandals* (*People's Conventions*) had been organised to increase democracy, a contentious debate opened over dissolving the very states India promised to officially recognise just months ago. Challenged by princes, Sardar Patel and V. P. Menon emphasized that without integration, the economies of states would collapse, and anarchy would arise if the princes were unable to provide democracy and govern properly. In December

1947, over 40 states in central and eastern India were merged into the Central Provinces and Orissa. Similarly, Patel also obtained the unification of 222 states in the Kathiawar peninsula of his native Gujarat. In a meeting with the rulers, Menon said:

"His Highness the Maharaja of Bhavnagar has already declared himself in favour of a United Kathiawar State. I may also remind you of the metaphor employed by Sardar Patel, of how a large lake cools the atmosphere while small pools become stagnant...It is not possible for 222 States to continue their separate existence for very much longer. The extinction of the separate existence of the States may not be palatable, but unless something is done in good time to stabilise the situation in Kathiawar, the march of events may bring more unpalatable results."

In Punjab, the Patiala and East Punjab States Union was formed. Madhya Bharat and Vindhya Pradesh emerged from the princely states of the former Central India Agency. Himachal Pradesh was created from 30 states of the former Punjab Hill States Agency. A few large states, including Mysore, Kutch, and Bilaspur, remained distinct, but a great many more were merged into the provinces. The Northeast Frontier Agency (present-day Arunachal Pradesh and Nagaland) was administered by the Ministry of External Affairs with the Governor of Assam.

The Constitution of India, adopted on January 26, 1950 gave the states many powers, but the Union government had superior powers – including dissolving state governments if law and order were disrupted. National institutions were emphasized to prevent factionalism and separatism. A common judiciary and the Indian Administrative Service and Indian Police Service were created to erect a single government infrastructure. The united leadership to fight social, economic challenges of India for the first time in thousands of years was welcomed by most Indians.

Pondicherry and Goa

In the 1950s, the regions of Pondicherry, Karikal, Yanaon, Mahe and Chandernagore were still colonies of France, and Daman and Diu, Dadra and Nagar Haveli and Goa remained as colonies of Portugal. The lodges in Machilipatnam, Kozhikode and Surat were ceded to India in October 1947. An agreement between France and India in 1948 agreed to an election in France's remaining Indian possessions to choose their political future. Chandernagore was ceded to India on May 2, 1950, and was merged with West Bengal on October 2, 1955. On November 1, 1954, the four enclaves of Pondicherry, Yanaon, Mahe, and Karikal were de facto transferred to the Indian Union and became the Union territory of Pondicherry. Portugal had resisted diplomatic solutions, and refused to transfer power. Dadra and Nagar Haveli were incorporated into India in 1953 after bands of Indian irregulars occupied the lands, but Goa, Daman and Diu remained a bone of contention.

Arbitration by the World Court and the United Nations General Assembly favoured self-determination, but Portugal resisted all overtures from India. On December 18, 1961, in what Prime Minister Nehru termed as a *police action*, the Indian Army liberated Goa, Daman and Diu. The Portuguese surrendered on December 19, and 3,000 Portuguese soldiers became prisoners of war. This take-over ended the last of the European colonies in India. In 1987, Goa achieved statehood.

States Reorganization

The Constitution did not re-shape India's map — it established three orders of states that preserved the territories and governing structures of the recent past. However, India's ethnically diverse population was dissatisfied with colonial-era arrangements and centralised authority, which disempowered ethnic groups that did not form a significant population in a province. The many regional languages of India were without official use and recognition. Political movements arose in the regions demanding official use and autonomy for the Marathi-, Telugu-, Tamil-speaking regions of the Bombay state and Madras state. Incidents of violence grew in cities like Bombay and Madras as the demands gained momentum and became a potential source of conflict. Potti Sreeramulu undertook a fast-unto-death, demanding an Andhra state. Sreeramulu lost his life in the protest, but Andhra State was soon created in 1953 out of the northern, Telugu-speaking districts of Madras state as a result of aroused popular support.

Prime Minister Nehru appointed the States Reorganisation Commission to recommend a reorganization of state boundaries along linguistic lines. The States Reorganisation Act of 1956, which went into effect on November 1, 1956, was the largest single change to state borders in the history of independent India. Bombay, Madhya Pradesh, Mysore, Punjab, and Rajasthan were enlarged by the addition of smaller states and parts of adjacent states. Hyderabad was partitioned among Bombay, Mysore, and Andhra Pradesh states, and the new linguistic state of Kerala was created by merging the Malayalam-speaking state of Travancore-Cochin with Malabar District of Madras state.

On May 1, 1960, Gujarat and Maharashtra were created out of Bombay State, which had been enlarged by the Act, as a result of conflicting linguistic movements. Violent clashes erupted in Mumbai and villages on the border with Karnataka over issues of Maharashtrian territory. Maharashtra still claims Belgaum as its own. In 1965, unrest broke out in Madras when Hindi was to take effect as India's national language.

Punjab and Northeastern India

A culture of centralization was resented across many regions — it stifled regional autonomy and cultural identity. Inefficiency, corruption and economic stagnation in 1960s and 1970s aided this argument. Although Punjab was one of the most prosperous states, demands for greater autonomy and statehood arose. In 1966, Punjab was divided into Sikh-majority Punjab and Hindu-majority Haryana, with their joint capital in Chandigarh, a union territory. Certain northern districts were allocated to Himachal Pradesh. Jawaharlal Nehru had opposed creating separate states for different religious communities, but it was carried out by Prime Minister Indira Gandhi, who faced pressure from the SGPC and leaders like Master Tara Singh.

When the Khalistan insurgency created turmoil in the 1980s, the Army attacked militant encampments in the Golden Temple. The bloody outcome outraged the Sikhs, who saw it as a desecration of their holiest shrine by the Government. Indira Gandhi was assassinated, which in turn resulted in communal violence in Delhi. The Government employed martial law and force to crush the militant groups, but also began a process of devolving powers to the states as a means to end separatism. Punjab today is one of the most peaceful and prosperous states.

China does not recognise the McMahon Line that is the framework of its boundary with India, and lays a claim to the territory of Arunachal Pradesh — briefly occupied by Chinese forces in the Sino-Indian War. In 1967, Chinese and Indian forces clashed at the Chola Border Post in Sikkim, whose merger with

India was disputed for long but resolved in 2003. Nagaland, Meghalaya, Mizoram, Arunachal Pradesh, Tripura, Manipur, and Assam, known as the *Seven Sisters*, became states between the 1970s and 1980s. In 1975, India under Indira Gandhi integrated Sikkim into the Union after a plebiscite resulted in an overwhelming vote in favour of merger with India, but the Army had to forcibly take control from the Chogyal. In the 1960-70s, violent militancy arose in Assam and Nagaland. Neglect and discrimination by the Union government, as well as poverty and cultural aversion resulted in violence against refugees from Bangladesh and other settlers. The ULFA insurgency paralyzed Assam in the 1980s. Similar tensions in Mizoram and Tripura forced the Indian government to impose a martial law environment. The decline of popular appeal, increased autonomy, economic development and rising tourism has helped considerably reduce violence across the region.

Modern Developments

Several new states were created in 2000 — Chhattisgarh (from Madhya Pradesh), Jharkhand (from Bihar) and Uttaranchal (from Uttar Pradesh). This resulted from a national debate concerning the purported need to partition large states burdened with socioeconomic challenges, including overpopulation and the political marginalisation of ethnic minorities. Such debate has not ceased: there are proposals for the creation of Vidarbha from Maharashtra, Telangana from Andhra Pradesh, Bundelkhand from parts of Madhya Pradesh and Uttar Pradesh, and Jammu and Laddakh from Kashmir.

Correspondingly, governments have begun devolving power to regional levels as a means of increasing popular representation and administrative efficiency, as well as alleviating social problems. These include disparities in economic growth — despite India's rapid economic development — and the corresponding easing of socioeconomic pressures faced by communities across these regions. Uttar Pradesh and Andhra Pradesh are forming special commissions for their Purvanchal, Rayalaseema, Telangana and Coastal Andhra regions. Groups, including self-appointed representatives of northeastern India's Bodo people, are pushing — often via violent insurgency — for either the formation of a Bodoland state or independence. In 2003, an agreement was signed between the Union government, the state of Assam and the main Bodo separatist groups. This created the *Bodoland Territorial Councils*, which granted autonomy to regions with significant Bodo populations. Other groups are pushing for the conferral of statehood upon Kutch, Cooch Behar, Gorkhaland, Kamtapur and Coorg.

Instrument of Accession (Jammu and Kashmir)

The Instrument of Accession is a legal document executed by Maharajah Hari Singh, ruler of the princely state of Jammu and Kashmir, on October 26, 1947. With the formal acceptance of the Governor General of India, it settled the question of the accession of the Jammu and Kashmir princely state (including Jammu, Kashmir, Northern Areas, Laddakh, Trans-Karakoram Tract and Aksai Chin) to the Dominion of India.

"Whereas the Indian Independence Act, 1947, provides that as from the fifteenth day of August, 1947, there shall be set up an Independent Dominion known as India, and that the Government of India Act 1935 shall, with such omission, additions, adaptations and modifications as the governor-general may by order specify, be applicable to the Dominion of India.

And whereas the Government of India Act 1935, as so adapted by the governor-general, provides that an Indian State may accede to the Dominion of India by an Instrument of Accession executed by the Ruler thereof.

Now, therefore, I Shriman Inder Mahander Rajrajeswar Maharajadhiraj Shri Hari Singhji, Jammu and Kashmir Naresh Tatha Tibbetadi Deshadhipathi, Ruler of Jammu and Kashmir (princely state), in the exercise of my sovereignty in and over my said State do hereby execute this my Instrument of Accession and I hereby declare that I accede to the Dominion of India with the intent that the governor general of India, the Dominion Legislature, the Federal Court and any other Dominion authority established for the purposes of the Dominion shall, by virtue of this my Instrument of Accession but subject always to the terms thereof, and for the purposes only of the Dominion, exercise in relation to the State of Jammu and Kashmir (hereinafter referred to as "this State") such functions as may be vested in them by or under the Government of India Act, 1935, as in force in the Dominion of India, on the 15th day of August, 1947, (which Act as so in force is hereafter referred to as "the Act")." It is further specified that. "I accept the matters specified in the schedule hereto as the matters with respect to which the Dominion Legislature may make law for this State." Thus the power of the Dominion to make laws was restricted to the matters mentioned in the Schedule namely Defence, Foreign Affairs and Communications and a few ancillary subjects specified in the schedule. For all other matters concurrence of the State Government was essential. The accession was accepted by Lord Mountbatten of Burma, Governor General of India, the following day (October 27, 1947). Mountbatten in his letter of acceptance wrote that "I do hereby accept this Instrument of Accession

Instrument of Accession

Various princely states existed in India during the period of the British Raj. After the British announced their imminent exit from India, it became necessary to place the future relations between these states and the government of free India on a regularized legal footing. The Instrument of Accession was the legal document designed to provide this legal basis for future relations. It was executed by the government of India on the one hand with the rulers of each of the princely states, individually, on the other hand. Among the more momentous such accessions was that executed by Maharaja Hari Singh, ruler of the State of Jammu and Kashmir, on October 26, 1947. It gave control of Jammu and Kashmir to the government of India. The accession of Jammu and Kashmir was accepted by Lord Mountbatten of Burma, Governor General of India, on October 27, 1947.

"Whereas the Indian Independence Act 1947, provides that as from the fifteenth day of August, 1947, there shall be set up an Independent Dominion known as India, and that the Government of India Act, 1935 shall, with such omission, additions, adaptations and modifications as the governor-general may by order specify, be applicable to the Dominion of India.

And whereas the Government of India Act, 1935, as so adapted by the governor-general, provides that an Indian State may accede to the Dominion of India by an Instrument of Accession executed by the Ruler thereof.

Now, therefore, I Shriman Inder Mahander Rajrajeswar Maharajadhiraj Shri Hari Singhji, Jammu and Kashmir Naresh

Tatha Tibbetadi Deshadhipathi, Ruler of Jammu and Kashmir State, in the exercise of my sovereignty in and over my said State do hereby execute this my Instrument of Accession and I hereby declare that I accede to the Dominion of India with the intent that the governor-general of India, the Dominion Legislature, the Federal Court and any other Dominion authority established for the purposes of the Dominion shall, by virtue of this my Instrument of Accession but subject always to the terms thereof, and for the purposes only of the Dominion, exercise in relation to the State of Jammu and Kashmir (hereinafter referred to as "this State") such functions as may be vested in them by or under the Government of India Act, 1935, as in force in the Dominion of India, on the 15th day of August, 1947, (which Act as so in force is hereafter referred to as "the Act").

Lord Mountbatten of Burma, the Governor-General of India, on conditionally accepting the Instrument of Accession wrote: "consistently with their policy that in the case of any state where the issue of accession has been the subject of dispute, the question of accession should be decided in accordance with the wishes of the people of

Instrument of Accession

Instrument of Accession Executed by Maharajah Hari Singh on October 26, 1947

Whereas the Indian Independence Act, 1947, provides that as from the fifteenth day of August, 1947, there shall be set up an independent Dominion known as INDIA, and that the Government of India Act 1935, shall with such omissions, additions, adaptations and modifications as the Governor General may by order specify, be applicable to the Dominion of India.

And whereas the Government of India Act, 1935, as so adapted by the Governor General, provides that an Indian State may accede to the Dominion of India by an Instrument of Accession executed by the Ruler thereof.

Now, therefore, I Shriman Inder Mahinder Rajrajeswar Maharajadhiraj Shri Hari Singhji, Jammu & Kashmir Naresh Tatha Tibbet adi Deshadhipati, Ruler of Jammu & Kashmir State, in the exercise of my Sovereignty in and over my said State do hereby execute this my Instrument of Accession and

1. I hereby declare that I accede to the Dominion of India with the intent that the Governor General of India, the Dominion Legislature, the Federal Court and any other Dominion authority established for the purposes of the Dominion shall by virtue of this my Instrument of Accession but subject always to the terms thereof, and for the purposes only of the Dominion, exercise in relation to the State of Jammu & Kashmir (hereinafter referred to as "this State") such functions as may be vested in them by or under the Government of India Act, 1935, as in force in the Dominion of India, on the 15th day of August 1947, (which Act as so in force is hereafter referred to as "the Act').
2. I hereby assume the obligation of ensuring that due effect is given to provisions of the Act within this State so far as they are applicable therein by virtue of this my Instrument of Accession.
3. I accept the matters specified in the schedule hereto as the matters with respect to which the Dominion Legislature may make law for this State.
4. I hereby declare that I accede to the Dominion of India on the assurance that if an agreement is made between the Governor General and the Ruler of this State whereby any functions in relation to the administration in this State of any law of the Dominion Legislature shall be exercised by the Ruler of the State, then any such agreement shall be construed and have effect accordingly.
5. The terms of this my Instrument of Accession shall not be varied by any amendment of the Act or the Indian Independence Act, 1947, unless such amendment is accepted by me by Instrument supplementary to this Instrument.
6. Nothing in this Instrument shall empower the Dominion Legislature to make any law for this State authorizing the compulsory acquisition of land for any purpose, but I hereby undertake that should the Dominion for the purpose of a Dominion law which applies in this State deem it necessary to acquire any land, I will at their

request acquire the land at their expense, or, if the land belongs to me transfer it to them on such terms as may be agreed or, in default of agreement, determined by an arbitrator to be appointed by the Chief Justice of India.

7. Nothing in this Instrument shall be deemed to commit in any way to acceptance of any future constitution of India or to fetter my discretion to enter into agreement with the Government of India under any such future constitution.
8. Nothing in this Instrument affects the continuance of my Sovereignty in and over this State, or, save as provided by or under this Instrument, the exercise of any powers, authority and rights now enjoyed by me as Ruler of this State or the validity of any law at present in force in this State.
9. I hereby declare that I execute this Instrument on behalf of this State and that any reference in this Instrument to me or to the Ruler of the State is to be construed as including a reference to my heirs and successors.

Given under my hand this 26th day of October, nineteen hundred and forty seven.

Hari Singh

Maharajadhiraj of Jammu and Kashmir State.

Schedule of Instrument of Accession the Matters with Respect to Which the Dominion Legislature May Make Laws for this State

A. Defence

1. The naval, military and air forces of the Dominion and any other armed forces raised or maintained by the Dominion; any armed forces, including forces raised or maintained by an acceding State, which are attached to, or operating with, any of the armed forces of the Dominion.
2. Naval, military and air force works, administration of cantonment areas.
3. Arms, fire-arms, ammunition.
4. Explosives.

B. External Affairs

1. External affairs; the implementing of treaties and agreements with other countries; extradition, including the surrender of criminals and accused persons to parts of His Majesty's Dominions outside India.
2. Admission into, and emigration and expulsion from, India, including in relation thereto the regulation of the movements in India of persons who are not British subjects domiciled in India or subjects of any acceding State; pilgrimages to places beyond India.
3. Naturalisation.

C. Communications

1. Posts and telegraphs, including telephones, wireless, broadcasting, and other like forms of communication.
2. Federal railways; the regulation of all railways other than minor railways in respect of safety, maximum and minimum rates and fares, station and services terminal charges, interchange of traffic and the responsibility of railway administrations as carriers of goods and passengers; the regulation of minor railways in respect of safety and the responsibility of the administrations of such railways as carriers of goods and passengers.
3. Maritime shipping and navigation, including shipping and navigation on tidal waters; Admiralty jurisdiction.
4. Port quarantine.
5. Major ports, that is to say, the declaration and delimitation of such ports, and the constitution and powers of Port Authorities therein.
6. Aircraft and air navigation; the provision of aerodromes; regulation and organisation of air traffic and of aerodromes.
7. Lighthouses, including lightships, beacons and other provisions for the safety of shipping and aircraft.
8. Carriage of passengers and goods by sea or by air.
9. Extension of the powers and jurisdiction of members of the police force belonging to any unit to railway area outside that unit.

D. Ancillary

1. Election to the Dominion Legislature, subject to the provisions of the Act and of any Order made thereunder.
2. Offences against laws with respect to any of the aforesaid matters.
3. Inquiries and statistics for the purposes of any of the aforesaid matters.
4. Jurisdiction and powers of all courts with respect to any of the aforesaid matters but, except with the consent of the Ruler of the acceding State, not so as to confer any jurisdiction or powers upon any courts other than courts ordinarily exercising jurisdiction in or in relation to that State.

1961 Indian Annexation of Goa

The Indian Annexation of Goa (also referred to as Invasion of Goa, the Liberation of Goa and the Portuguese-Indian War), was an action by India's armed forces that ended Portuguese rule in its Indian enclaves in 1961. The armed action, codenamed Operation Vijay by Indian government, involved air, sea and land strikes for over 36 hours, and was a decisive victory for India, ending 451 years of Portuguese colonial rule in Goa. Thirty-four Indians and thirty-one Portuguese were killed in the fighting. The brief war drew a mixture of worldwide praise and condemnation. In India, the action was seen as a liberation of historically Indian territory, while Portugal viewed it as aggression against a long-held colonial possession.

Background

Goa, Western India

Goa, Daman, Diu, and Dadra and Nagar Haveli had been Portuguese colonies since the 16th century. After having won independence from the British Empire in 1947, the Republic of India, under the leadership of Prime Minister Jawaharlal Nehru presented an ultimatum to the government of Portugal, led by dictator Antonio de Oliveira Salazar, for the immediate and peaceful hand over of all colonial enclaves held by the Portuguese on the Indian subcontinent. On, September 17, 1955, Nehru stated in

Indian Parliament that reliance on peaceful methods to bring Goa into India "is not only a sound policy, but the only possible policy."

Diplomatic efforts towards this goal by the Indian government failed, because Portugal asserted that the Estado da India was not a colony and was a part of metropolitan Portugal and hence its transfer was non-negotiable; and that the Indian Union had no rights to this territory since the Indian union did not exist at the time Goa came under Portuguese rule. The positions of both governments were irreconcilable, leading to enmity between the two countries. India attempted to use its position in the Non-Aligned Movement to gain support for its demands, while Portugal, as a founding member of NATO attempted to seek support amongst Western nations, as well as with India's rivals, Pakistan and China.

In Goa, a popular support had been built up against Portuguese rule by civil leaders like Ram Manohar Lohia who advocated the use of nonviolent Gandhian techniques to oppose the government. A major popular protest against rule on the 18th of June 1946 was suppressed by the Portuguese. Similarly, in 1954, the Portuguese used force to put down an attempt by nonviolent Satyagrahi activists to march into Goa. A similar and simultaneous effort in Dadra and Nagar Haveli was successful, however, and it was incorporated into the Indian Union in 1962. The Portuguese followed their actions up with a purge of supporters of independence, many of whom were jailed. This action led to the closure of the Indian consulate in the city of Panjim in Goa in 1955 and the imposition of economic sanctions against Portuguese-held territories.

In addition to nonviolent protests, aggressive groups such as the Azad Gomantak Dal (The Free Goa Party) and the United Front of Goans conducted aggressive attacks aimed at weakening Portuguese rule in Goa. These organisations – along with Indian volunteers – were also involved in the liberation of Dadra and Nagar Haveli from Portuguese rule in 1954.

Commenting on the armed resistance, Capt. Carlos Azaredo (now retired General) stationed with the army in Goa states in Portuguese newspaper O Expresso: "To the contrary to what is being said, the most evolved guerilla warfare which our Armed Forces encountered was in Goa. I know what I'm talking about, because I also fought in Angola and in Guine. In 1961 alone, until

December, around 80 policemen died. The major part of the terrorists of Azad Gomantak Dal were not Goans. Many had fought in the British Army, under General Montgomery, against the Germans."

In 1957, the Indian army deployed anti-aircraft batteries near the Daman and Diu airfields and threatened to shoot down any aircraft that strayed into Indian airspace whilst taking off or landing at the newly built airports at these locations.

By October 1961, the decision was taken to use military force to oust the Portuguese from their Indian enclaves, and accordingly military resources were allocated for Operation Vijay.

Events Preceding the Hostilities

Attack on the Sabarmati

On 24 November 1961, the *Sabarmati*, a passenger boat passing between the Portuguese-held island of Anjidiv and the Indian port of Kochi, was fired upon by Portuguese ground troops, resulting in injuries to the chief engineer of the boat, as well as the death of a passenger. The action was precipitated by Portuguese fears that the boat carried a military landing team intent on storming the island. A Portuguese investigation into the matter revealed that the boat had also been fired upon a seven days earlier, when it accidentally strayed into Portuguese waters. The incidents lent themselves to foster widespread public support in India for military action in Goa.

Indian Military Build-up

On receiving the go-ahead for military action and the mandate of the capture of all occupied territories for the Indian government, Lt. Gen. Chaudhari of India's Southern Army fielded the 17th Infantry Division and the 50th Parachute Brigade commanded by Major General K.P. Candeth. The assault on the enclave of Daman was assigned to the 1st Maratha Light Infantry while the operations in Diu were assigned to the 20th Rajput and 4th Madras battalions. Meanwhile, the Commander in Chief of India's Western Air Command, Air Vice Marshal Erlic Pinto, was appointed as the commander of all air resources assigned to the operations in Goa. Air resources for the assault on Goa were concentrated in the bases at Pune and Sambra.

The Indian navy deployed two warships—the INS *Rajput*, an 'R' Class destroyer, and the INS *Kirpan*, a Blackwood class anti-submarine frigate—off the coast of Goa. The actual attack on Goa was delegated to four task groups: a Surface Action Group comprising five ships: *Mysore*, *Trishul*, *Betwa*, *Beas* and *Cauvery*; a Carrier Group of five ships: *Delhi*, *Kuthar*, *Kirpan*, *Khukri* and *Rajput* centred around the light aircraft carrier *Vikrant*; a Mine Sweeping Group consisting of mine sweepers including *Karwar*, *Kakinada*, *Cannonore* and *Bimilipatan* and a Support Group which consisted of the *Dharini*.

International Efforts at Peace

Portugal's prime minister, Antonio de Oliveira Salazar, alarmed by India's hinted threats at armed action against its presence in Goa, first asked the United Kingdom to mediate, then protested through Brazil and eventually asked the UN Security Council to intervene. Meanwhile on 6 December, Mexico offered the Indian government its influence in Latin America to bring pressure on the Portuguese to relieve tensions.

Meanwhile, India's defence minister, Krishna Menon, and head of India's UN delegation, stated in no uncertain terms that India had not "abjured the use of force" in Goa, and went on to link Goa to Angola, condemning Portugal's anti decolonization policies in both cases. Indian forces were, at the time, serving in Congo as part of a UN operation and had been involved in the fighting.

American diplomatic initiatives to prevent an armed conflict in India had to balance its relationship with India, as well as its NATO alliance with Portugal, as well as dispel the idea that such initiatives were being made under pressure from the Portuguese government, while avoiding any NATO involvement in the issue. The U.S. government stopped short of suggesting self determination for the people of Goa, as this, they realized, would be needed to apply to all other Portuguese holdings worldwide, and would damage U.S.–Portugal relations.

The American ambassador to India, John Kenneth Galbraith, requested the Indian government on several occasions to resolve the issue peacefully through mediation and consensus rather than armed conflict. Indian prime minister Jawaharlal Nehru postponed the invasion of Goa and expressed his willingness to come to the negotiating table, on the condition that Portugal first announce its intentions to withdraw from Goa. This condition was however rejected by the Portuguese as contrary to the spirit of a negotiation.

President John F. Kennedy, in a message to Nehru, argued that if India used force against Goa, this, along with its military presence in Congo, would make an otherwise Gandhian nation look belligerent.

On 8 December, C.S. Jha, India's delegate at the United Nations Security Council, expressed India's disregard for international pressure by stating: "(The invasion of Goa) is a question of getting rid of the last vestiges of colonialism in India. That is a matter of faith with us. Whatever anyone else may think, Charter or no Charter, Council or no Council, that is our basic faith which we cannot afford to give up at any cost."

On December 14, Acting UN Secretary-General U Thant addressed identical letters to Indian Prime Minister Nehru and Portuguese Prime Minister Antonio Salazar. He urged them to "ensure that the situation does not deteriorate to the extent that it might constitute a threat to peace and security," and to enter into negotiations to seek a solution to the problem.

Eventually, on 10 December, nine days prior to the invasion, Nehru stated to the press that "Continuance of Goa under Portuguese rule is an impossibility". America's response was to warn India that if and when India's armed action in Goa was brought to the UN security council, it could expect no support from the U.S. delegation.

The Portuguese Mandate

Portuguese Prime Minister Antonio de Oliveira Salazar, sent the following message to Governor General Vassalo e Silva in Goa on 14 December, in which he ordered the Portuguese forces in Goa to fight till the last man.

Radio 816/Lisbon 14-Dec.1961: You understand the bitterness with which I send you this message. It is horrible to think that this may mean total sacrifice, but I believe that sacrifice is the only way for us to keep up to the highest traditions and provide service to the future of the Nation. Do not expect the possibility of truce or of Portuguese prisoners, as there will be no surrender rendered because I feel that our soldiers and sailors can be either victorious or dead. These words could, by their seriousness, be directed only to a soldier of higher duties fully prepared to fulfil them. God will not allow you to be the last Governor of the State of India.

Portuguese military preparations

Portuguese military preparations began in the earnest in 1954 following the Indian economic blockade when three army battalions were transported to Goa, raising the Portuguese military presence there to 12,000 men. However, by late 1960 the under-secretary of the Army Staff, Lt Col Costa Gomes, conducted a survey visit to Goa and proposes a reduction in the military grouping reducing the strength from 12,000 men to around 3,500.

In accordance with Prime Minister Salazar's instructions to resist the Indian invasion, the Portuguese administration in Goa prepared for war.

One Portuguese Navy sloop, the NRP *Afonso de Albuquerque,* was present in Goa at the time of invasion. The vessel was armed with four 120 mm guns capable of two shots per minute, and four automatic rapid firing guns. In addition to the sloop, there were five merchant navy ships in Goa, as well as three light patrol boats (Lancha de Fiscalizaçao) each armed with a 20mm Oerlikon gun.

Portuguese ground defences consisted of a total of 3,995 men, including infantry troops and 810 native soldiers, many of whom had little military training and were utilized primarily for security and anti-terrorist operations. In addition there were about 1,040 police officers and 400 border guards divided amongst the three Portuguese enclaves in India. The strategy employed to resist Indian invasion was centred around the *Plano Sentinela* which called for the concentration of all defences in the port town of Mormugao, and the *Plano de Barragens* which envisaged the demolishing of all bridges and links to delay the invading army, as well as the mining of approach roads and beaches. These plans were however inviable due to the desperate shortage of mines and ammunition.

Commenting on the Plano Sentinela, Capt. Carlos Azaredo who was stationed in Goa at the time of hostilities states in Portuguese newspaper *O Expresso* on 8 Dec 2001, "It was a totally unrealistic and unachievable plan, which was quite incomplete. It was based on exchange of ground with time. But, for this purpose, portable communication equipment was necessary".

On the December 16, the Portuguese Air Force was placed on alert to transport ten tons of anti tank grenades in two DC6 aircraft from Monjito Air Base in Portugal to Goa assist in its defence. However the aircrafts were denied stop over facilities at the US Air Base at Weelhus in Libya. When the Portuguese Air Force was unable to obtain such facilities at any other air base along the way-most nations including Pakistan denying passage of Portuguese military aircraft-the mission was passed on to the civilian airline TAP which offered a Lockheed Constellation (registration CS-TLA) on charter for the job. However, when permission to transport weapons through Karachi was denied by the Pakistani Government, the Lockheed Constellation landed in Goa at 1800 hours on December 17 with a consignment of half a dozen bags of sausages as food supplies instead of the intended grenades. However the aircraft also arrived with a contingent of female paratroopers to assist in the evacuation of Portuguese civilians.

The Portuguese air presence in Goa was thus limited to the presence of two transport aircraft, one belonging to the Portuguese international airline (TAP) and the other to the Goan airline Portuguese India airlines (TAIP): a Lockheed Constellation and a Douglas DC4 Skymaster aircraft. The Indians claimed that the Portuguese had a squadron of F-86 Sabres stationed at Dabolim Airport—which later turned out to be false intelligence. Air defence was limited to a few obsolete anti aircraft guns manned by two artillery units who had been smuggled into Goa disguised as soccer teams.

On the December 14, the Portuguese administration in Goa receives orders from the Ministry for Overseas Affairs in Lisbon to transfer the relics of St. Francis Xavier, Patron saint of Goa, to Lisbon. Orders are also received ordering the Portuguese forces in Goa to destroy any buildings of non-military Portuguese heritage in Goa. Accordingly, barrels filled with petrol are transported to the Idalcao Palace in Pangim, which serves as the administrative headquarters, but are removed on orders from Governor Vassalo Da Silva who states "I cannot destroy the evidence of our greatness in the Orient".

Portuguese Civilian Evacuation

The military buildup created panic amongst Europeans in Goa, who were desperate to evacuate their families before the commencement of hostilities. On 9 December, the vessel *India* arrived at Goa's Mormugao port en route to Lisbon from Timor. Despite orders from the Portuguese government in Lisbon not to allow anyone to embark on this vessel, the Governor General of Goa, Manuel Vassalo e Silva, allowed 700 Portuguese civilians of European origin to board the ship and flee Goa. The ship had had capacity for only 380 passengers, and was filled to its limits, with evacuees occupying even the ship's toilets. On arranging this evacuation of women and children, Vassalo e Silva remarked to the press, "If necessary, we will die here." Evacuation of European civilians continued by air even after the commencement of Indian air strikes.

Indian Reconnaissance Operations

Indian reconnaissance operations had commenced on 1 December, when two Indian Leopard class frigates, the INS *Betwa* and the INS *Beas*, undertook linear patrolling of the Goan coast at a distance of 8 miles (13 km). By 8 December, the Indian Air Force had commenced baiting missions and fly-bys to lure out Portuguese air defences and fighters, but to no avail.

On December 17, a tactical reccee flight conducted by Sqn Ldr I S Loughran in a Vampire NF.54 Night Fighter over Dabolim Airport in Goa was met with 5 rounds fired from a ground anti aircraft gun. The aircraft took evasive action by drastically dropping altitude and escaping out to sea. The anti aircraft gun was later recovered near the ATC building with a round jammed in its breach.

The Indian light aircraft carrier INS *Vikrant* was deployed 75 miles (121 km) off the coast of Goa to head a possible amphibious operation on Goa, as well as to deter any foreign military intervention.

Timeline

The Air War

The mandate handed to Air Vice Marshal Erlic Pinto by the Indian Air Command was listed out as follows:

1. The destruction of Goa's lone airfield in Dabolim, without causing damage to the terminal building and other airport facilities.

2. Destruction of the wireless station at Bambolim, Goa.
3. Denial of airfields at Daman and Diu, which were, however, not to be attacked without prior permission.
4. Support to advancing ground troops.

The Goa Raids

The first Indian raid was conducted on 18 December on the Dabolim Airfield and was in the form of 12 Canberra aircraft led by Wing Commander N.B. Menon. The raid resulted in the dropping of 63,000 pounds of explosives within minutes, rendering the runway unusable. In line with the mandate given by the Air Command, structures and facilities at the airfield were left undamaged.

The second Indian raid was conducted on the same target by eight Canberra aircraft led by Wing Commander Surinder Singh, which again left the airport's terminal and other buildings untouched.

Two transport aircraft-a Lockheed Constellation belonging to the Portuguese airline, TAP and a Douglas DC-4 Skymaster belonging to the Goan airline TAIP were parked on the apron.

A third Indian raid was carried out by six Hawker Hunters, and was targeted at the wireless station at Bambolim, which was successfully attacked with a combination of rockets and gun cannon ammunition.

On the night of the 18th December, the Portuguese used both aircraft to evacuate the families of some government and military officials in spite of the heavily damaged runway. During the first hours of the evening, airport workers hastily recovered part of the runway. The first aircraft to leave was the Lockheed Constellation commanded by Manuel Correia Reis which took off using only 700 metres; the debris from the runway damaged the fuselage with 25 holes and a flat tire. The second to leave was the TAIP DC-4 Skymaster, piloted by TAIP Director Major Solano de Almeida, both aircraft used the cover of night and a very low altitudes to break through Indian aerial patrols and escape to Karachi, Pakistan.

The mandate to support ground troops was served by the No. 45 squadron of de Havilland Vampires which patrolled the sector but did not receive any requests into action. In an incident of friendly fire, two Vampires fired rockets into the positions of the 2nd Sikh Light Infantry injuring two soldiers, while elsewhere, an Indian Harvard was attacked by friendly ground troops and sustained nominal damage.

The Daman and Diu raids

In the Daman sector, Indian Mysteres flew 14 sorties, continuously harassing Portuguese artillery positions.

In the Diu Sector, air operations were entrusted to the Armaments Training Wing led by Wg Cdr Micky Blake. The first air attacks were made at dawn, December 18, by and were aimed at destroying Diu's fortifications facing the mainland. Throughout the rest of the day, the Air Force had at least two aircrafts in the air ant any time giving close support to advancing Indian infantry. During the morning, the air force attacked and destroyed Diu Airfield's ATC as well as parts of Diu Fort. On orders from Tactical Air Command located at Pune, a sortie of two Toofanis attacked and destroyed the airfield runway with 4 1000 lb Mk 9 bombs. A second sortied aimed at the runway and piloted by Wg Cdr Blake himself was aborted when Blake detected what he reported as people waving white flags. in subsequent sorties, the Indian Air Force attacked and destroyed the Portuguese ammunition dump as well a patrol boat that attempted to escape from Diu.

In the absence of any Portuguese air presence, Portuguese ground based anti-aircraft units attempted to offer resistance to the Indian raids, but were overwhelmed and quickly silenced, leaving complete air superiority to the Indians. Continued air attacks forced the Portuguese governor of Diu to surrender.

In later years, commentators have maintained that India's intense air strikes against the airfields were uncalled-for, since none of the targeted airports had any military capabilities and did not cater to any military aircraft. As such, the airfields were defenceless civilian targets. To this day, the Indian navy continues to control the Dabolim Airport, although this is now used as a civilian airport as well.

The Naval War

The Storming of Anjidiv Island

The Indian Naval Command assigned the task of securing the

island of Anjidiv to the INS *Trishul* and the INS *Mysore*. Under covering fire from the ships, Indian marines under the command of Lt. Arun Auditto stormed the island at 1425 hours on the 18th of December, and engaged the Portuguese defenders. The Portuguese ceased fire, and raised a white flag (it is claimed in some quarters that the "white flag" was in fact bedsheets drying in the windows, which the Indian army mistook for a white flag of surrender), thus luring the Indian marines out of their cover, before opening fire again. The Indian marines lost 7 killed and 19 wounded. Among the wounded were two officers. The Portuguese defences were eventually overpowered after a fierce barrage of shells from the Indian ships and the island was secured by the Indians at 1400 hours on the next day.

Naval Battle at Mormugao Harbour

On the morning of 18 December, the Portuguese sloop NRP Afonso de Albuquerque was anchored off Mormugao Harbour. Three Portuguese patrol boats were also present at Goa Daman and Diu. Besides engaging Indian naval units, the *Afonso de Albuquerque* was also tasked with providing a coastal artillery battery for the defence of the harbour and adjoining beaches, as well as providing vital radio communications with Lisbon after on-shore radio facilities had been destroyed in Indian air-strikes.

At 0900 hours, three Indian frigates led by the INS *Betwa* took up position off the Harbour, awaiting orders to attack the NRP *Afonso* and secure sea access to the port. At 1100 hours, the Indian Air Force raided the Mormugao harbour, strafing the area with bombs. At 1200 hours, upon receiving its clearance from HQ, the INS *Betwa,* accompanied by the INS *Beas* entered the harbour and opened fire on the NRP *Afonso* with their 4.5-inch guns while transmitting requests to surrender in between shots in morse code. In response, the NRP Afonso lifted anchor, headed out towards the enemy and returned fire with its 120 mm guns.

Besides being outnumbered by the Indians, the *Afonso* was also at a severe disadvantage since it was in a confined position that restricted its maneuverability, and also because its four 120 mm guns were capable of a mere two rounds a minute, as compared to the 60 rounds per minute cadence of the guns aboard the Indian frigates. A few minutes into the exchange of fire, at 1215, the *Afonso* took a direct hit in its control tower, injuring its weapons officer. At 1225 hours, an anti-personnel Shrapnel bomb fired from an Indian vessel exploded directly over the ship, killing its radio officer and severely injuring its Commander, Captain Antonio da Cunha Aragao, after which the First Officer Pinto da Cruz took command of the vessel. The ships propulsion system was also badly damaged in this attack. Indian naval artillery also hit the British merchant vessel "Ranger".

At 1235, the NRP Afonso swerved 180 degrees and was run aground against Bambolim beach. At that time, against the commander's orders, a white flag was hoisted under instructions from the segeant in charge of signals. But the flag coiled itself around the mast and as a result was not spotted by the Indians, who continued their barrage. The flag was immediately lowered.

Eventually at 1250 hours, after having fired nearly 400 rounds at the Indians, hitting two of the Indian vessels, and having taken severe damage, the order was given to initiate the abandonment of the ship. Under heavy fire, directed both at the ship as well as at the coast, non essential crew including weapons staff leave the ship and make their way to the shore. They are followed at 1310 hours by the rest of the crew, who along with their injured commander, disembarked directly onto the beach after setting fire to the ship. Following this, the commander was transferred by car to the hospital at Panjim.

In all the NRP Afonso suffered 5 dead and 13 men wounded in the battle.

The sloop's crew formally surrendered with the remaining Portuguese forces on December 19 at 2030 hours.

As a gesture of goodwill, the commanders of the INS *Betwa* and the INS *Beas* later visited Captain Aragao as he lay recuperating in bed at Panjim.

The *Afonso*-having been renamed as 'Sarasvati' by the Indian Navy-lay grounded at the beach near Dona Paula, until 1962 when it was towed to Bombay and sold for scrap. Parts of the ship were recovered and are on display at the Naval Museum in Bombay.

The Action at Diu

The Indian naval cruiser "New Delhi" was anchored off the coast of Diu and offered a continuous barrage of artillery at the Diu Fortress where the Portuguese were holed up. Commanding

Officer of the Indian Air Force operating in the area reported that some of the shells fired from the New Delhi were bouncing off the beach and exploding on the Indian mainland. However no casualties were reported from this.

At 0400 hours on the 18th of December, a Portuguese patrol boat *Vega* encountered the New Delhi around 12 miles (19 km) off the coast of Diu, and was attacked with heavy machine gun fire. Taking no casualties and minimal damage, the boat managed to withdraw to the port at Diu.

At 0700 hours, news was received that the Indian invasion had commenced, and the commander of the *Vega,* 2nd Lt Oliveira e Carmo was ordered to sail out and fight until the last round of ammunition. At 0730 hours the crew of the *Vega* spotted two Indian aircraft on patrol missions and opened fire on them with the ship's 20 mm gun. In retaliation the Indian aircraft attacked the *Vega* twice, killing the captain and the gunner and forcing the rest of the crew to abandon the boat and swim ashore, where they were later taken prisoner.

Action at Daman

Like the Vega in Diu, the patrol boat *Antares* at Daman under the command of 2nd Lt. Abreu Brito was ordered to sail out and fight the imminent Indian invasion. The boat stayed in position from 0700 hours on 18 December and remained a mute witness to repeated air strikes followed by ground invasion until 1920 hours when it lost all communications with land.

With all information pointing to total occupation of all Portuguese enclaves in India, Lt. Brito attempted to save his crew and boat by escaping to Karachi in Pakistan. The boat traversed 530 miles (850 km), escaping detection by Indian forces to arrive at Karachi at 2000 hours on 20 December.

The Ground War

The target of the Indian ground attack in Goa was the securing of the capital town of Panjim as well as the harbour of Mormugao and the airport at Dabolim, and was a task assigned to the 17th Infantry Division under Major Gen. KP Candeth, and the 50 Para Brigade-one of the Indian army's most elite airborne units-under Brigadier Sagat Singh.

The Attack on Goa: the Northern Prong

Although the 50 Para Brigade-also called the Pegasus Brigade-was charged with merely assisting the main thrust conducted by the 17th Infantry, its units moved rapidly across minefields, roadblocks and four riverine obstacles to be the first to reach Panjim.

On the morning of 18 December, the 50 Para Brigade moved into Goa in three columns.

1. The eastern column comprised the 2nd Para Maratha advanced via the town of Ponda in central Goa.
2. The central column consisting of the 1st Para Punjab advanced via the village of Banastari.
3. The western column-the main thrust of the attack-comprised the 2nd Sikh Light Infantry as well as an armoured division which crossed the border at 0630 hours in the morning and advanced along Tivim.

The western column, facing no resistance, reached the town of Betim at 1700 hours, just a 500 metre wide river crossing away from Panjim, the capital town. In the absence of orders, the units set camp at Betim and proceeded to secure areas up and down the riverfront.

The order to cross the river was received on the morning of the 19th of December, upon which two rifle companies advanced on Panjim at 0730 hours and secured the town without facing any resistance. On orders from Brigadier Sagat Singh, the troops entering Panjim removed their steel helmets and donned the Parachute Regiment's maroon berets. As the men marched into the town, they were welcomed as liberators by the locals.

The Advance from the East

Meanwhile, in the east, the 63rd Indian Infantry Brigade advanced in two columns. The right column comprising the 2nd Bihar and the left column consisting of the 3rd Sikh linked up at the border town of Mollem and then advanced upon the town of Ponda taking separate routes. By night fall, the 2nd Bihar had reached the town of Candeapur, while the 3rd Sikh had reached Darbondara. Although neither column had encountered any resistance, their further progress was hampered because all bridges spanning the river had been destroyed.

The rear battalion comprised the 4th Sikh Infantry, which reached Candeapur in the small hours of the 19th of December, and not to be bogged down by the absence of the bridge, waded across the river in chest high water, to reach Margao-the administrative centre of Southern Goa-by 1200 hours. From here, the column advanced on the harbour of Mormugao. En route to this target, the column encountered armed resistance from a unit of the Portuguese Army at the village of Verna, where it was joined by the 2nd Bihar. The 500 strong Portuguese unit at Verna surrendered at 1530 hours after a fierce resistance, and the 4th Sikh then proceeded to Mormugao and Dabolim Airport, where the main body of the Portuguese army awaited the Indians.

A decoy attack was staged south of Margao by the 4th Rajput company to mislead the Portuguese. This column overcame minefields, roadblocks and demolished bridges, and eventually went on to help secure the town of Margao.

The expected defence of Mormugao never occurred, and the Portuguese troops holed up at the harbour surrendered without a fight in a formal ceremony at 2030 hours on December the 19th.

The Attack on Daman

The advance on the enclave of Daman was conducted by the 1st Maratha Light Infantry in a pre dawn operation on the 18th of December. By 1700 hours, in the absence of any resistance, the Indians had managed to occupy most of the territory, with the exception of the airfield where the Portuguese were making their last stand.

The Indians assaulted the airfield the next morning upon which the Portuguese surrendered at 1100 hours without a fight. Approximately 600 Portuguese soldiers were taken prisoner.

The Attack on Diu

Diu was attacked on 18 December from the north west along Kob Forte by two companies of the 20th Rajput and from the northeast along Amdepur by the Rajput B Company with the capture of the Diu Airfield being the primary objective.

These Indian Army units ignored requests from the Indian Air Force to attack only on first light when close air support would be available. Instead, attempts were made to cross a water channel separating them from the Portuguese forces under cover of dark on rafts made of bamboo cots tied to oil barrels. This attack was repulsed by around 125 or 130 Portuguese soldiers armed with small automatic weapons and inflicting fairly heavy losses.

The assault was made afresh at dawn in the presence of air support. Whereas the 20th Rajput was bogged down in their assault by the well entrenched machine gun positions of the Portuguese, the B Company was able to advance under heavy artillery cover and take the town of Gogal. The constant barrage of artillery fire as well as continuous air strikes eventually led to the surrender of the Portuguese garrison later that day. In surrendering to three officers of the Indian Air Force, the Diu Governor informed them that he could have kept the Army out for a few weeks but he had no answer to the Air Force. The Indians suffered 4 dead and 14 wounded, while the Portuguese suffered 10 dead and 2 wounded.

On 19 December, the 4th Madras C Company landed on the island of Panikot off Diu and accepted the surrender of a small troop of 13 Portuguese soldiers there.

Portuguese Surrender

By the evening 19 December, most of Goa had been taken over by advancing Indian infantry forces, and a large party of more than two thousand Portuguese soldiers had taken position at the military base at Alparqueiros at hte entrance to the port town of Vasco Da Gama. Per the Portuguese strategy code named *'Plano Sentinela'* the defending forces were to make their last stand at the harbour, holding out against the Indians until Portuguese naval reinforcements could arrive. Orders delivered from the Portuguese President called for a scorched earth policy-that Goa was to be destroyed before it was given up to the Indians. Commentators have argued that Salazar wanted to sacrifice his troops in Goa, in order to attract international condemnation of India's invasion of Goa. Despite these orders, Governor General Manuel Antonio Vassalo e Silva took stock of the numerical superiority of the Indian troops, as well as the food and ammunition supplies available to his forces and took the decision to offer surrender. He later described his orders to destroy Goa as *"um sacrificio inútil"* (a useless sacrifice).

In a communication to all Portuguese forces under his command, he stated, "Having considered the defence of the Peninsula of Mormugao... from aerial, naval and ground fire of the enemy and ... having considered the difference between the forces and the resources... the situation does not allow myself to proceed with the fight without great sacrifice of the lives of the inhabitants of Vasco da Gama, I have decided with ... my patriotism well present, to get in touch with the enemy ... I order all my forces to cease-fire." The official Portuguese surrender was conducted in a formal ceremony held at 2030 hours on the 19th of December when Governor General Manuel Antonio Vassalo e Silva signed the instrument of surrender bringing to an end 451 years of Portuguese Rule in Goa. In all, 4668 personnel were taken prisoner by the Indians-a figure which included military and civilian personnel, Portuguese, Africans and Indians (Goans). This comprised 3412 prisoners in Goa, 853 in Daman and 403 in Diu.

Portuguese non-combatants present in Goa at the time of the surrender-which included Mrs Vasalo D'Silva, wife of the Portuguese Governor General of Goa-were transported by December 29 to Bombay from where they were repatriated to Portugal. Manuel Vassalo, however remained along with approximately 3300 Portuguese combatants as POWs in Goa.

Upon the surrender of the Portuguese governor general, Goa, Daman and Diu was declared a federally administered Union Territory placed directly under the President of India, and Maj. Gen. K. P. Candeth was appointed as its military governor. The war had lasted two days. India lost 34 killed and 51 wounded. Portugal lost 31 killed, 57 wounded, and 4668 captured. Those Indian forces who served within the disputed territories for 48 hours, or flew at least one operational sortie during the conflict, received a General Service Medal 1947 with the *Goa 1961* bar.

Portuguese Actions Post-hostilities

On 18 December, even as Indian forces were rolling into Goa, a special emergency session of the United Nations Security Council was convened at the request of the Portuguese Government. At the meeting, called to consider the Indian invasion of Portuguese territories in Goa, Daman and Diu, Adlai Stevenson, the US representative to the UN, criticized the Indian military action. He then submitted a draft resolution that called for a cease fire, a withdrawal of all Indian forces from Goa, and the resumption of negotiations. This resolution was co-sponsored by France, UK and Turkey, but failed after the Soviet Union, India's long time cold war ally, exercised its veto. Upon receiving news of the fall of Goa, the Portuguese government formally severed all diplomatic links with India and refused to recognize the incorporation of the seized territories into the Indian Republic. An offer of Portuguese citizenship was instead made to all Goan natives who wished to emigrate to Portugal than remain under Indian rule. This was amended in 2006 to include only those who had been born before 19 December 1961. Later, in the show of defiance, Salazar's government placed a reward of US$10,000 for the capture of Brigadier Sagat Singh, the commander of the maroon berets of India's parachute regiment who were the first troops to enter Panjim, Goa's capital.

Relations between India and Portugal thawed only in 1974, when, following a military coup d'etat and the fall of the authoritarian corporatist rule in Lisbon, Goa was finally recognised as part of India, and steps were taken to re-establish diplomatic relations with India. In 1992, Portuguese President Mário Soares became the first Portuguese head of state to visit Goa after its annexation by India. This followed Indian President R. Venkataraman's visit to Portugal in 1990.

Internship and Repatriation of POWs

Following their surrender, the Portuguese soldiers were interned by the Indian Army at their own military camps at Navelim, Aguada, Ponda and Alparqueiros and were kept under harsh conditions which included sleeping on cement floors and hard manual labour. By January 1962, most POWs had been transferred to the newly established detainees camp at Ponda where conditions were substantially better.

In one incident, recounted by Lt. Francisco Cabral Couto (now retired general), an attempt was made on January 17, by some of the prisoners to escape the camp. The attempt was foiled, and the officers in charge of the escapees were threatened with court martial and execution by the Indians. This situation was defused by the timely intervention of a Jesuit military chaplain.

The captivity lasted for six months *"thanks to the stupid stubbornness of Lisbon"*. The Portuguese Government insisted that the POWs be repatriated by Portuguese aircraft-a demand that was rejected by the Indian Government who instead insisted on aircraft from a neutral country. The negotiations were delayed even further when Salazar ordered the detention of 1200 Indians in Mozambique allegedly as a bargaining chip in exchange for Portuguese POWs.

By May 1962, most of the POWs had been repatriated—being first flown to Karachi, in chartered French aircraft, and then sent off to Lisbon by 3 ships: The Vera Cruz, The Pátria and The Moçambique. On arrival at Tejo in Portugal, returning Portuguese servicemen were taken into custody by military police at gunpoint and without immediate access to their families who had arrived to receive them. Following intense questioning and interrogations, the officers were charged with direct insubordination on having refused to comply with directives not to surrender to the Indians. On 22 March 1963, the punishments were announced: 10 officers were expelled from the Armed forces with compulsory retirement for 5 and half a year's suspension from military service for 9.

Ex-governor Manuel Antonio Vassalo e Silva was greeted with a hostile reception when he returned to Portugal. He was subsequently court martialed for failing to follow orders, expelled from the military and was sent into exile. He returned to Portugal only in 1974, after the fall of the regime, and was given back his military status. He was later able to conduct a state visit to Goa, where he was given a warm reception.

International Reaction to the Capture of Goa

"The casualties were minimum. I am in favour of all wars being like the war between India and Portugal — peaceful and quickly over!"-J. K. Galbraith, former US ambassador to India

United States of America

The United States' official reaction to the invasion of Goa was delivered by Adlai Stevenson in the UN Security Council, where he condemned the armed action of the Indian government and demanded that all Indian forces be unconditionally withdrawn from Goan soil.

To express its displeasure with the Indian action in Goa, the US Senate Foreign Relations Committee attempted, over the objections of President John F. Kennedy, to cut the 1962 foreign aid appropriation to India by 25 percent. Referring to the perception, especially in the West, that India had previously been lecturing the world about the virtues of nonviolence, US President

Kennedy told the Indian ambassador to the US, "You spend the last fifteen years preaching morality to us, and then you go ahead and act the way any normal country would behave.... People are saying, the preacher has been caught coming out of the brothel."

In an article titled "India, The Aggressor", *The New York Times* on 19 December 1961, stated "With his invasion of Goa Prime Minister Nehru has done irreparable damage to India's good name and to the principles of international morality."

Life International, in its issue dated 12 February 1962, carried an article titled "Symbolic pose by Goa's Governor" in which it expressed its vehement condemnation of the military action.

The world's initial outrage at pacifist India's resort to military violence for conquest has subsided into resigned disdain. And in Goa, a new Governor strikes a symbolic pose before portraits of men who had administered the prosperous Portuguese enclave for 451 years. He is K. P. Candeth, commanding India's 17th Infantry Division, and as the very model of a modern major general, he betrayed no sign that he is finding Goans less than happy about their "liberation". Goan girls refuse to dance with Indian officers. Goan shops have been stripped bare by luxury-hungry Indian soldiers, and Indian import restrictions prevent replacement. Even in India, doubts are heard. "India", said respected Chakravarti Rajagopalachari, leader of the Swatantra Party, "has totally lost the moral power to raise her voice against the use of military power" – Symbolic pose by Goa's Governor, Life International, *February 12, 1962*

Soviet Union

The head of state of Soviet Union, Leonid Brezhnev, who was touring India at the time of the war, made several speeches applauding the Indian action. In a farewell message, he urged Indians to ignore western indignation as it came "from those who are accustomed to strangle the peoples striving for independence... and from those who enrich themselves from colonialist plunder". Nikita Khrushchev, the de facto Soviet leader, telegraphed Nehru stating that there was "unanimous acclaim" from every Soviet citizen for "Friendly India". The USSR had earlier vetoed a UN security council resolution condemning the Indian invasion of Goa.

China

In an official statement, released long after the action in Goa, Peking stressed the support of the Chinese government for the struggle of the people of Asia, Africa and Latin America against "imperialist colonialism". China neither condemned nor applauded the invasion, despite Portuguese rule of Macau, as at the time, it was enjoying cordial relations with India, although the Sino-Indian War would begin only months later.

Pakistan

In a letter to the US President on 2 January 1962, the Pakistani President General Ayub Khan stated: "My Dear President, The forcible taking of Goa by India has demonstrated what we in Pakistan have never had any illusions about—that India would not hesitate to attack if it were in her interest to do so and if she felt that the other side was too weak to resist."

Manipur Accession to India

The cremation of Maharaja Bodhchandra Singh was delayed from the early morning to late dark evening quite unusually as the decision of the Government of India for his immediate successor was awaited which could not be decided and given by the then Chief Commissioner of Manipur, PC Matthew, ICS. The decision of succession came however in the late afternoon from New Delhi in a "crash" wireless message flashed selecting his 'legitimate eldest young son, Okendrajit Singh of some 5 years old, the younger brother of Princes Tamphasana Devi to succeed his late father as was decided and recommended in a decision taken in a very prolonged meeting held at the Chief Commissioner's House after examining very thoroughly and carefully all the "nooks and corners" of the very very delicate issue that had come up in between the Chief Commissioner, PC Matthew, Maharaj Kumar Priya Brata Singh, ex-Chief Minister and Customs Secretary to His Highness the Maharaja, Waikhom Chaoba Singh, former Darbar Member (Minister) and was also the "guardian-tutor" of Maharaja Bodhchandra Singh during the time of his yubrajship.

The Rajmata, Kamlavati Devi (Sangai Devi), the second Rani of Maharaja Bodhchandra Singh had been also made the "regent" of the young and minor king duly assisted by a 'court of ward" headed by late Salam Tombi Singh, Member of the then Manipur

Territorial Council and later on became Speaker of the Manipur Legislative Assembly and a Minister, for as per standing tradition of Manipur in regard to royal cremations, it cannot be carried out unless the name of a successor of the deceased king is announced and made publicly known.

The queen of Manipur then was Nepali princess, Iswari Devi, eldest daughter of Prince Ramraja of Ramnagar of the then United Provinces and a cousin of His Majesty Maharaja Dhiraj, the king of Nepal. Iswari Devi was also a grand daughter of His Highness the Maharaja (then Prime Minister) of Nepal, and also a cousin sister of Nepali Brigadier, Kali Bahadur of the Royal Nepal Army whose brigade of warrior Gorkhas was in Manipur during 1942/43 participating in the fighting of the British against the Japanese as one of its loyal Allies.

Maharani Iswari Devi had no issue. Actually, the third Oriya daughter of Raja of Bodo Khimdi in Ganjam district of the erstwhile Madras Presidency, Ram Priya Devi whom Maharaja Bodhachandra Singh married in 1929 when he was the Yubraj should have been the Queen of Manipur had she not been untimely divorced in 1941 due to a 'point of no return' very strained relationship developed in between the father king of Manipur, Maharaja Sir Churachand Singh and the Raja of Bodo Khimdi on the issue of much less unexpected "royal dowry" received by the former from the latter.

Of course, as had been mentioned earlier the option on the part of Manipur was either to merge with the Dominion of India or with the Dominion of Pakistan. Considering her very unfavourable geographical and other political considerations, and also cultural and religious conditions, in particular, joining with the Dominion of Pakistan by Manipur was straightaway very much out of question and hence Maharaja Bodhchandra Singh very thoughtfully and rightly "paved the way" for finally merging with the Dominion of India by his signing during the early stage in the so called instrument of Accession and the Standstill Agreement on 11 August, 1947.

In fact, the British Government had already given their green signal in the year 1935 to Maharaja Sir Churachand Singh for the State of Manipur to join with the Dominion of Burma (now Myanmar) when it was being carved out by separating it from the British India if he was willing to do so to which, the Maharaja, far sightedly was thoughtful in his thinking or otherwise, had kept "mum" on the very tricky issue-the seemingly generous offer of the British Government was actually nothing but for keeping the most strategic State of Manipur as a "buffer state" on the eastern most fringe of India for serving their interest.

Had Manipur joined with Burma, as was very much desired and worked upto the last for last for it by Neta Hijam Irabot Singh much later on, what would have been the conditions of the State-could they have been politically and economically in a much better off state or in a much worsened condition than the present one which is very much like living in a "big frying cauldron" placed above a very violently burning fire? Really it is also a billion dollar question that may not be very easily answered even by a political 'genius'.

While such far-sighted views of the kings of Manipur are something very much appreciable the hasty and highly dictating manner on the part of the then Government of India adopted in forcing the helpless king, Maharaja Bodhchandra Singh to sign the Merger Agreement on 21 September 1949 at Governor's House at Shillong without the due approval of his Cabinet is still considered by many, particularly by the legal experts, to be very "untactful" and "undemocratic" act on the part of the Government of India.

The feelings of great sadness are still there in the humble minds of the people of Manipur of the high-handed act of the then Government of India, particularly of the Union Home Minister, Sardar Vallavbhai Patel by which the king of Manipur and his party were put under some sort of a House arrest as some war "captives at the royal residency at Red Lands, Shillong from 18 to 20 September, 1949 and of the unbearable news of humiliations underwent by the highly religious and very peaceful king. Maharaja Bodhchandra Singh at the hands of the Governor of Assam, Prakasa and his Advisor, Nari K Rustomji.

Maharaja Bodhchandra Singh became so desperate by the unexpected humiliations done to him that he became almost "insane" at one point of time and had secretly and most unbelievably told his private Secretary late Sanasam Gourahari Singh of Singjamei Makha who accompanied in the royal journey to be ready even to murder the Governor and his Advisor, Nari K Rustomji when they meet them again on the next day of 19.9.1949 for further negotiation to be carried out by shooting the former by the Maharaja and the latter by Gourahari Singh and then both

Maharaja Bodhchandra Singh and the private secretary Gourahari Singh to end their lives then and there in the Governor's House Shillong by shooting each other for the sake of keeping up the age-old prestige and territorial integrity of their beloved mother land, independent, Manipur".

The kings of Manipur played important roles in framing Manipur history. The kingdom of Manipur has been known by various names like Tilli-Koktong, Sanna-Leipak, Poirei-Lam, Mitei-Leipak, Meitrabak and the present day Manipur during the reign of a total of 109 rulers. From as early as 33 AD, Lord Pakhangba and his dynasty continued to rule the kingdom directly in chronological order and it was Pakhangba himself who introduced Kangla in Manipur. Their rule lasted till 1949 AD when the merger of Manipur with the Indian Union came into effect.

The kingdom of Manipur lost its sovereignty in the year 1891 AD after the Britishers defeated Manipur in the Anglo-Manipuri war in Khongjom. The Britishers ruled Manipur till the Indian independence in 1947, followed by the annexation of the state in the Indian Territory. Famous Manipuri kings, Khagemba (Sana Hihonhan) in the 16th century and Pamheiba (Garib Niwaz) during 17th century further extended the kingdom of Manipur by storming deep into the neighbouring kingdom of Burma.

Among the vast chronicle of the Manipur kingdom, Maharaja Bhagyachandra (1762-1798 A.D.) deserves special mention. The famous dance form, Ras Lila, was fabricated by Maharaja Bhagyachandra. The legendary Maharajah spread Vaishnavism in a large scale in Manipur. Credit also goes to the Maharajah for fighting and defending Manipur from the Burmese invasions time and again. The merger of Manipur with the Dominion of India came with Maharaja Bodhchandra Singh, who continued to enjoy his authority on Manipur for his lifetime as per the agreement.

4

The Question of National Language of India

Languages with Official Status in India

The official language of the Union is Hindi with English as a secondary official language; states in India can legislate their own official languages. Neither the Constitution of India, nor any Indian law defines any *national language*.

States specify their own official language(s) through legislation. The section of the Constitution of India dealing with official languages therefore includes detailed provisions which deal not just with the languages used for the official purposes of the union, but also with the languages that are to be used for the official purposes of each state and union territory in the country, and the languages that are to be used for communication between the union and the states *inter se*.

At the time the constitution entered into force, English was used for most official purposes both at the federal level and in the various states. The constitution envisaged the gradual phasing in of local languages, principally Hindi, to replace English over a fifteen-year period, but gave Parliament the power to, by law, provide for the continued use of English even thereafter. Accordingly, English continues to be used today, in combination with Hindi (at the central level and in some states) and other languages (at the state level).

The legal framework governing the use of languages for official purpose currently includes the Constitution, the Official Languages

Act, 1963, Official Languages (Use for Official Purpose of the Union) Rules, 1976, and various state laws, as well as rules and regulations made by the central government and the states.

Official Languages of the Union

The Indian constitution, in 1950, declared Hindi in Devanagari script to be the official language of the union. Unless Parliament decided otherwise, the use of English for official purposes was to cease 15 years after the constitution came into effect, i.e., on 26 January 1965. The prospect of the changeover, however, led to much alarm in the non Hindi-speaking areas of India. As a result, Parliament enacted the Official Languages Act, 1963, which provided for the continued use of English for official purposes along with Hindi, even after 1965.

In late 1964, an attempt was made to expressly provide for an end to the use of English, but it was met with protests from states such as Tamil Nadu, Kerala, West Bengal, Karnataka, Pondicherry and Andhra Pradesh. Some of these protests also turned violent. As a result, the proposal was dropped, and the Act itself was amended in 1967 to provide that the use of English would not be ended until a resolution to that effect was passed by the legislature of every state that had not adopted Hindi as its official language, and by each house of the Indian Parliament.

The current position is thus that the Union government may continue to use English in addition to Hindi for its official purposes as a "subsidiary official language," but is also required to prepare and execute a programme to progressively increase its use of Hindi. The exact extent to which, and the areas in which, the Union government uses Hindi and English, respectively, is determined by the provisions of the Constitution, the Official Languages Act, 1963, the Official Languages Rules, 1976, and statutory instruments made by the Department of Official Language under these laws.

The Language of Parliamentary Proceedings and Laws

The Indian constitution draws a distinction between the language to be used in Parliamentary proceedings, and the language in which laws are to be made. Parliamentary business, according to the Constitution, may be conducted in either Hindi or English. The use of English in parliamentary proceedings was to be phased out at the end of fifteen years unless Parliament chose to extend its use, which Parliament did through the Official Languages Act, 1963. In addition, the constitution permits a person who is unable to express himself in either Hindi or English to, with the permission of the Speaker of the relevant House, address the House in his mother tongue.

In contrast, the constitution requires the authoritative text of all laws, including Parliamentary enactments and statutory instruments, to be in English, until Parliament decides otherwise. Parliament has not exercised its power to so decide, instead merely requiring that all such laws and instruments, and all bills brought before it, also be translated into Hindi, though the English text remains authoritative.

The Language of the Judiciary

The constitution provides that all proceedings in the Supreme Court of India, the country's highest court, shall be in English. Parliament has the power to alter this by law, but has not done so.

The Language of Administration

The Union government is required by law to progressively increase the use of Hindi in its official work, which it has sought to do through "persuasion, incentive and goodwill."

The Official Language Act provides that the Union government shall use both Hindi and English in most administrative documents that are intended for the public. The Official Languages Rules, in contrast, provide for a higher degree of use of Hindi in communications between offices of the central government (other than offices in Tamil Nadu, to which the rules do not apply). Communications between different departments within the central government may be in either Hindi or English, although a translation into the other language must be provided if required.

Communications within offices of the same department, however, must be in Hindi if the offices are in Hindi-speaking states, and in either Hindi or English otherwise with Hindi being used in proportion to the percentage of staff in the receiving office who have a working knowledge of Hindi. Notes and memos in files may be in either Hindi or English, with the Government having a duty to provide a translation into the other language if required. In addition, every person submitting a petition for the redress of a grievance to a government officer or authority has a constitutional right to submit it in any language used in India.

Official Language Implementation

Various steps have been taken by the Indian government to implement the use and familiarisation of Hindi extensively. Regional Hindi implementation offices at Bangalore, Cochin, Mumbai, Kolkata, Guwahati, Bhopal, Delhi and Ghaziabad have been established to monitor the implementation of Hindi in Central government offices and PSUs. Annual targets are set by the Department of Official Language regarding the amount of correspondence being carried out in Hindi.

A Parliament Committee on Official Language constituted in 1976 periodically reviews the progress in the use of Hindi and submits a report to the President. Kendriya Hindi Samiti chaired by the Prime Minister was established in 1967. This apex policy making body lays down the guidelines for the propagation of Hindi. Town Official Language Implementation Committees are constituted in towns having ten or more Central Government offices. Cash awards are given to the employees of the Central Government, for writing books in Hindi. All Central government offices and PSUs are to establish Hindi Cells for implementation of Hindi in their offices.

Official Languages at the State Level

The Indian constitution does not specify the official languages to be used by the states for the conduct of their official functions, and leaves each state free to, through its legislature, adopt Hindi or any language used in its territory as its official language or languages. The language need not be one of those listed in the Eighth Schedule, and several states have adopted official languages which are not so listed. Examples include Kokborok in Tripura; Mizo in Mizoram; Khasi, Garo, and Jaintia in Meghalaya; and French in Pondicherry.

The Language of the Legislature and Administration

The constitutional provisions in relation to use of the official language in legislation at the State level largely mirror those relating to the official language at the central level, with minor variations. State legislatures may conduct their business in their official language, Hindi or (for a transitional period, which the legislature can extend if it so chooses) English, and members who cannot use any of these have the same rights to their mother tongue with the Speaker's permission. The authoritative text of all laws must be in English, unless Parliament passes a law permitting a state to use another language, and if the original text of a law is in a different language, an authoritative English translation of all laws must be prepared.

The state has the right to regulate the use of its official language in public administration, and in general, neither the constitution nor any central enactment imposes any restriction on this right. However, every person submitting a petition for the redress of a grievance to an officer or authority of the state government has a constitutional right to submit it in any language used in that state, regardless of its official status.

In addition, the constitution grants the central government, acting through the President, the power to issue certain directives to the government of a state in relation to the use of minority languages for official purposes. The President may direct a State to officially recognise a language spoken in its territory for specified purposes and in specified regions, if its speakers demand it and satisfy him that a substantial proportion of the State's population desire its use. Similarly, States and local authorities are required to endeavour to provide primary education in the mother tongue for all linguistic minorities, regardless of whether or not their language is official in that State, and the President has the power to issue directions he deems necessary to ensure that they are provided these facilities.

The Language of the Judiciary

States have significantly less freedom in relation to determine the language in which judicial proceedings in their respective High Courts will be conducted. The constitution gives the power to authorise the use of Hindi, or the state's official language in proceedings of the High Court to the Governor, rather than the state legislature, and requires the Governor to obtain the consent of the President of India, who in these matters acts on the advice of the Government of India. The Official Languages Act gives the Governor a similar power, subject to similar conditions, in relation to the language in which the High Court's judgments will be delivered. Four states-Bihar, Uttar Pradesh, Madhya Pradesh and Rajasthan-have been granted the right to conduct proceedings in their High Courts in their official language, which, for all of them, was Hindi. However, the only non-Hindi state to seek a similar power-Tamil Nadu, which sought the right to conduct proceedings in Tamil in its High Court-had its application rejected by the central government earlier, which said it was advised to do so by the Supreme Court. In 2006, the law ministry said that it would not object to Tamil Nadu state's desire to conduct Madras High Court proceedings in Tamil.

Anti-Hindi Agitations of Tamil Nadu

The Anti-Hindi agitations of Tamil Nadu are a series of agitations that happened in the Indian state of Tamil Nadu (formerly Madras State and part of Madras Presidency) during both pre-and post-Independence periods. The agitations involved several mass protests, riots, student and political movements in Tamil Nadu, and concerned the official status of Hindi in the state and in the Indian Republic.

The first anti-Hindi agitation was launched in 1937, in opposition to the introduction of compulsory teaching of Hindi in the schools of Madras Presidency by the first Indian National Congress government led by C. Rajagopalachari (Rajaji). This move was immediately opposed by Periyar E. V. Ramasamy and the opposition Justice Party (later Dravidar Kazhagam). The agitation, which lasted three years, was multifaceted and involved fasts, conferences, marches, picketing and protests. The government responded with a crackdown resulting in the death of two protesters and the arrest of 1,198 persons including women and children. The mandatory Hindi education was later withdrawn by the British Governor of Madras Lord Erskine in February 1940 after the resignation of the Congress Government in 1939.

Adoption of an official language for the Indian Republic was a hotly debated issue during the framing of the Indian Constitution after India's independence from Britain. After an exhaustive and divisive debate, Hindi was adopted as the official language of India with English continuing as an associate official language for a period of fifteen years, after which Hindi would become the sole official language. The new Constitution came into effect on 26 January 1950. Efforts by the Indian Government to make Hindi the sole official language after 1965 were not acceptable to many non-Hindi Indian states, who wanted the continued use of English. The Dravida Munnetra Kazhagam (DMK), a descendant of Dravidar Kazhagam, led the opposition to Hindi. To allay the fears of the opposition, Prime Minister Jawaharlal Nehru enacted the Official Languages Act in 1963 to ensure the continuing use of English beyond 1965. The text of the Act did not satisfy the DMK and increased their skepticism that his assurances might not be honoured by future administrations.

As the day (26 January 1965) of switching over to Hindi as sole official language approached, the anti-Hindi movement gained momentum in Tamil Nadu with increased support from college students. On 25 January, a full-scale riot broke out in the southern city of Madurai, sparked off by a minor altercation between agitating students and Congress party members. The riots spread all over Tamil Nadu, continued unabated for the next two months, and were marked by acts of violence, arson, looting, police firing and lathi charges. The Congress Government of the Madras State, called in paramilitary forces to quell the agitation; their involvement resulted in the deaths of about seventy persons (by official estimates) including two police men. To calm the situation, Indian Prime Minister Lal Bahadur Shastri gave assurances that English would continue to be used as the official language as long the non-Hindi speaking states wanted. The riots subsided after Shastri's assurance, as did the student agitation.

The agitations of 1965 led to major political changes in Tamil Nadu. The DMK won the 1967 assembly election and the Congress Party never managed to recapture power in the state since then. The Official Languages Act was eventually amended in 1967 by the Congress Government headed by Indira Gandhi to guarantee the indefinite use of Hindi and English as official languages. This effectively ensured the current "virtual indefinite policy of bilingualism" of the Indian Republic.

Background

The Republic of India has hundreds of languages. According to the Census of 2001, there are 1,635 rationalized mother tongues and 122 languages with more than 10,000 speakers. During the British Raj, English was the official language. When the Indian Independence Movement gained momentum in the early part of the 20th Century, efforts were undertaken to make Hindustani (an amalgam of Hindi and Urdu) as a common language to unite various linguistic groups against the British Government. As early as 1918, Mahatma Gandhi established the *Dakshin Bharat Hindi Prachar Sabha* (Institution for the Propagation of Hindi in South India). In 1925, the Indian National Congress switched to Hindustani from English for conducting its proceedings. Both Gandhi and Jawaharlal Nehru were supporters of Hindustani and Congress wanted to propagate the learning of Hindustani in non-Hindi speaking Provinces of India. The idea of making Hindustani or Hindi the common language, was not acceptable to Periyar E. V. Ramasamy, who viewed it as an attempt to make Tamils subordinate to North India.

Agitation of 1937-40

The Indian National Congress won the 1937 elections in Madras Presidency. C. Rajagopalachari (Rajaji) became the Chief Minister on 14 July 1937. He was a supporter of propagating Hindi in South India. Even before the elections, he had expressed support for Hindi in a newspaper article (*Sudesamithran*, 6 May 1937): "Government employment is limited. All cannot get it. Therefore one has to search for other jobs. For that and for business, knowledge of Hindi is necessary. Only if we learn Hindi, the south Indian can gain respect among the others." On 11 August 1937, within a month of coming to power, he announced his intention to introduce Hindi language teaching in secondary schools by issuing a policy statement.

This move followed lobbying by pro-Hindi organisations like *Hindustani Seva Dal* and *Hindustani Hitashi Sabha*. These organisations had earlier convinced many Congress led local governments to introduce compulsory Hindi in schools in the early 1930s. Periyar E. V. Ramasamy and the opposition Justicy Party led by A. T. Panneerselvam immediately opposed the move. An Anti-Hindi conference was organised on 4 October 1937 to protest the announcement. On 21 April 1938, Rajaji went ahead and passed a government order (G.O) making the teaching of Hindi compulsory in 125 Secondary schools in the Presidency. Rajaji's persistence was viewed by opponents as an attempt to destroy Tamil and promote Hindi. They started state wide protests against Rajaji and Hindi. The agitation was marked by protest marches, anti-Hindi conferences, observing a anti-Hindi day (1 July and 3 December 1938), fasts against government policies, black flag demonstrations and picketing of government offices and institutions. It was active in Tamil speaking districts of the Presidency-Ramnad, Tinnevely, Salem, Tanjore and North Arcot. The agitation lasted till the order was withdrawn in February 1940. Two persons-Thalamuthu and Natarajan-lost their lives. Around 1,200 people including Periyar were imprisoned.

Support for the Agitation

The anti-Hindi agitation was backed by Periyar's Self-Respect Movement and the opposition Justice Party. Periyar eventually became the President of the Justice Party during the course of the agitation. The agitation was also supported by Tamil scholars like Maraimalai Adigal, Somasundara Bharathi, K. Appadurai, Mudiyarasan and Ilakkuvanar. In December 1937, Tamil Saivite scholars were among the first to announce their opposition to the Hindi teaching in the *Saiva Sidhandha Maha Samaja* meeting at Velur. Women also participated in the agitation in large numbers.

Moovalur Ramamirtham, Narayani, Va. Ba. Thamaraikani, Munnagar Azhagiyar, Dr. Dharmambal, Malar Mugathammaiyar, Pattammal and Seethammal were some of the women who were arrested for participating in the agitation. On 13 November 1938, the Tamil Nadu Women's Conference was convened to demonstrate women's support for the movement. Despite the anti-Brahmin sentiments espoused by the backers of the agitation a, few Brahmins like Kanchi Rajagopalachari also participated in the movement.

The Tamil speaking Muslims in the Madras presidency supported the agitation (as opposed to the Urdu speaking Muslims, who supported the propagation of Hindi). P. Kaliffulah, a Muslim League member representing Trichy in the Legislative Assembly, declared "I may at once say that I am a Rowther myself; my mother tongue is Tamil and not Urdu. I am not ashamed of it; I am proud of it.. We have not been told why Hindi after all has been chosen as the common language of India". Acknowledging the agitation's popular support, Lord Erskine, the then Governor of Madras wrote to Viceroy Linlithgow in July 1938 that "Compulsory Hindi has been the cause of great trouble in this province and is certainly contrary to the wishes of the bulk of the population..."

Fasts

On 1 May 1938, a young man named Stalin Jagadeesan went on a fast demanding the withdrawal of compulsory Hindi teaching. He became a symbol for the anti-Hindi agitators. In an interview published in Periyar's magazine *Viduthalai* he declared that his fast was to prove that *Tamil thai* (lit.Mother Tamil) still had loyal sons. On 1 June, another man named Ponnusamy began a fast in front of Rajaji's house. Periyar did not approve of fasting as a form of protest. But other leaders of the agitation like C. N. Annadurai used Jagadeesan as an example. Annadurai declared in an anti-Hindi meeting that "If Jagadeesan dies, I am ready to take his place, and die along with ten others. As soon as Jagadeesan dies, you should also be prepared to die". Jagadeesan's fast was called off after ten weeks and it was reported that he had been eating regularly during the nights.

Tamil Brigade

In August-September 1938, a protest march was jointly organised by Periyar's Self-Respect movement and the Muslim league. It was flagged of by Periyar and Khaliffullah. The marchers who called themselves *Tamilar Padai* (lit. Tamil brigade), started from Trichy on 1 August 1938. They were led by Kumarasamy Pillai and Moovalur Ramamirtham Ammal. In the next 42 days, the marchers covered 234 villages and 60 towns. They addressed 87 public meetings and received widespread coverage in the Press. They reached Madras on 11 September 1938 and were arrested for picketing government offices. The march succeeded in raising anti-Hindi and pro-Tamil support in smaller towns and villages they covered.

Thalamuthu and Natarajan

Two persons died during the agitation and were claimed as martyrs by the agitators. Their deaths fueled the protests further. Natarajan (a Dalit) was arrested On 5 December 1938. He was admitted to the hospital on the 30 December and died on 15 January 1939. On 13 February 1939, Thalamuthu Nadar was arrested with others for picketing the Hindu Theological High School in Madras. While imprisoned, he fell ill on 6 March and died on 11 March. The government claimed that his death was due to Cellulitis and Amoebic dysentery and he was already in poor health when he died. It dismissed their deaths and claimed they were illiterates. When the issue was raised in the Assembly, Rajaji dismissed it casually. The agitators were incensed by the government attitude and turned the dead men into martyrs. Their funeral processions in Madras were attended by hundreds of mourners and witnessed fiery speeches denouncing the government. Annadurai proclaimed that Natarajan's name and deeds should be inscribed in gold in the history of the world. The agitators praised their sacrifices and claimed that the dead men had refused early release in exchange for ending their activities. In an interview given to the *Sunday Observer* on 27 January 1939, Natarajan's father K. Lakshmanan said when his son was hospitalized he refused to apologize to get an early release.

Anti Brahminism

The anti-Hindi movement viewed the Hindi legislation as an attempt by Brahmins to impose Hindi and Sanskrit over Tamil. Rajaji's earlier attempt to translate an English Language Physics book into Tamil using Sanskrit words was viewed as proof of his preference of Sanskrit over Tamil. The anti-Hindi movement portrayed the Brahmin dominated Tamil Nadu Congress party as a stooge of "Hindi Imperialists" from the North. The resistance of the Brahmin Tamil scholars for removing Sanskrit words from Tamil was viewed by some in the agitation as proof of Brahmin complicity in the attempt to destroy Tamil.

Rajaji was identified as an enemy of Tamil. Dravidian movement newspapers carried cartoons depicting Rajaji hurling a dagger at *Tamil Thai* and disrobing her. Similar banners were displayed in the processions taken out by anti-Hindi agitators. In an anti-Hindi meeting organised in August 1938, Pavalar Balasundaram accused the Brahmin community of "killing Tamil Thai". Rajaji's dismissal of Natarasan's death in the Assembly was denounced as "Aryans laughing while Tamils shed tears for their hero".

Government Response

The ruling Congress Party was divided on the Hindi issue. While Rajaji and his supporters stuck to their position, Sathyamurti and Sarvepalli Radhakrishnan were against it. They wanted Rajaji to make Hindi optional or to provide a conscience clause for allowing parents to withhold their children from Hindi Classes. Satyamurti also disagreed with the use of Criminal Law Amendment Act of 1932 against the anti-Hindi agitators. In a letter written to Mahatma Gandhi on 7 July 1938, he wrote:

I personally believe that where a parent or guardian swears an affidavit before a magistrate stating his reasons that it is against his conscience that his boy or girl should learn Hindustani compulsorily, the child may be exempted. I personally believe very few parents or guardians will claim this exemption. This will expose the hollowness of the agitation and kill it. I wish you to write to Sri. C. Rajagopalachari suggesting this to him. Moreover, I am not very happy over the use by the Madras Government of the Criminal Law Amendment Act against these picketers..

Rajaji defended his action in another G.O issued on 14 June 1938:

The attainment by our Province of its rightful place in the national life of India requires that our educated youth should possess a working knowledge of the most widely spoken language in India. Government have therefore decided upon the introduction of Hindustani in the secondary school curriculum of our province. Government desire to make it clear that Hindi is not to be introduced in any elementary school whatsoever, the mother tongue being the only language taught in such schools. Hindi is to be introduced only in secondary schools and there too only in the 1st, 2nd and 3rd forms, that is to say in the 6th, 7th and 8th years of school life. It will not therefore interfere in any way with the teaching of the mother tongue in the secondary schools....Hindi will be compulsory only in the sense that attendance in such classes will be compulsory and pupils cannot take Hindi as a substitute for Tamil, Telugu, Malayalam or Kannada, but must learn Hindi only in addition to one of these languages

He refused to give in to the demands of the agitators. He claimed they were motivated by their "prejudices of anti-Aryanism" and "Hatred of the Congress". He used the Criminal Law Amendment Act against the agitators. 1,198 protesters were arrested and out of them 1,179 were convicted (73 of those jailed were women and some of them went to jail with their children; 32 children accompanied their mothers to prison). Periyar was sentenced to one year of rigorous imprisonment (he was released within six months on 22 May 1939 citing medical grounds) and Annadurai was jailed for four months. On 7 June 1939, all those arrested for participating in the agitations were released without explanation. Rajaji also organised pro-Hindustani meetings to counter the agitators.

Cancellation

On 29 October 1939, Rajaji's Congress Government resigned protesting the involvement of India in the Second World War. Madras provincial government was placed under Governor's rule. On 31 October, Periyar suspended the agitation and asked the Governor to withdraw the compulsory Hindi order. On 21 February 1940, Governor Erskine, issued a press communique withdrawing compulsory Hindi teaching and making it optional.

Agitations of 1940-1950

During 1940-46, there were sporadic agitations against Hindi by the Dravidar Kazhagam (DK) and Periyar. Whenever the government introduced Hindi as a compulsory language in schools, anti-Hindi protests happened and succeeded in stopping the move. The largest anti-Hindi agitations in this period occurred in 1948-50. After India obtained independence in 1947, the Congress Government at the Centre urged all states to make Hindi compulsory in schools. The Congress Government of Madras Presidency under Omandur Ramasamy Reddiar complied and made Hindi compulsory from the academic year 1948-49.

It also introduced a minimum mark qualification in Hindi for the promotion of students to higher standards (grades). Periyar once again launched a anti-Hindi agitation. The 1948 agitation was supported by former Congress nationalists like M. P. Sivagnanam and Thiru. Vi. Ka, who recanted their earlier pro-Hindi policies. On 17 July, the DK convened an all party anti-Hindi conference to oppose the compulsory Hindi teaching. As in the agitation of 1938-40, this agitation was also characterized by strikes, black flag demonstrations and anti-Hindi processions. When Rajaji (then the Governor-General of India) visited Madras on 23 August, the DK staged a black flag demonstration protesting against his visit.

On 27 August, Periyar and Annadurai were arrested. The Government did not change its position on Hindi and the agitation continued. On 18 August Periyar and other DK leaders were arrested again. A compromise was reached between the government and agitators. The government stopped the legal action against the agitators and they in turn dropped the agitation on 26 December 1948. Eventually, the government made Hindi teaching optional from the academic year 1950-51. Students who did not want to learn Hindi were allowed to participate in other school activities during Hindi classes.

Language and Indian Constitution

The Indian Constituent Assembly was established on 9 December 1946, for drafting a Constitution when India became independent. The Constituent Assembly witnessed fierce debates on the language issue. The adoption of a "National Language", the language in which the constitution was to be written in and the language in which the proceedings of the assembly were to be conducted were the main questions debated by the framers of the Constitution. On one side were the members from the Hindi speaking provinces like Algu Rai Sastri, R.V. Dhulekar, Balkrishna Sharma, Purushottam Das Tandon, (all from United Provinces), Babunath Gupta (Bihar), Hari Vinayak Pataskar (Bombay) and Seth Govind Das (Central Provinces and Berar).

They moved a large number of pro-Hindi amendments and argued for adopting Hindi as the sole National Language. On 10 December 1946, Dhulekar declared "People who do not know Hindustani have no right to stay in India. People who are present in the House to fashion a constitution for India and do not know Hindustani are not worthy to be members of this assembly. They had better leave."

The pro-Hindi block was further divided into two camps: 1) The Hindi faction comprising Tandon, Govind Das, Sampurnanand, Ravishankar Shukla and K. M. Munshi and 2)the Hindustani faction represented by Jawaharlal Nehru and Abul Kalam Azad. The adoption of Hindi as the national language was opposed by members from South India like T.T. Krishnamachari, G. Durgabai, T. A. Ramalingam Chettiar, N. G. Ranga, N. Gopalaswamy Ayyangar (all belonging to Madras) and S. V. Krishnamurthy Rao (Mysore). This anti-Hindi block favoured retaining English as official language. Their views were reflected in the following pronouncement of Krishnamachari: We disliked the English language in the past. I disliked it because I was forced to learn Shakespeare and Milton, for which I had no taste at all. If we are going to be compelled to learn Hindi, I would perhaps not be able to learn it because of my age, and perhaps I would not be willing to do it because of the amount of constraint you put on me. This kind of intolerance makes us fear that the strong Centre which we need, a strong Centre which is necessary will also mean the enslavement of people who do not speak the language at the centre. I would, Sir, convey a warning on behalf of people of the South for the reason that there are already elements in South India who want separation..., and my honourable friends in U.P. do not help us in any way by flogging their idea of "Hindi Imperialism" to the maximum extent possible. So, it is up to my friends in Uttar Pradesh to have a whole India; it is up to them to have a Hindi-India. The choice is theirs.

After three years of debate, the assembly arrived at a compromise at the end of 1949. It was called the Munshi-Ayyangar compromise (after K.M. Munshi and Gopalaswamy Ayyangar) and it struck a balance between the demands of all groups. Part XVII of the Indian Constitution was drafted according to this compromise. It did not have any mention of a "National Language". Instead, it defined only the "Official Languages" of the Union:

Hindi in Devanagari script would be the official language of the Indian Union. For fifteen years, English would also be used for all official purposes (Article 343). A language commission could be convened after five years to recommend ways to promote Hindi as the sole official language and to phase out the use of English (Article 344). Official communication between states and between states and the Union would be in the official language of the union (Article 345).English would be used for all legal purposes-in court proceedings, bills, laws, rules and other regulations (Article 348).The Union was duty bound to promote the spread and usage of Hindi (Article 351).

India became independent on 15 August 1947 and the Constitution was adopted on 26 January 1950.

The Language Commission

The adoption of English as official language along with Hindi was heavily criticized by pro-Hindi politicians like Jana Sangh's founder Syama Prasad Mookerjee, who demanded that Hindi should be made National language. Soon after the Constitution was adopted on 26 January 1950, efforts were made to propagate Hindi for official usage. In 1952, the Ministry of Education launched a voluntary Hindi teaching scheme. On 27 May 1952, use of Hindi was introduced in warrants for judicial appointments. In 1955, in-house Hindi training was started for all ministries and departments of the central government. On 3 December 1955, the government started using Hindi (along with English) for *"specific purposes of the Union"*

As provided for by Article 343, Nehru appointed the First Official Language Commission under the chairmanship of B. G. Kher on 7 June 1955. The commission delivered its report on 31 July 1956. It recommended a number of steps to eventually replace English with Hindi (The report had dissenting notes from two non-Hindi members-P. Subbarayan from Tamil Nadu and Suniti Kumar Chatterji from West Bengal). The Parliamentary Committee on Official Language, chaired by Govind Ballabh Pant was constituted in September 1957 to review the Kher commission report. After two years of deliberations, the Pant Committeee submitted its recommendations to the President on 8 February 1959.

It recommended that Hindi should be made the primary official language with English as the subsidiary one. The Kher Commission and the Pant Committee recommendations were condemned and opposed by from non Hindi politicians like Suniti Kumar Chatterji, Frank Anthony and P. Subbarayan. The Academy of Telugu opposed the switch from English to Hindi in a convention held in 1956. Rajaji, once a staunch supporter of Hindi, organised a All India Language Conference (attended by representatives of Tamil, Malayalam, Telugu, Assamese, Oriya, Marathi, Kannada and Bengali languages) on 8 March 1958 to oppose the switch and declared *"Hindi is as much foreign to non-Hindi speaking people as English is to the protagonists of Hindi."*

As the opposition to Hindi grew stronger, Nehru tried to reassure the concerns of non-Hindi speakers. Speaking in the parliamentary debate on the Pant committee report Nehru gave an assurance to them (in September 1959) :

For an indefinite period-I do not know how long-I should have, I would have English as an associate, additional language not because of facilities and all that but because I do not wish the people of Non-Hindi areas to feel that certain doors of advance are closed to them because they are forced to correspond-the Government, I mean-in the Hindi language. They can correspond in English. So I could have it as an alternate language as long as people require it and the decision for that-I would leave not to the Hindi-knowing people, but to the non Hindi-knowing people. This assurance momentarily allayed the fears of the South Indians.

DMK's anti-Hindi Policies

The Dravida Munnetra Kazhagam (DMK) which split from the Dravidar Kazhagam in 1949, inherited the anti-Hindi policies of its parent organisation. DMK's founder Annadurai had earlier participated in the anti-Hindi agitations during 1938-40 and in the 1940s. In July 1953, the DMK launched an agitation for changing the name of a town-Dalmiapuram-to Kallakudi. They claimed that the town's name (after Ramakrishna Dalmia) symbolised the exploitation of South India by the North. On 15 July 1953, M. Karunanidhi (later Chief Minister of Tamil Nadu) and other DMK members erased the Hindi name in Dalmiapuram railway station's name board and lay down on the tracks. In the altercation with the Police that followed the protests, two DMK members lost their lives and several others including Karunanidhi were arrested.

In the 1950s DMK continued its anti-Hindi policies along with the secessionist demand for Dravidistan. On 28 January 1956, Annadurai along with Periyar and Rajaji signed a resolution passed by the Academy of Tamil Culture endorsing the continuation of English as the official language. On 21 September 1957 the DMK convened a anti-Hindi Conference to protest against the imposition of Hindi. It observed 13 October 1957 as "anti-Hindi Day". On 31 July 1960, another open air anti-Hindi conference was held at Kodambakkam, Madras. In November 1963, DMK dropped its secessionist demand in the wake of the Sino-Indian War and the passage of the anti-secessionist 16th Amendment to the Indian Constitution. But the anti-Hindi stance remained and hardened with the passage of Official Languages Act of 1963. The DMK's view on Hindi's qualifications for official language status were reflected in Annadurai's response to the "numerical superiority of Hindi" argument: "If we had to accept the principle of numerical superiority while selecting our national bird, the choice would have fallen not on the peacock but on the common crow."

Official Languages Act of 1963

As the deadline stipulated in Part XVII of the Constitution for switching to Hindi as primary official language approached, the Central Government stepped up its efforts to spread Hindi's official usage. In 1960, compulsory training for Hindi typing and stenography was started. The same year, India's president Rajendra Prasad acted on the Pant Committee's recommendations and issued orders for preparation of Hindi glossaries, translating procedural literature and legal codes to Hindi, imparting Hindi education to government employees and other efforts for propagating Hindi.

To give legal status to Nehru's assurance of 1959, the Official Languages Act was passed in 1963. In Nehru's own words :

This is a Bill, in continuation of what has happened in the past, to remove a restriction which had been placed by the Constitution on the use of English after a certain date i.e. 1965. It is just to remove that restriction that this is placed.

The bill was introduced in Parliament on 21 January 1963. Opposition to the Bill came from DMK members who objected to the usage of the word "may" instead of "shall" in section 3 of the bill ("the English language may, as from the appointed day, continue to be used in addition to Hindi"). DMK 's argument was that the term "may" could be interpreted as "may not" by future administrations. They feared that minority opinion will not be considered and non Hindi speakers' views would be ignored. On 22 April, Nehru assured the parliamentarians that, for that particular case "may" had the same meaning as "shall". The DMK then demanded, if that was the case why "shall" was not used instead of "may".

Leading the opposition to the bill was Annadurai (then a Member of the Rajya Sabha). He pleaded for the indefinite continuation of the *status quo*. He argued for the continuation of English as official Language as it "distributes advantages or disadvantages evenly". The Bill was passed on 27 April without any change in the wording. As he had warned earlier, Annadurai launched state wide protests against Hindi. In November 1963, Annadurai was arrested along with 500 DMK members for burning part XVII of the Constitution at an anti-Hindi Conference.

Nehru died in May 1964 and Lal Bahadur Shastri became Prime Minister of India. Shastri and his senior cabinet members

Morarji Desai and Gulzari Lal Nanda were strong supporters of Hindi being the sole official language. This increased the apprehension that Nehru's assurances of 1959 and 1963 will not be kept despite Shastri's assurances to the contrary.

Concerns over the preference of Hindi in central government Jobs, civil service examinations and the fear that English will be replaced with Hindi as medium of instruction brought students into the Anti-Hindi Agitation camp in large numbers. On 7 March 1964, the chief minister of Madras State, M. Bhaktavatsalam at a session of the Madras Legislative Assembly recommended the introduction of Three-language formula (English, Hindi and Tamil) in the state. Apprehension over the Three-language formula increased student support for the Anti-Hindi cause

Agitation of 1965

Events Leading up to January 26

As January 26, 1965 approached, the Anti Hindi agitation in Tamil Nadu grew in numbers and urgency. The Tamil Nadu Students Anti Hindi Agitation Council was formed in January as an umbrella student organisation to coordinate the Anti Hindi efforts. The office beares of the council were student union leaders from all over Tamil Nadu including P. Seenivasan, K. Kalimuthu, Na. Kamarasan, Seyaprakasam, Ravichandran, Tiruppur. S. Duraiswamy, Sedapatti Muthaiah, Durai Murugan, K. Raja Mohammad, Navalavan, M. Natarajan and L. Ganesan. Explaining the anxiety of the students, *The Indian Express* noted in its editorial on 6 February 1965:

It was inevitable that the Madras students should have taken the lead in opposing the elevation of Hindi. After all a decision whether Hindi or English is to be the official language of the country affects them much more than any other section of the population. It is the students of the South who stand to lose most, when Hindi alone becomes the official language.

Several student conferences (sponsored by industrialists like G. D. Naidu and Karumuttu Thiagarajan Chettiar) were organised throughout the state to protest against Hindi imposition.. On 17 January, The Madras State Anti-Hindi Conference was convened in Trichy. Participants included Rajaji (Swatantara Party), V. R. Nedunchezhiyan (DMK), P. T. Rajan (Justice Party), G. D. Naidu, Karumuthu Thyagaraja Chettiar, S. P. Adithan (We Tamils Party) and Muhammad Ismail (Muslim League) In the Conference Rajaji declared that the Part XVII of the Constitution should "be heaved and thrown into the Arabian Sea." On 16 January, Annadurai announced that 26 January (also the Republic Day of India) would be observed as a day of mourning. He wrote to Shastri asking for the language transition to be postponed by a week so that Tamils could celebrate Republic Day with the rest of the country. Shastri refused and the stage was set for the confrontation.

"Day of Mourning"

Madras State's Chief Minister M. Bhaktavatsalam warned that the state government would not tolerate the sanctity of the Republic day blasphemed and threatened the students with "stern action" if they participated in politics. The DMK advanced the "Day of Mourning" by a day. On 25 January, Annadurai was taken into preventive custody along with 3000 DMK members to forestall the agitations planned for the next day.

Madurai Incident

In the morning of 25 January, students in Madurai took out a procession toward the Thilagar *thidal* (lit. Grounds) at the centre of the city. Their intention was to stage a public burning of Part XVII of the constitution. They burned a huge effigy of "Hindi Demoness" and shouted slogans against Hindi like "Down with Hindi" and "Hindi Never, English Ever". As the procession approached the Congress Party district office at North Masi Street, some Congress "volunteers" who had arrived in a Jeep shouted insults and obscenities at the students.

A volley of sandals from the students returned the insult. The provoked Congress volunteers, who ran back into the Party's office, returned with knives and attacked students, wounding seven. As the riot broke out, students set fire to the pandal in the Congress office, constructed for the Republic day celebrations. When news of the attack spread riots broke out in Madurai and other parts of the State. In retaliation for the attack, students cut down flag poles of the Congress party all over Madurai.

Two Months of Riots

As the riots spread, police responded with lathi charges and firing on student processions. This further inflamed the situation. Acts of arson, looting and damage to public property became common. Railway cars and Hindi name boards at railway stations were burned down. The Bhaktavatsalam Government considered the situation as a law and order problem and brought in para military forces to quell the agitation.

Incensed by police action, violent mobs killed two police men. Five agitators (Sivalingam, Aranganathan, Veerappan, Muthu, and Sarangapani) committed suicide by pouring gasoline and setting themselves on fire and three more (Dandapani, Muthu, and Shanmugam) died by consuming poison.

In two weeks of riots, around 70 people were killed (by official estimates). Some unofficial reports put the death toll as high as 500. A large number of students were arrested. The damage to property was assessed as one Crore (1,00,00,000) Rupees.

On 28 January, classes in Madras University and Annamalai University were suspended indefinitely. Within the Congress, opinion was divided-On 31 January, a group of Congress leaders including Mysore Chief minister S.Nijalingappa, Bengal Congress leader Atulya Ghosh, Union Minister Sanjeeva Reddy and Congress president K. Kamaraj met in Bangalore and issued an appeal not to force Hindi on non-Hindi speaking areas as they believed it might endanger the unity of the country.

Morarji Desai refused their demands regretting that Hindi was not made official before the anti-Hindi protests crystallized. He said Congress leaders in Madras should convince people there and no regional sentiments should come in the move to forge the integration of the country. Union Home Minister Gulzari Lal Nanda agreed with Bhaktavatsalam's handling of the agitation and commended him for standing "hard as a rock".

Rioting continued through out the first week of February. On February 6, student representatives met Bhatavatsalam to find a compromise.

But the talks failed and violence continued unabated. Processions, fasts, general strikes, burning of Hindi books, destruction of Hindi name boards, agitations in front of Post offices became commonplace. In a Union cabinet meeting on 11 February, C. Subramaniam, the Minister for Food, demanded statutory recognition for English as official Language. When he was voted down, he resigned along with another minister from Tamil Nadu (O. V. Alagesan).

Impact of 1965 Agitation

Immediate Impact

Faced with open revolt in his cabinet, Shastri buckled down and made a broadcast through All India Radio on February 11. Expressing shock over the riots, he promised to honour Nehru's assurances. Further he made four assurances of his own:

Every state will have complete and unfettered freedom to continue to transact its own business in the language of its own choice, which may be the regional language or English. Communications between one State to another will either be in English or will be accompanied by authentic English translation. The non-Hindi states will be free to correspond with the Central Government in English and no change will be made in this arrangement without the consent of the non-Hindi States. In the transaction of business at the Central level, English will continue to be used.

Later he added a fifth assurance: The All India Civil Services examination would continue to be conducted in English rather than in Hindi alone.

His assurances calmed down the volatile situation. On 12 February, the students council postponed the agitation indefinitely and on 16 February, C. Subramaniam and O. V. Alagesan withrew their resignations. Sporadic acts of protests and violence continued to happen throughout February and early March. On 7 March, the administration withdrew all the cases filed against the student leaders and on 14 March, the Anti-Hindi Agitation Council dropped the agitation.. Shastri's climbdown angered the pro-Hindi activists in North India. Members of Jan Sangh went about the streets of New Delhi, blackening out English signs with tar.

Impact on 1967 Election

After dropping the agitation in March 1965, the Tamil Nadu Students Anti-Hindi Agitation council continued to push for the scrapping of the Three Language formula and for a constitutional amendment to drop part XVII. On 11 May, a three-person delegation of the student council met with Prime minister Shastri to press their demands. The Anti-Hindi agitation slowly changed into a general anti-Congress organisation with the goal of defeating the congress in the 1967 election. On 20 February 1966, the first statewide conference of the council was held. It was attended by Rajaji, who asked the students to work toward defeating the Congress. In the 1967 elections, student leader P. Seenivasan contested against Kamaraj in the Virudunagar constituency. A large number of students from all over Tamil Nadu campaigned for him and ensured his victory: the Congress party was defeated and DMK came to power for the first time in Tamil Nadu.

Offical Languages (Amendment) Act of 1967

Amendment Efforts in 1965

Efforts to amend the Official Languages Act according to Shastri's assurances given in February 1965 faced stiff resistance from the pro-Hindi lobby. On 16 February, 55 MPs from 8 different states publicly expressed their disapproval of any change in the Language policy. On 19 February, 19 MPs from Maharashtra and Gujarat voiced their opposition for change and on 25 February, 106 Congress MPs met the Prime Minister to request him not to amend the Act. However, Congress MPs from Madras did not debate the issue on the Parliament floor but met the Prime Minister on 12 March. Congress and opposition parties hesitated to debate the issue in Parliament as they did not wish to make their bitter divisions on public.

On 22 February at a meeting in Congress Working Committee, K. Kamaraj pressed for the amendment to Official Languages Act, but received instant opposition from Morarji Desai, Jagjivan Ram and Ram Subhag. The Congress working committee finally agreed to a resolution which amounted to slowing down of Hindi-isation, strong implementation of three language formula in Hindi and non-Hindi speaking states, conduction of public services exam in all regional languages. These decisions were agreed upon during the Chief Minister meeting which was held on February 24.

The three language formula was not strictly enforced either in South or Hindi-speaking areas. The changes to public services exams were impractical and not well received by government officials. The only real concession to the south was the assurance that the Official Languages Act would be modified. However, any effort to follow through with that pledge received stiff resistance. In April 1965, a meeting of a cabinet sub-committee comprising Gulzari Lal Nanda, A. K. Sen, Satyanarayan Sinha, Mahavir Tyagi, M. C. Chagla and S. K. Patil and but no southern members debated the issue and could not come to any agreement. The sub-committee recommended the continuation of English and Hindi as joint link languages and was not in favour of either quota system or use of regional languages in public services exams. They drafted an amendment to Official Languages Act incorporating Nehru's assurances explicitly. This bill guaranteeing the use of English in interstate and state-Union communications as long as desired by Non-Hindi states was approved for discussion by the Speaker on August 25. But it was withdrawn after a bitter debate citing inopportune time due to the ongoing Punjabi Suba movement and Kashmir crisis at that time.

Amendment in 1967

Shastri died in January 1966 and Indira Gandhi became prime minister. The election of 1967 saw Congress retaining power with a reduced majority. In Tamil Nadu, Congress was defeated and DMK came to power. In November 1967, a new attempt to amend the bill was made. On 27 November, the bill was tabled in parliament; it was passed on 16 December (by 205 votes to 41 against). It received presidential assent on 8 January 1968 and came into effect. The Amendment modified section 3 of the 1963 Act to guarantee the "virtual indefinite policy of bilingualism" (English and Hindi) in official transactions.

Agitation of 1968

The Anti-Hindi activists from Tamil Nadu were not satisfied with the 1967 Amendment, as it did not address their concerns about the Three language Formula. However with DMK in power, they hesitated to restart the agitation. The Tamil Nadu Students' Anti-Hindi Agitation council split into several factions. The moderate factions favoured letting Annadurai and the government to deal with the situation. The extremist factions restarted the agitations. They demanded scrapping of the three language formula and an end to teaching of Hindi, abolishing the use of Hindi commands in the National Cadet Corps (NCC), banning of Hindi films and songs and closure of the *Dakshina Bharat Hindi Prachara Sabha*-the Institution for propagation of Hindi in South India.

On 19 December 1967, the agitation was restarted. It turned violent in 21 December and acts of arson and looting were reported in the state. Annadurai defused the situation by accepting most of their demands. On 23 January 1968, a resolution was passed in the Tamil Nadu Legislative Assembly. It accomplished the following: The Three-Language policy was scrapped and Hindi was eliminated from the curriculum. Only English and Tamil were to be taught, the use of Hindi commands in NCC was banned, Tamil was to be introduced as medium of instruction in all colleges and as the language of administration within five years, the Central Government was urged to end the special status accorded to Hindi in the Constitution and treat all languages equally, It was urged to provide financial assistance for development of all languages mentioned in the Eighth Schedule of the Constitution. These measures satisfied the agitators and normality returned by February 1968.

Agitation of 1986

In 1986, Indian Prime minister Rajiv Gandhi introduced the "National Education Policy". This education policy provided for setting up Navodaya Schools, where the DMK claimed teaching of Hindi would be compulsory. The Anna Dravida Munnetra Kazhagam (ADMK) led by M. G. Ramachandran (which had split from the DMK in 1972), was in power in Tamil Nadu and the DMK was the main opposition party. Karunanidhi announced an agitation against the opening of Navodaya Schools in Tamil Nadu. On 13 November, the Tamil Nadu Legislative Assembly unanimously passed a resolution demanding the repeal of Part XVII of the constitution and for making English the sole official language of the union.

On 17 November 1986, DMK members protested against the new education policy by burning Part XVII of the Constitution. 20,000 DMK members including Karunanidhi were arrested. 21 persons committed suicide by self immolation. Karunanidhi was sentenced to ten weeks of rigorous imprisonment. Ten DMK MLAs including K. Anbazhagan were expelled from the Legislative Assembly by the speaker P. H. Pandian. Rajiv Gandhi assured Members of Parliament from Tamil Nadu that Hindi would not be imposed. As part of the compromise, Navodhaya schools were not started in Tamil Nadu. Currently, Tamil Nadu is the only state in India without Navodhaya schools.

Legacy

The anti-Hindi agitations of 1937-40 and 1940-50 led to a change of guard in the Madras Presidency. The main opposition party to the Indian National Congress in the state, the Justice Party, came under Periyar's leadership on 29 December 1938. In 1944, the Justice Party was renamed as Dravidar Kazhagam.

The political careers of many later leaders of the Dravidian Movement, such as C. N. Annadurai and M. Karunanidhi, started with their participation in these agitations.

The agitations stopped the compulsory teaching of Hindi in the state. The agitations of the 1960s played a crucial role in the defeat of the Tamil Nadu Congress party in the 1967 elections and the continuing dominance of Dravidian parties in Tamil Nadu politics.

Many political leaders of the Dravida Munnetra Kazhagam and Anna Dravida Munnetra Kazhagam, like P. Seenivasan, K. Kalimuthu, Durai Murugan, Tiruppur. S. Duraiswamy, Sedapatti Muthaiah, K. Raja Mohammad, M. Natarajan and L. Ganesan, owe their entry and advancement in politics to their stints as student leaders during the agitations, which also reshaped the Dravidian Movement and broadened its political base, when it shifted from its earlier pro-Tamil (and anti-Brahmin) stance to a more inclusive one, which was both anti-Hindi and pro-English.

Finally, the current two-language education policy followed in Tamil Nadu is also the direct result of the agitations.

In the words of Sumathi Ramaswamy: [The anti-Hindi agitations knit] together diverse, even incompatible, social and political interests...

Their common cause against Hindi had thrown together religious revivalists like Maraimalai Atikal (1876-1950) with avowed atheists like Ramasami and Bharathidasan (1891-1964); men who supported the Indian cause like T.V. Kalyanasundaram (1883-1953) and M.P. Sivagnanam with those who wanted to secede from India like Annadurai and M. Karunanidhi (b.1924); university professors like Somasundara Bharati (1879-1959) and M.S. Purnalingam Pillai (1866-1947) with uneducated street poets, populist pamphleteers and college students.

The anti-Hindi agitations ensured the passage of Official Languages Act of 1963 and its amendment in 1967, thus ensuring the continued use of English as an official language of India. They effectively brought about the "virtual indefinite policy of bilingualism" of the Indian Republic.

Official Language

Official Language-Constitutional/Statutory Provisions

Article 343(1) of the Constitution provides that Hindi in Devanagari script shall be the Official Language of the Union. Article 343(2) also provided for continuing the use of English in official work of the Union for a period of 15 years (i.e., up to 25 January 1965) from the date of commencement of the Constitution. Article 343(3) empowered the parliament to provide by law for continued use of English for official purposes even after 25 January 1965. Accordingly, section 3(2) of the Official Languages Act, 1963 (amended in 1967) provides for continuing the use of English in official work even after 25 January 1965. The Act also lays down that both Hindi and English shall compulsorily be used for certain specified purposes such as Resolutions, General Orders, Rules, Notifications, Administrative and other Reports, Press Communiques; Administrative and other Reports and Official Papers to be laid before a House or the Houses of Parliament; Contracts, Agreements, Licences, Permits, Tender Notices and Forms of Tender, etc.

In 1976, Official Language Rules were framed under the provisions of section 8(1) of the Official Languages Act, 1963. Its salient features are as under:

i. They apply to all Central Government Offices, including any office of a Commission, Committee or Tribunal appointed by the Central Government and Corporation or Company owned or controlled by it;

ii. Communications from a Central Government Office to State/Union Territories or to any person in Region "A" comprising the States of Uttar Pradesh, Uttarakhand, Himachal Pradesh, Madhya Pradesh, Chhattisgarh, Bihar, Jharkhand, Rajasthan, Haryana and UTs of Andaman and Nicobar Islands and Delhi, shall be in Hindi;

iii. Communications from a Central Government Office to States/UTs in Region "B" comprising the States of Punjab, Gujarat, Maharashtra and the Union Territory of Chandigarh, shall ordinarily be in Hindi. However, communication to any person in Region "B" may be either in English or Hindi;

iv. Communications from a Central Government Office to a State Government Office in region 'C' comprising all other States and UTs not included in region 'A' & 'B' or to any office (note being a Central Government Office) or person shall be in English;

v. Communications between Central Government Offices and from Central Government Offices to the Offices of the State Governments/Union Territories and individuals, etc., will be in Hindi in such proportions as may be determined from time to time;

vi. All Manuals, Codes and other Procedural literature relating to Central Government Offices are required to be prepared both in Hindi and English. All Forms, Headings of Registers, Name Plates, Notice Boards and various items of stationery, etc., are also required to be in Hindi and English;

vii. It shall be the responsibility of the officer signing the documents specified in section 3(3) of the Act to ensure that these are issued both in Hindi and English

viii. Shall be the responsibility of the administrative head of each Central Government Office to ensure that the provisions of the Act, the Rules and directions issued under Sub-Rule-2 are properly complied with and to devise suitable and effective check points for this purpose

Policy

In compliance with the Official Language Resolution, 1968, an Annual Programme is prepared by the Department of Official Language in which targets are set for the offices of the Central Government with regard to originating correspondence, telegrams, telex, etc., in Hindi. A Quarterly Progress Report is called for from the offices of the Central Government regarding achievements vis-à-vis the said targets. An Annual Assessment Report is prepared on the basis of the Quarterly Progress Reports, which is laid on the Tables of both Houses of the Parliament and copies endorsed to State Governments and the Ministries/Departments of the Central Government.

Eight Regional Implementation Offices have been established at Bangalore, Cochin, Mumbai, Kolkata, Guwahati, Bhopal, Delhi and Ghaziabad to monitor the implementation of Official Language Policy of the Union.

Committees/Samities

A Committee of Parliament on Official Language was constituted in 1976 under section 4 of the Official Languages Act, 1963 to periodically review the progress in the use of Hindi as the Official Language of the Union and to submit a report to the President. The Committee consists of 20 Members of the Lok Sabha and 10 of the Rajya Sabha. The Committee have decided to submit its report in parts. It has so far submitted to the President eight parts of its report. The Presidential Orders on seven parts of its report have been issued and work is in progress on the eighth part.

The Kendriya Hindi Samiti was constituted in the year 1967. It is chaired by the Prime Minister. It is the apex policy making body which lays down the guidelines for the propagation and progressive use of Hindi as Official Language of the Union.

Under the directions of the Kendriya Hindi Samiti, Hindi Salahakar Samitis have been constituted in all Ministries/ Departments under the chairmanship of the Ministers concerned. These Samitis periodically review the progress in the use of Hindi in their respective Ministries/Departments and the offices/ undertakings and suggest measures to promote the use of Hindi.

Besides, the Central Official Language Implementation Committee [headed by Secretary, Department of Official Language and consisting of Joint Secretaries (In-charge Official Language) of all the Ministries/Departments as ex-officio members] reviews the status of use of Hindi for official purposes of the Union, training of its employees in Hindi and implementation of instructions issued from time to time by the Department of Official Language and suggests measure for removing the shortcomings and difficulties noticed in implementing these instructions.

Town Official Language Implementation Committees are constituted in different towns having ten or more Central Government offices, etc., to review the progress made in the use of Hindi in their member offices and exchange experiences. So far 255 Town Official Language Implementation Committees have been constituted all over the country.

Award Schemes

The Indira Gandhi Rajbhasha Awards Scheme has been in operation since 1986-87. Shields are given every year to Ministries/ Departments, Banks and Financial Institutions, Public Sector Undertakings and Town Official Language Implementation Committees for outstanding achievements in the implementation of the Official Language Policy of the Union. Cash awards are given to the working/retired employees of the Central Government, Banks, Financial Institutions, Universities, Training Institutions and Autonomous Bodies of the Central Government for writing original books in Hindi.

The National Awards Scheme for Original Book writing on Gyan-Vigyan has been renamed as Rajiv Gandhi National Awards Scheme for Original Book Writing in Hindi for promoting writing of books in Hindi on all branches of modern Science/Technology and contemporary subjects. This Scheme is open to all citizens of India.

At Regional level, Regional Official Language Awards are given each year to the Regional/Subordinate Offices, Public Sector Undertakings, Town Official Language Implementation Committees, Banks and Financial Institutions of the Central Government for outstanding achievements in implementing the Official Language Policy of the Union and accelerating the progressive use of Hindi.

Training

Under the Hindi Teaching Scheme, administered by the Department of Official Language, training in Hindi language is being imparted through 119 full-time and 49 part-time centres throughout the country. Likewise, training in Hindi Stenography and Hindi Typing is being provided through 23 full-time and 38 part-time centres. Thus, training in Hindi is being provided in 229 centres located in different parts of the country. Five Regional Offices of Hindi Teaching Scheme at Kolkata, Mumbai, Delhi, Chennai and Guwahati are providing academic and administrative support to the Hindi Teaching Scheme in the East, West, North-Central, South and North-East Regions. To fulfil the increasing demand of Hindi training of North Eastern region a new Regional Headquarter has been established at Guwahati and new Hindi training centres have been established at Imphal, Aizwal and

Agartala. The Kendriya Hindi Prashikshan Sansthan was established on 31 August 1985, as a subordinate office of the Department of Official Language, with the objective of providing Hindi Training through condensed courses in Hindi language/typing and stenography as also training through correspondence in Hindi language and Hindi Typewriting. Its sub-institutes were opened in Mumbai, Kolkata and Bangalore in 1988 and in Chennai and Hyderabad in 1990. Training of Hindi typing on computers is being imparted at almost all the typing/stenography centres in the country.

The Central Translation Bureau was set up in March 1971 for translation of different types of non-statutory literature, manuals/codes, forms, etc., of various Ministries/Departments, Offices of the Central Government and Public Sector Undertakings, Banks, etc. The Bureau has also been entrusted with the responsibility of conducting translation training courses for the officers/employees associated with the translation work. Initially, translation training courses of 3 months were being conducted at the Headquarters in New Delhi. In order to strengthen training facilities and meet regional requirements, Translation Training Centres have been established in Mumbai, Bangalore and Kolkata. Besides, Central Translation Bureau also conducts short-term translation courses for Central Government employees.

Technical

In order to facilitate the use of Official Language with the help of Mechanical and Electronic equipment, especially computers, a Technical Cell was set up in the Department of Official Language in October 1983. The main activities of the Cell are as under:

- Development of "Language application tools"-Under this programme LILA Rajbhasha, a self-learning package through the medium of Bangla, English, Kannada, Malayalam, Tamil and Telugu has been developed, MANTRA Rajbhasha, an aid tool for English to Hindi translation has also been developed
- Organising computer training programmes in Hindi-Every year around 100 training programmes are conducted to impart training for the use of Hindi on computers
- Organising exhibitions and seminars on bilingual computing-Technical seminars are held to help the users

and manufacturers come face to face to discuss the use of Hindi software, etc.

The Department of Official Language has now set up its portal www.rajbhasha.gov.in (External website that opens in a new window).

Publications

The Department of Official Language brings out 'Rajbhasha Bharati', a quarterly magazine, dedicated for encouraging writings in the field of Official Language, literature, technology, information technology, etc., in Hindi and also to give wide publicity to the efforts being made in different Central Government Offices for the use and propagation of Official Language Hindi. So far 112 issues of Rajbhasha Bharati have been published. Likewise, Annual Programme for implementation of the Official Language policy is brought out every year.

Annual Assessment Report regarding the use of Official Language in different Ministries/Departments and offices of the Central Government/Public Sector Undertakings, etc., is also brought out every year and laid on the tables of both the houses of Parliament. Official Language Manual, Calendars, Films, Posters, etc., are also brought out to give information regarding the activities relating to propagation and progressive use of Hindi as the Official Language.

Official Language

One of the main political issues in Indian politics is connected to language problem. After India's independence the government decided that the official language of India will be Hindi. Hindi belongs to the family of Aryan languages. Speakers of other languages, especially the Dravidian languages, saw in this decision an attempt to erase their language cultures. But the Indian constitution has declared that English can also be used for official purposes. Hindi has at least 13 different dialects and she is the most commonly spoken language in India. But the reason Hindi was chosen to be the official language of India wasn't because it is the most commonly spoken language in India, but it has connection with India history before it's independence.

Before its independence, most of India was a British colony. Before the British the most dominant Empire of north India was the Moghul Empire. The Moghuls were Muslim invaders who arrived in India from the present day Afghanistan. The official language of the Moghul courts was Persian. The Moghuls, like other residents who lived to the west of the Indian sub-continent named India as 'Hind' or 'Hindustan', after the river Indus which flows in the present day Pakistan. The language spoken in 'Hind' was called by them Hindi or Hindustani. This language and its script were based on an ancient Indian language called Sanskrit. Most of the sacred books of Hinduism are written in Sanskrit and the script is called Devanagiri.

Some of the Moghul family members were great patrons of poetry and music. Slowly there developed a 'Hindustani' poetry, based on Hindustani language which used words from Arabic and Persian and was written in Perso-Arabic script. This language was called Urdu. Urdu also replaced Persian as the language of the Moghul courtyards. And so there developed two languages with different writings but were actually one language when spoken except for their higher vocabularies. For example, rulers were titled in Urdu language as Shah, Nawab or Nizam. While in Hindi they were called Raja or Maharaja. Among the Hindustani speakers of north India, Urdu became the language of the Muslims while Hindi became the language of others.

After the collapse of the Moghuls the British became the rulers of north India. The British introduced English to India and continued using Urdu for official purposes. But nationalist Hindus demanded from the British to change the official language from Urdu to Hindi which is written in Indian script. Even Hindus whose mother tongue were not Hindi supported this argument. This debate between the Hindus and the Muslims continued right up to the independence of India.

Against this stand of two different languages two of India's notable leaders, Jawaharlal Nehru and Mahatma Gandhi, supported the idea of one Hindustani language which could be written in both forms. But when British India was divided in two countries, India and Pakistan. Muslims who got Pakistan made Urdu their official language and Indians made Hindi with Devanagiri script as their official language. But the debate over the official language didn't end up with choosing Hindi with Devanagiri script as the official language. New debates occurred because of this decision. One problem was connected to the different dialects of Hindi and the second problem was connected to other languages which exist in India. The first problem was which dialect of Hindi is the right Hindi. Hindi has at least 13 dialects, some of them completely different from each other. Two reasons caused to it that Hindi language includes in it so many different dialects. One reason was related to the fact that India is called Hind in many languages spoken west from it up to the Middle East.

Muslim invaders of India like the Moghuls came from these regions and called the language spoken in 'Hind' as Hindi. The Indians also began calling their different languages as 'Hindi'. The other reason which concerns to the fact that Hindi has so many different dialects is related to the independence period of India and the debate of the official language of India.

Most of the Indians belong religiously to Hinduism and they perceive Urdu, written in Perso-Arabic script as Muslim language. Before the independence of India the Muslims supported the continuation of Urdu as the official language of India, while the Hindus supported Hindi. In order to secure Hindi's position as the sole official language of India the political leaders convinced the north Indians to claim that they speak a Hindi dialect and so different dialect speakers were put together in the Hindi speaking category by the British bureaucrats. After India's independence when Hindi was chosen as the official language of India, different 'Hindi' language speakers began demanding official recognition of their languages. Maithali and Punjabi speakers also demanded to recognize their languages as separate languages from Hindi. Of the different 'Hindi' languages, only Punjabi got this recognition. Other 'Hindi' languages are considered dialects of Hindi and their status in the different states of India isn't clear and is interpreted differently by different parties.

The official Hindi is based on the dialect which was spoken in the Delhi-Agra region with a Sanskrit vocabulary. While the popular Hindi spoken by majority of Indians is based on this dialect, it is also affected by the different cultures of India mainly the Hindi cinema based in Mumbai(formerly Bombay) in west India and it includes many English words.

Among the other language speakers of India, the decision to choose Hindi as the official language was seen as an attempt to erase their cultures. After different struggles – political, violent and passive – the central government decided to allow the state governments to pick their official languages and recognized constitutionally other languages of India. For now the Indian constitution recognizes 18 Indian languages. One of meanings of the constitutional recognition is the right to use any of these languages for government service examinations. But, in reality this possibility isn't always given to the examinee.

The different states of India have different official languages, some of them not recognized by the central government. Some states have more then one official language. Bihar in east India has three official languages-Hindi, Urdu and Bengali – which are all recognized by the central government. But Sikkim, also in east India, has four official languages of which only Nepali is recognized by the central government. Besides the languages officially recognized by central or state governments, there are other languages which don't have this recognition and their speakers are running political struggles to get this recognition. Anyway as stated earlier the central government decided that Hindi is the official language of India and therefore it has also the status of official language in the states. Another language that has a official status in all states is English.

The Official Languages Act, 1963

[ACT No 19 OF 1963]

[10th May, 1963]

An Act to provide for the languages which may be used for the official purpose of the Union, for transaction of business in Parliament, for Central and State Acts and for certain purpose in High Courts. BE it enacted by Parliament in the Fourteenth Year of the Republic of India as follows:—

1. Short title and Commencement-
   (1) This Act may be called the Official Languages Act, 1963.
   (2) Section 3 shall come into force on the 26th day of Januray, 1965 and the remaining provisions of this Act shall come into force on such date as the Central Government may, by notification in the Official Gazette, appoint and different dates may be appointed for different provisions of this Act.

2. Definitions.

In this Act, unless the context otherwise requires,—

(a) "Appoint day", in relation to section 3, means the 26th day of January, 1995 and in relation to any other provision of this Act, means the day on which that provision comes into force;

(b) "Hindi" means Hindi in Devanagari script.

3. Continuance of English language for official purposes of the Union and for use in Parliament.

Notwithstanding the expiration of the period of fifteen ears from the commencement of the Constitution, the English language may, as from the appointed day, continue to be used, in addition to Hindi,—

(a) For all the official purpose of the Union for which it was being used immediately before that day; and

(b) For the transaction of business in Parliament.

4. Committee on official Language.

(1) After the expiration of ten years from the date on which section 3 comes into force, there shall be constituted a Committee on Official Language, on a resolution to that effect being moved in either House of Parliament with the previous sanction of the President and passed by both Houses.

(2) The Committee shall consist of thirty members, of whom twenty shall be members of the House of the People ad ten shall be members of the council of States, to be elected respectively by the members of the House of the People and the members of the Council of States in accordance with the system of proportional representation by means of the single transferable vote.

(3) It shall be the duty of the Committee to review the progress made in the use of Hindi for the official purposes of the Union and submit a report to the President making recommendations thereon and the President shall cause the report to be laid before each House of Parliament, and sent to all the State Governments.

(4) The President may, after consideration of the report referred to in sub-section (3), and the views, if any, expressed by the State Governments thereon, issue directions in accordance with the whole or any part of that report.

5. Authorised Hindi translation of Central Acts, etc.

(1) A translation in Hindi published under the authority of the President in the Official Gazette on and after the appointed day

(a) Of any Central Act or of any Ordinance promulgated by the President, or

(b) Of any order, rule, regulation or bye-law issued under the Constitution or under any Central Act. shall be deemed to be the authoritative text thereof in Hindi.

(2) As from the appointed day, the authoritative text in the English language of all Bills to be introduced or amendments thereto to be moved in either House of Parliament shall be accompanied by a translation of the same in Hindi authorised in such manner as may by prescribed by rules made under this Act.

6. Authorised Hindi translation of State Acts in certain cases.

Where the Legislature of a State has prescribed any language other than Hindi for use in Acts passed by the Legislature of the State or in Ordinances promulgated by the Governor of the State, a translation of the same in Hindi, in addition to a translation thereof I the English language as required by clause (3) of article 348 of the Constitution, may be published on or after the appointed day under the authority of the Governor of the State in Official Gazette of that State and in such a case, the translation in Hindi of any such Act or Ordinance shall be deemed to be the authoritative text therefore in the Hindi language.

7. Optional use of Hindi or other official language in judgments, etc., of High Courts.

As from the appointed day or any day thereafter, the Governor of a State may, with the previous consent of the President, authorised the use of Hindi or the official language of the State, in addition to the English language, for the purpose of any judgment, decree or order passed or made by the High court for that State and where any judgment, decree or order is passed or made in any such language (other than the English language), it shall be accompanied by a translation of the same in the English language issued under the authority of the High Court.

8. Power to make rules.

   (1) The Central Government may, by notification in the Official Gazette, make rules for carrying out the purposes of this Act.

   (2) Every rule made under this section shall be laid, as soon as my be after it is made, before each House of Parliament while it is in session for a total period of thirty days which may be comprised in one session or in two successive sessions, and if before the expiry of the session in which it is so laid or the session immediately following, both Houses agree in making any modification in the rule shall or both Houses agree that the rule should not b made, the rule shall thereafter have effect only in such modified form or be of no effect, as the case may be, so however, that any such modification or annulment shall be without prejudice to the validity of anything previously done under that rule.

9. Certain provisions not to apply to Jammu and Kashmir.

The provision of section 6 and section 7 shall not apply to the State of Jammu.

The Official Languages Act, 1963

Year : 1963

Act : The Official Languages Act, 1963.act No. 19 of 1963.[10th May, 1963.]

An Act to provide for the languages which may be used for the official purposes of the Union, for transaction of business in Parliament, for Central and State Acts and for certain purposes in High Courts.

BE it enacted by Parliament in the Fourteenth Year of the Republic of India as follows:—

1. Short title and commencement.

(1) This Act may be called the Official Languages Act, 1963.

(2) Section 3 shall come into force on the 26th day of January, 1965 and the remaining provisions of this Act shall come into force on such date1* as the Central Government may, by notification in the Official Gazette, appoint and different dates1* may be appointed for different provisions of this Act.

2. Definitions. In this Act, unless the context otherwise requires,—

(a) "appointed day", in relation to section 3, means the 26th day of January, 1965 and in relation to any other provision of this Act, means the day on which that provision comes into force;

(b) "Hindi" means Hindi in Devanagari script.

3. Continuance of English language for official purposes of the Union andfor use in Parliament. 2*[3. Continuance of English language for official purposes of the Union and for use in Parliament.

(1) Notwithstanding the expiration of the period of fifteen years from the commencement of the Constitution, the English language may, as from the appointed day, continue to be used, in addition to Hindi,—

(a) for all the official purposes of the Union for which it was being used immediately before that day; and

(b) for the transaction of business in Parliament:

Provided that the English language shall be used for purposes of communication between the Union and a State which has not adopted Hindi as its official language: Provided further that where Hindi is used for purposes of communication between one State which has adopted Hindi as its official Provided also that nothing in this sub-section shall be construed as preventing a State which has not adopted Hindi as its official language from using Hindi for purposes of communication with the Union or with a State which has adopted Hindi as its official language, or by agreement with any other State, and in such a case, it shall not be obligatory to use the English language for purposes of communication with that State.

(2) Notwithstanding anything contained in sub-section (1), where Hindi or the English language is used for purposes of communication—

(i) between one Ministry or Department or office of the Central Government and another;

(ii) between one Ministry or Department or office of the Central Government and any corporation or company owned or controlled by the Central Government or any office thereof;

(iii) between any corporation or company owned or controlled by the Central Government or any office therof and another, a translation of such communication in the English language or, as the case may be, in Hindi shall also be provided till such date as the staff of the concerned Ministry, Department, Office or Corporation or company aforesaid have acquired a working knowledge of Hindi.

(3) Notwithstanding anything contained in sub-section (1), both Hindi and the English language shall be used for—

(i) resolutions, general orders, rules, notifications, administrative or other reports or press communiques issued or made by the Central Government or by a Ministry, Department or office thereof or by a corporation or company owned or controlled by the Central Government or by any office of such corporation or company;

(ii) administrative and other reports and official papers laid before a House or the Houses of Parliament;

(iii) contracts and agreements executed, and licences, permits, notices and forms of tender issued, by or on behalf of the Central Government or any Ministry, Department or office thereof or by a corporation or company owned or controlled by the Central Government or by any office of such corporation or company.

(4) Without prejudice to the provisions of sub-section (1) or sub-section (2) or sub-section (3), the Central Government may, by rules made under section 8, provide for the language or languages to be used for the official purpose of the Union, including the working of any Ministry, Department, section or office, and in making such rules, due consideration shall be given to the quick and efficient disposal of the official business and the interests of the general public and in particular, the rules so made shall ensure that persons serving in connection with the affairs of the Union and having proficiency either in Hindi or in the English language may function effectively and that they are not placed at a disadvantage on the ground that they do not have proficiency in both the languages.

(5) The provisions of clause (a) of sub-section (1), and the provisions of sub-section (2), sub-section (3) and sub-section (4) shall remain in force until resolutions for the discontinuance of the use of the English language for the purposes mentioned therein have been passed by the Legislatures of all the States which have not adopted Hindi as their official language and until after considering the resolutions aforesaid, a resolution for such discontinuance has been passed by each House of Parliament.]

4. Committee on Official Language.

(1) After the expiration of ten years from the date on which section 3 comes into force, there shall be constituted a Committee on Official Language, on a resolution to that effect being moved in either House of Parliament with the previous sanction of the President and passed by both Houses.

(2) The Committee shall consist of thirty members, of whom twenty shall be members of the House of the People and ten shall be members of the Council of States, to be elected, respectively by the members of the House of the People and the members of the Council of States in accordance with the system of proportional representation by means of the single transferable vote.

(3) It shall be the duty of the Committee to review the progress made in the use of Hindi for the official purposes of the Union and submit a report to the President making recommendations thereon and the President shall cause the report to be laid before each House of Parliament, and sent to all the State Governments.

(4) The President may, after consideration of the report referred to in sub-section (3), and the views, if any, expressed by the State Governments thereon, issue directions in accordance with the whole or any part of that report:

5. Authorised Hindi translation of Central Acts, etc.

(1) A translation in Hindi published under the authority of the President in the Official Gazette on and after the appointed day,—

(a) of any Central Act or of any Ordinance promulgated by the President, or

(b) of any order, rule, regulation or bye-law issued under the Constitution or under any Central Act, shall be deemed to be the authoritative text thereof in Hindi.

(2) As from the appointed day, the authoritative text in the English language of all Bills to be introduced or amendments thereto to be moved in either House of Parliament shall be accompanied by a translation of the same in Hindi authorised in such manner as may be prescribed by rules made under this Act.

6. Authorised Hindi translation of State Acts in certain cases.

Where the Legislature of a State has prescribed any language other than Hindi for use in Acts passed by the Legislature of the State or in Ordinances promulgated by the Governor of the State, a translation of the same in Hindi, in addition to a translation thereof in the English language as required by clause (3) of article 348 of the Constitution, may be published on or after the appointed day under the authority of the Governor of the State in the Official Gazette of that State and in such a case, the translation in Hindi of any such Act or Ordinance shall be deemed to be the authoritative text thereof in the Hindi language.

7. Optional use of Hindi or other official language in judgments, etc., of High Courts.

As from the appointed day or any day thereafter, the Governor of a State may, with the previous consent of the President, authorise the use of Hindi or the official language of the State, in addition to the English language, for the purposes of any judgment, decree or order passed or made by the High Court for that State and where any judgment, decree or order is passed or made in any such language (other than the English language), it shall be accompanied by a translation of the same in the English language issued under the authority of the High Court.

8. Power to make rules:

   (1) The Central Government may, by notification in the Official Gazette, make rules for carrying out the purposes of this Act.

   (2) Every rule made under this section shall be laid, as soon as may be after it is made, before each House of Parliament while it is in session for a total period of thirty days which may be comprised in one session or 1*[in two or more successive sessions, and if, before the expiry of the session immediately following the session or the successive sessions aforesaid] both Houses agree in making any modification in the rule or both Houses agree that the rule should not be made, the rule shall thereafter have effect only in such modified form or be of no effect, as the case may be, so however, that any such modification or annulment shall be without prejudice to the validity of anything previously done under that rule.

9. Certain provisions not to apply to Jammu and Kashmir. The provisions of section 6 of sectin 7 shall not apply to the State of Jammu and Kashmir.

Three-Language Formula

The Three-language formula is a formula of language learning formulated by the Union Education Ministry of the Government of India in consultation with the states. The formula was enunciated in the 1968 National Policy Resolution. It provides that children in the Hindi-speaking states are to be taught three languages, namely Hindi, English and another modern Indian language (preferably one of the southern languages). The children in non-Hindi-speaking states are to be taught Hindi, English, and the regional language. The formula was formulated in response to demands from non-Hindi speaking states, mainly Tamil

Three Language Formula

In order to provide facilities for teaching a minority language or mother tongue, State Education Ministers evolved a scheme in 1949. Subsequently, the Union Education Ministry in consultation with States formulated a Three Language Formula. This Formula as enunciated in the National Policy Resolution of 1968 and reiterated in the National Policy on Education 1986 provides Hindi, English and modern Indian language (preferably one of the southern languages) in the Hindi speaking states and Hindi. English and the Regional language in the non-Hindi speaking States.

This Formula has created many difficulties for Urdu speakers. The major grievance of Urdu speaking linguistic minority is that their children have been denied the facility of mother tongue instruction. The result is that a large number children of Urdu speakers are learning the regional language instead of the mother tongue as the first language.

Accordingly, the Gujral Committee recommended the following modified form of three language formula:

(i) In Hindi speaking States:

(a) Hindi (with Sanskrit as part of the composite course);

(b) Urdu or any other modern Indian language excluding (a) and

(c) English or any other modern European language.

(ii) In non-Hindi speaking States:

(a) Regional language;

(b) Hindi;

(c) Urdu or any other modern Indian language excluding (a) and (b); and

(d) English or any other modern European language. (4.240).

The Three Language formula, at present in vogue in Andhra Pradesh with a degree of success, may also be adopted as an alternative by the non-Hindi speaking States for Urdu speaking population.

The formula is:

(a) Urdu and Hindi (a composite course);

(b) Regional language;

(c) English or any other modern European language. (4.241).

The Gujral Committee felt that in any formula that is worked out, it should be ensured that students are able to study their mother tongue as well as the official language of the State.

The Statewise position of the languages and the stages at which they are taught is as under:

Andhra Pradesh

According to Government Statement the Three Language Formula in Urdu medium schools is as follows:

Urdu : From Class I to X

Telugu : From VI to X. Option to take it in Class III

English/Hindi : Class VIII to X.

But the formula is sought to be amended as follows:

Mother tongue : From Class I to X (Urdu)

Telugu : Class V to X

English/Hindi : Class VI to X.

However, United Action Committee for Urdu has demanded as follows:

Urdu : Class I to X

Telugu : Class III onwards

English : From Class VI for all.

Urdu/Hindi : From Class VIII (80+20)

In the case of Urdu mother tongue students learning through Telugu or English medium Urdu should be introduced from Class III. Bihar.

Bihar State has modified the Three Language Formula in the following manner:

First Language : Hindi, Urdu, Bengali, Oriya, Maithali and Santhali

Second Language : Hindi for non-Hindi students or Sanskrit (for Hindi students)

Third Language : English

Department of Education is trying to provide teachers for teaching Urdu under Three Language Formula in Secondary schools. Urdu as first language is taught under Three Language Formula from classes I to class X in Urdu medium schools. Some witnesses demanded that Urdu should also be taught in classes XI and XII also. It was also demanded by many witnesses that the facility for teaching Urdu should be provided in non-Urdu medium schools.

Delhi

Three Language Formula implemented in Delhi is as follows:

First Language : Hindi

Second Language : English

Third Language : Sanskrit or any minority language.

Urdu, Punjabi, Sindhi, Bengali, Malyalam, Gujarati, Tamil, Telugu, Persian, Kannada, Arabic and Marathi, are taught as minorities languages. In schools run by minority managements where the medium of instruction is also the minority language concerned, the 1st language taught is the minority language.

The complaint made by the Urdu representatives against the implementation of Three Language Formula is that the facility for teaching Urdu is generally provided only to the students whose mother tongue is Urdu. There are very few non-Urdu medium schools where Urdu is being taught as a modern Indian Language under Three Language Formula.

Gujarat

Three Language Formula in force in Gujarat in Urdu medium schools is as follows:

1. Mother tongue (Urdu) : From Class I
2. Gujarati : From Class III
3. Hindi/English : From Class V
4. English : From Class VIII
5. Classical language : From Class VIII.

(Sanskrit, Persian or Arabic)

Thus the students have to learn five languages including a classical language. Option between Hindi and English in Class V and compulsory English from class VIII appears paradoxical.

It is necessary that in Gujarati medium schools, Urdu minorities should learn Urdu from class III.

Haryana

Following Three Language Formula is in vogue in Haryana:

First Language : Hindi from Class I

Second Language : English from Class VI

Third Language : Any of the following languages Telugu, Sanskrit, Urdu or Punjabi from classes VII to VIII Urdu as a subject under three language formula is being taught in the schools which are located in Urdu speaking areas.

Currently, Urdu is being taught in Class VII and VIII.

Himachal Pradesh

First Language : Hindi

Second Language : English

Third Language : Urdu, Tamil, Telugu, Malayalam and Bengali

Urdu is taught in Classes IX and X under Three Language Formula. Although Malayalam, Tamil, Kannada and Bengali are also taught under this Formula but the Sub-Committee was told that there were only 4 schools teaching these modern Indian Languages. The Sub-Committee is happy to note that Himachal Pradesh is the only state where most of the students whose mother tongue is other than Urdu are learning Urdu under Three Language Formula. All the witnesses were, however, of the opinion that as Urdu is presently taught only in Classes IX and X, the students do not acquire reasonable proficiency in the language. They demanded that Urdu should be taught for three years i.e. from Classes VIII to X.

Madhya Pradesh

According to material secured by the Sub-Committee, Three Language Formula implemented in Madhya Pradesh is as follows:

First Language : Hindi, English, Marathi, Urdu, Punjabi, Sindhi, Bengali, Gujarati, Tamil, Telugu, and Malayalam Second Language: Hindi/English Third Language : Hindi, English, Sanskrit, Marathi,

Urdu, Punjabi, Sindhi, Gujarati, Telugu, Tamil, Malayalam, Arabic, Persian, French and Russian. Although Urdu has been included in three language formula, Urdu teachers have been provided in very few non-Urdu medium schools. Urdu representatives demanded that Urdu teachers should be appointed in such schools as per requirement.

Karnataka

The Three Language Formula as in force in Karnataka is as follows: For Kannada Students:

First Language : Kannada from Class I

Second Language : English from Class V

Third Language : Hindi from Class V

For Urdu medium students:

First Language : Urdu from Class I

Second Language : Kannada from Class III

Third Language : English or Hindi from Class V

The defect about this formula as pointed out by the non officials is:

(i) for Kannada medium, two languages are introduced in Class V. when Urdu students take a language (Kannada) in class III. Kannada students could also be brought on par with regard to equitable load distribution;

(ii) Urdu medium students are given option between English and Hindi. This keeps them ignorant of one or the other language. Some have proposed Urdu-Hindi composite course from Class V and English from VI for all students; and

(iii) Kannada is optional from class III and no examinations is prescribed. The consensus among non-officials was that Kannada should be compulsory from class III and examination should be held at least from Class IV.

The other point they raised was that the pupils should pass in second and third languages as well as Hindi but the marks should not be counted for determining the rank.

However, the consensus among both officials and non-officials was that a uniform load pattern and stages of introduction of languages should be adopted for the entire country.

Karnataka Rajya Urdu Teachers' Association in a memorandum stated that to make the teaching of Kannada Language effective and favourite in Urdu schools, it is essential to prepare syllabus and text-books of Kannada with easy language and keeping the cultural background of Urdu speaking minority. (This demand was accepted by the previous government on May 23, 1985, in a discussion with this Association, and formed a Committee for this purpose under the Chairmanship of the Director of Public Instruction (PE) in Karnataka, but no work has been done).

The memorandum also stated that to make Kannada Language study effectively implemented, sufficient number of Kannada teachers should be appointed in Urdu schools on par with the pupil-teacher ratio. Presently, irrespective of the strength of section, only one Kannada teacher is posted in Urdu schools. Hence, the Kannada teachers express their inability to cope up with the work

Maharashtra

The Director of Education told the sub-Committee that all the students were given primary education (from Classes I to V) only in mother tongue. Three Language Formula is strictly implemented from Classes VIII to Class X. For the students whose mother tongue is Urdu, Three Language Formula in the Urdu medium schools is as under:

First Language : Urdu.

Second Language : For Classes VI to VIII, a composite course of Hindi and Marathi.

Third Language : English.

If a student does not offer this group he can have:

First Language : Urdu

Second Language : Marathi or Marathi+Hindi.

(Composite) or Marathi+Sanskrit

(Composite) or Marathi + Pali

(Composite) or Marathi+Ardhamgadhi

(Composite) or a Classical language or Marathi+Arabic.

Third Language : English.

Facility of teaching Urdu under Three Language Formula is not available in Marathi medium schools.

Rajasthan

Three Language Formula is implemented in Rajasthan as follows:

First Language : Hindi.

Second Language : English.

Third Language : Any of the following languages: Sanskrit, Urdu, Sindhi, Punjabi and Gujarati.

Uttar Pradesh

Following is the Three Language Formula implemented in Uttar Pradesh:

First Language : Hindi Classes (VI to VII).

Second Language : English or any other Modern.

European Language Classes VI to VIII.

Third Language : Any language from amongst languages mentioned in Eighth Schedule of the Constitution Classes VI to VIII. Facility for teaching Urdu under Three Language Formula has been provided only in a few schools. A large number of office bearers of Urdu organisations and Urdu writers, poets, journalists expressed their discontentment about the attitude of the Department of Education in this regard. It was brought to the notice of the sub-Committee that there was a large number of schools where the number of students willing to learn Urdu is quite sizeable. But the teachers have not been provided by the Department of Education. It was alleged that learning through Urdu medium or studying Urdu as a subject is not encouraged by the Department. It was also complained that there was not a single non-Urdu medium school in which facility of Urdu teaching is provided.

West Bengal

Three Language Formula in West Bengal is as follows:

First Language : Bengali, Hindi, English, Nepali, Urdu, Assamese, Gujarati, Malayalam, Marathi, Modern Tibetan, Oriya, Punjabi (Gurmukhi), Santhali, Tamil, Telugu, Lushai, Sudani-Classes VI to X

Second Language : English, Bengali, Nepali-Classes VI to X

Third Language : Bengali, Hindi, Sanskrit, Pali, Persian, Arabic,

Latin, Greek, Classical Armenian, French, Russian, Portuguese, Spanish and Italian

Regionalisam and Regional Inequality

The Plight of the 'Bihar migrants' in Maharashtra was undoubtedly not a pleasing sight for any right minded citizen residing in any part of the country. The atrocities unleashed by Maharashtra Navnirman Sena (MNS) led by Raj Thakeray on the North Indian population in Maharashtra violated Article 19 of the Indian Constitution that ensures the individual the freedom to reside in any part of the country on free will.

What began on December 15, 1953 as a fast unto death by Telugu nationalist leader Potti Sriramulu turned out as a launch pad for 'Political Regionalism' in India that has changed the course of politics and regionalism in the country?

Although it is important to understand the socio-economic-political scenario post independence. The brand of regionalism that evolved post Independence was more justifiable, indisputable and rational. It echoed the voices, views and aspirations of the people in the country. The struggle stood for long standing wishes of the people to be divided on linguistic basis.

Thus, Andhra Pradesh courtesy Potti Sriramulu became the first state to be reorganised on linguistic basis. The States Reorganisation Committee suggested the formation of 16 states and 3 Union Territories based on linguistic preferences. Thus began the politics of Regionalism in India.

In order to understand the politics of regionalism in India, it is extremely important to understand the term Regionalism. Regionalism can be defined as a political ideology of a particular group of people belonging to one community. Regionalism often relates to strengthening politics or economic power in order to influence the autonomy over different states. Regionalism post independence meant constant struggle of each state to overpower the other. India has witnessed a tremendous growth of regionalism and struggles post independence era.

The recent MNS attacks on North Indians from Bihar and UP added fuel to the existing fire of regionalism. According to the claims put forth by Raj Thackerey, chief of MNS, the adding migrant population in Maharashtra had resulted in a lot of Maharashtrians remaining unemployed. This resulted in chaos in

Maharashtra and MNS activists took to the streets. They beat up several north Indians and forced them to go out of the state. However, this hasn't been the first case of regionalist claims. One of the earliest regionalist claims was made by Maharashtra Shiv Sena against Kannadigas on the pretext of Marathi pride. Andhra Pradesh has been one of the states that has been under the scanner for its regionalist claims for quite some time now. For long the people residing in the Telengana region have felt neglected by the Andhra Pradesh government. Telangana has till date remained a backward region whereas the Andhra region had been progressing quite well. Thus the people of Telangana demanded separation of Telangana and Andhra. This gave rise to debates and arguments on the proposal. While the people of Telangana welcomed the idea, the people of Andhra protested against it vehemently. The demands had died down till Chandrababu Naidu; the former Chief Minister of Hyderabad started executing his plans of Cyberabad. This infuriated the people in Telangana and the demands resurfaced. Regionalism in Andhra Pradesh meant demands of a separate state in order to ensure equal justice done to all the citizens of the state. It meant ensuring all the citizens were equal in terms of socioeconomic and political status.

The United Liberation Front of Assam (ULFA) too had launched an attack on Biharis and Bengalis was yet another example of strong regionalist sentiments. The clashes were a result of clash of interests between the Biharis, Bengali community and the Assamese interests. Thus the ULFA intervened and adopted violent methods to drive out the migrants from the state of Assam.

Regionalism has witnessed a drastic change in the means and methods adopted to achieve the same. From the nonviolent means like fasting unto death by Potti Sriramulu to extreme violent means adopted by the ULFA and MNS today.

However, formation of regional parties at the centre and state level has proved to be a boon for the country. They voice the opinion of the region at the centre level and ensure that their voices are heard. Growing regionalism is therefore not a cause of worry for India since in spite of regionalism every individual who resides in India remains a citizen of India irrespective from which state he belongs to. Thus India should not worry too much about the issue of regionalism so long as it brings regional development.

5

Jawaharlal Nehru's Foreign Policy

Jawaharlal Nehru is considered to be the architect of modern India. Apart from his careful handling of India's tumultuous domestic situation in the years immediately after the Independence, Nehru's major contribution lies in the field of foreign policies. In fact, Nehru determined India's international profile to a great degree in the post-independence years, in his capacity as the foreign minister of India. Jawaharlal Nehru's foreign policy has been made subject to much controversy and debate, like his economic policies. However, taken in the context of India's newly found status as a democratic republic, Nehru's foreign affairs policies seem to be extremely apt.

Socialism can be said to be one of the greatest international influences on Nehru, but Gandhi's ideals of Satyagraha also influenced him to a great degree. But he committed himself to neither point of view in framing his foreign policy. Nehru's foreign policies were characterized by two major ideological aspects. First, he wanted India to have an identity that would be independent of any form of overt commitment to either power bloc, the USA or the Soviet. Secondly, he had an unshaken faith in goodwill and honesty in matters of international affairs. The first policy led ultimately to the founding of the Non-Alignment Movement (NAM). His second faith was terribly shaken by the Chinese attack of 1962, openly disobeying all the clauses of the Panchsheel or five-point agreement of 1954 between New Delhi and Peking. This breach of faith was a major psychological shock for Nehru, and was partially the reason for his death.

The Founding Principles of Nehru's Foreign Policy: Nehru saw war and violent insurgency from very close quarters as a freedom fighter, and he believed in neither. In his foreign policies, Nehru tried to guide India in such a way, so as to steer clear from any form of violence and militarism. He rightly believed that a newly decolonized nation must invest all its economic and logistic resources towards development and not defence and armament. Just like his economic policies, which were non-committal towards any ideological position, Nehru wanted to bring in a healthy level of pragmatism in his dealings of India's foreign affairs as well. He understood that overt commitment to any of the two major power blocs to emerge in the aftermath of World War II, would not serve India's path. He therefore wanted to tread a third path, which was not necessarily the middle path.

It should be remembered that this dogged non-commitment of Nehru was not seen sympathetically by any of the super powers of either East or West at its initial stage. It was frequently termed as a kind of international opportunism and was accused of 'neutralism'-a stance reckoned to be not only dangerous but also equally immoral in the world of International politics. However, the increasing popularity of NAM among various Asian and African countries and Nehru's growing stature as a statesman situation changed their views. India too benefited from this position, as it managed to secure rebuilding grants from member countries of either bloc. After Nehru's successful mediation in the Korean War and the Congo problem, putting an end to a long and violent struggle, his status as a commendable and efficient statesman reached new heights. Jawaharlal Nehru's theory of ideological non-commitment in a world that was rendered dangerous by the Cold War was appreciated by one and all.

Nehru and the Non-Alignment Movement: The greatest success of Jawaharlal Nehru's non-committal international politics was the formation of the Non-Alignment Movement (NAM). Nehru found allies in Tito, Nasser, Soekarno, U Nu and Nkrumah at a later stage in his formation of this new alliance. An alliance of newly independent and long colonized nations was not taken seriously in the beginning, either by the Eastern or the Western bloc. However, the importance of the alliance was soon felt, and initially led to a great degree of international pressure from both parts of the globe. However, Nehru proceeded with his mission undaunted. It was great test for his courage and it was soon found out that the NAM was not merely a passive platform of neutral and inactive nations. It had clear objectives that included the gradual decolonization of the world, and a strong statement that the member countries were not party to the ever escalating tension of the Cold War. The favoured process of decolonization as adopted by the NAM member countries was one of discussion and peaceful agreement. On many occasions, NAM met with success, often under the leadership of Nehru. Whoever supported its cause was an ally and a friend. Nehru preached a policy of issue based alliance and not one based on political and economic dogmas. He was proud of being an Asian, and wanted Asian nations to be the primary determinants of their political fate, not always guided by Western forces.

Nehru's unshaken belief in the force of international brotherhood was attested with his decision to continue with India's Commonwealth status. He was made subject to much criticism back home because of the support he extended towards the Commonwealth, particularly after the complication of the independence issue by the British government in the post World War II years, leading to the unwanted partition. However Nehru, always the believer in peaceful alliances and solution of international affairs based on discussions, went on with his ideals.

Nehru and the Kashmir Problem: Nehru's Foreign policies did not augur well when it came to deal with the neighbours. Kashmir was a perpetual problem, and he failed to reach any successful negotiation regarding Kashmir with the neighbour Pakistan. Nehru had an innate belief in honest fellow-feeling and political generosity. He tried to force a negotiation with the Pakistani government through the United Nations. But the Pakistani military rulers denied any peaceful agreement. The offer of a possible plebiscite was also taken off in 1950. After India's dogged denial of the two-nation theory, a result in favour of Kashmir in the Muslim dominated Kashmir would be a strategic disaster for India. The Kashmir problem remained unresolved, and not even Nehru's diplomatic expertise could give any positive direction to the problem. It still continues to be the one of the key international problems in South Asia.

Nehru and the China Crisis: Nehru's foreign policies concerning China have been made subject to much criticism. However, even in this case, it was Nehru's faith in transparency in the handling of International relations that is seen to be the root of all problems. Nehru was intent on a very warm and mutually beneficial relationship between India and China. The five-point agreement or the Panchsheel between New Delhi and Peking initiated in 1954 was a result of these negotiations. However, China started patrolling certain parts of the Indian border from 1955 onwards. Delhi started negotiations to solve the problem in a peaceful way. India, under the leadership of Nehru wanted to take one issue at a time and begin the discussions. The Chinese government, under Chou En-lai wanted to treat the border issue in its entirety at one go. It was gross violation of the five-point agreement. The Chinese denial for the arbitration from the International Court of Justice complicated the problem. Amidst such tensions, the Chinese suddenly started a full-scale invasion in 1962. It was a rude shock, not only to Nehru, but to the entire international society. The Indian military was unprepared and also unequipped. Both USA and the Soviet extended token help. Soviet was quite busy with the Cuban crisis, however soon after the problem subsided, President Kruschev did extend some help. American help was minimum, compared to the massive military help that was extended to Pakistan in 1954. On top of that, the Sandys-Rusk team visited India to hold talks in order to make India concede certain areas of Kashmir to Pakistan, a claim that was squarely denied. Nehru stood firm with this faith in the five-point principle. The international community stood by him, as China withdrew under growing international pressure, fearing isolation and global antagonism. Nehru played his last masterstroke in international policy, as he turned the military defeat in a moral victory for India.

The Chinese invasion had far reaching effects on India's foreign policy. It forced Nehru to change his stance on international affairs. He realized that unmitigated goodwill was not necessary the way the business of foreign affairs was conducted. Nehru's dreams were more or less shattered. It was also a great eye-opener. It made India to see that it is important to strengthen one's military strength and not overtly depend on peaceful negotiations in matters of international affairs. The Chinese invasion was a shock to Nehru, almost shaking his idealistic foundation to the very base. Domestic problems also kept escalating, putting a great degree of mental and physical stress on Nehru.

National Security and Foreign Policy

Nehru led newly independent India from 1947 to 1964, during its first years of freedom from British rule. Both the United States and the Union Soviet Socialist Republic competed to make India an ally throughout the Cold War.

On the international scene, Nehru was a champion of pacifism and a strong supporter of the United Nations. He pioneered the policy of non-alignment and co-founded the Non-Aligned Movement of nations professing neutrality between the rival blocs of nations led by the U.S. and the U.S.S.R. Recognising the People's Republic of China soon after its founding (while most of the Western bloc continued relations with the Republic of China), Nehru argued for its inclusion in the United Nations and refused to brand the Chinese as the aggressors in their conflict with Korea. He sought to establish warm and friendly relations with China despite the invasion of Tibet in 1950, and hoped to act as an intermediary to bridge the gulf and tensions between the communist states and the Western bloc.

Meanwhile, Nehru had promised in 1948 to hold a plebiscite in Kashmir under the auspices of the U.N. but, as Pakistan failed to pull back troops in accordance with the UN resolution and as Nehru grew increasingly wary of the U.N., he declined to hold a plebiscite in 1953. He ordered the arrest of the Kashmiri politician Sheikh Abdullah, whom he had previously supported but now suspected of harbouring separatist ambitions; Bakshi Ghulam Mohammad replaced him.

His policy of pacifism and appeasement with respect to China also came unraveled when China annexed Aksai Chin, the region of Kashmir adjoining Tibet in 1962 that led to the Sino-Indian war.

Nehru was hailed by many for working to defuse global tensions and the threat of nuclear weapons. He commissioned the first study of the human effects of nuclear explosions, and campaigned ceaselessly for the abolition of what he called "these frightful engines of destruction." He also had pragmatic reasons for promoting de-nuclearisation, fearing that a nuclear arms race would lead to over-militarisation that would be unaffordable for developing countries such as his own.

In 1956 he had criticised the joint invasion of the Suez Canal by the British, French and Israelis. Suspicion and distrust cooled relations between India and the U.S., which suspected Nehru of tacitly supporting the Soviet Union. Accepting the arbitration of the UK and World Bank, Nehru signed the Indus Water Treaty in 1960 with Pakistani ruler Ayub Khan to resolve long-standing disputes about sharing the resources of the major rivers of the Punjab region.

Final Years

Nehru had led the Congress to a major victory in the 1957 elections, but his government was facing rising problems and criticism. Disillusioned by intra-party corruption and bickering, Nehru contemplated resigning but continued to serve. The election of his daughter Indira as Congress President in 1959 aroused criticism for alleged nepotism, although actually Nehru had disapproved of her election, partly because he considered it smacked of "dynastism"; he said, indeed it was "wholly undemocratic and an undesirable thing", and refused her a position in his cabinet. Indira herself was at loggerheads with her father over policy; most notably, she used his oft-stated personal deference to the Congress Working Committee to push through the dismissal of the Communist Party of India government in the state of Kerala, over his own objections. Nehru began to be frequently embarrassed by her ruthlessness and disregard for parliamentary tradition, and was "hurt" by what he saw as an assertiveness with no purpose other than to stake out an identity independent of her father.

Although the Pancha Sila (Five Principles of Peaceful Coexistence) was the basis of the 1954 Sino-Indian treaty over Tibet, in later years, Nehru's foreign policy suffered through increasing Chinese antagonism over border disputes and Nehru's decision to grant asylum to the Dalai Lama. After years of failed negotiations, Nehru authorized the Indian Army to annex Goa from Portugal in 1961.

In the 1962 elections, Nehru led the Congress to victory yet with a diminished majority. Opposition parties ranging from the right-wing Bharatiya Jana Sangh and Swatantra Party, socialists and the Communist Party of India performed well.

In a matter of months, the border disputes with China turned into open conflict. Nehru assumed that as former victims of imperialism (India being a colony itself) they shared a sense of solidarity, as expressed in the phrase "Hindi-Chini bhai bhai"

(Indians and Chinese are brothers). He was dedicated to the ideals of brotherhood and solidarity among developing nations. Nehru, credulously, did not believe that one fellow Socialist country would attack another; and in any event, he felt secure behind the impregnable wall of ice that is the Himalayas. Both proved to be severe miscalculations of China's intentions and military capabilities. Following reports of his intention to confront Chinese occupation of the disputed areas—summarised in a memorable statement that he had asked the Army to "throw them (Chinese) out"-China launched a pre-emptive attack.

In a matter of days, a Chinese invasion of northeastern India exposed the weaknesses of India's military as Chinese forces came as far as Assam. Widely criticised for his government's insufficient attention to defence, Nehru was forced to sack the defence minister Krishna Menon and seek U.S. military aid. Nehru's health began declining steadily, and he was forced to spend months recuperating in Kashmir through 1963. Some historians attribute this dramatic decline to his surprise and chagrin over the invasion of India by the Chinese, which he perceived as a betrayal of trust. Upon his return from Kashmir in May 1964, Nehru suffered a stroke and later a heart attack. He died in the early hours of 27 May 1964. Nehru was cremated in accordance with Hindu rites at the Shantivana on the banks of the Yamuna River, witnessed by hundreds of thousands of mourners who had flocked into the streets of Delhi and the cremation grounds.

The foundations of India's foreign policy were laid during the freedom movement when our leaders, even when fighting for independence, were engaged with the great causes of the time. The principles of India's foreign policy, that emerged then, have stood the test of time: a belief in friendly relations with all countries of the world, the resolution of conflicts by peaceful means, the sovereign equality of all states, independence of thought and action as manifested in the principles of Non-alignment, and equity in the conduct of international relations.

Under the leadership of Jawaharlal Nehru, India was the founder member of the Non-aligned Movement. India has played an active role in strengthening the Movement and making it an effective voice in representing the collective aspirations and interests o the developing countries on such vital issues as development, peace and stability. India hosted the 7th NAM

Summit in New Delhi in 1983. In recent years, after the end of the Cold War, our foreign policy has been focused on strengthening the Movement by redefining its priorities in keeping with the changing times.

India has also been in the forefront of the world community in the struggle against colonialism. Indeed, the Independence of India itself played the role of a catalyst in removing the vestiges of colonialism in other parts of the developing world, particularly in Africa. India was also the first country to raise the question of racial discrimination in South Africa in 1946. It was at India's initiative that the AFRICA (Action for Resistance to Invasion, Colonialism and Apartheid) Fund was set up at the 8th NAM Summit in Harare in 1986. India was the Chairman of the AFRICA Fund Committee, which wound up in 1993.

A notable feature of Indian foreign policy has been its strong advocacy of general and complete disarmament, with nuclear disarmament being accorded the highest priority. Towards this end, India has taken several initiatives within the United Nations and outside. In 1988, India presented to the 3rd Session of the UN General Assembly devoted to Disarmament an Action Plan for Ushering in a Nuclear Weapons Free and Non-Violent World Order. In order to highlight international concern about the unprecedented nuclear arms race, India was also a member of the Six-Nation Five-Continent joint Initiative in the 1980s. But while India has, and will, remain committed to nuclear disarmament, to be achieved in a time-bound framework, it has consistently and in a principled manner opposed such discriminatory treaties as the Nuclear non-Proliferation Treaty (NPT) and Comprehensive Nuclear Test Ban Treaty (CTBT) and has refused to give up its nuclear options until all countries in the world including nuclear weapon states embrace the idea of nuclear disarmament in a phased manner.

As a founder member of the United Nations, India has been firmly committed to the purposes and principles of the United Nations and has made significant contributions to its various activities, including peace-keeping operations. India has been a participant in all its peace-keeping operations including those in Korea, Egypt and Congo in earlier years and in Somalia, Angola and Rwanda in recent years. India has also played an active role in the deliberations of the United Nations on the creation of a more equitable international economic order. It has been an active member of the Group of 77, and later the core group of the G-15 nations. Other issues, such as environmentally sustainable development and the promotion and protection of human rights, have also been an important focus of India's foreign policy in international forums.

Commensurate with national interests and security, the improvement of bilateral relations is an important component of any foreign policy, and India has succeeded in establishing a network of mutually beneficial relations with all countries of the world.

In particular, the improvement of relations with our neighbours has always been one of the pillars of India's foreign policy. India played an historic and unique role in the liberation of Bangladesh which emerged as a sovereign nation in 1971. Through the implementation of the 1964 and 1974 Agreements, the issues of the stateless people of Indian origin in Sri Lanka were resolved. In 1988, India helped preserve the integrity of Maldives by coming to the assistance of that country and preventing an attempted take over by armed mercenaries. The Indian government has taken recent initiatives to further strengthen ties with our neighbours, which have won international appreciation. These initiatives are based on five clear principles: First, with neighbours like Bangladesh, Bhutan, Maldives, Nepal and Sri Lanka, India does not ask for reciprocity but gives all that it can in good faith and trust. Secondly, no South Asian country should allow its territory to be used against the interests of another country of the region. Thirdly, none will interfere in the internal affairs of another. Fourthly, all South Asian countries must respect each other's territorial integrity and sovereignty. And finally, they should settle all their disputes through peaceful bilateral negotiations.

These tenets have paid rich dividends. A landmark Treaty has been signed with Bangladesh on the sharing of waters of the Ganga. With Bhutan and Nepal, major projects of economic collaboration have been advanced. Our relations with Sri Lanka have shown steady improvement. With Pakistan, India ha consistently pursued a policy seeking to improve relations under the framework of the Simla Agreement signed in 1972 which provided for the resolution of outstanding issues peacefully and bilaterally and for establishing durable peace in the Sub-continent.

Bilateral discussions with Pakistan have resumed recently and India would continue efforts to have good neighborly relations with Pakistan.

An important achievement of India's foreign policy has been the strengthening of regional cooperation. India is an active member of the South Asian Association for Regional Cooperation (SAARC) which was launched in December 1985. With India's full support, SAARC has recently taken significant steps in accelerating the pace of economic cooperation. The South Asian Preferential Trade Arrangement (SAPTA) became operational in December 1995. At the 9th SAARC Summit in Male in May 1997, which was chaired by India, a historical decision has also been taken to strive for a South Asian Free Trade Area (SAFTA) latest by the year 2001 AD. The emergence of the Indian Ocean Rim Association for Regional Cooperation (IOR-ARC) in March 1997, as a major instrument of cooperation in the larger region, has also had the active support of India.

India's foreign policy has always regarded the concept of neighborhood as one of widening concentric circles, around a central axis of historical and cultural commonalties. From this point of view, it has always given due priority to the development of relations with South East Asia. In 1947, India organized the Asian Relations Conference. It chaired the International Control Commission in 1954 and was a major player in the organization of the Bandung Conference in 1955. Today, India is implementing a 'Look East' policy which is underpinned by important economic considerations. Some significant steps in the pursuance of this policy have been taken with the admission of India as a full dialogue partner of ASEAN and a member of the ASEAN Regional Forum, in 1996.

An attribute of a dynamic foreign policy is the ability to respond to changing developments. The emergence of the Central Asian Republics in the aftermath of the break up of the Soviet Union was one such recent development, and India, given the strategic and economic importance of this region, has been quick to strengthen its bilateral relations with each of these Republics. The shift in recent years by the countries of Central and East Europe to political pluralism and market-oriented structures has also seen India trying to build upon existing business and institutional linkages so as to further strengthen the traditional ties of friendship with the countries of this region. The countries of the Gulf have a political and strategic importance for India. The region is a major market for Indian exports. Three million Indians are employed in these countries. The strengthening of ties with this region, therefore, has been a priority of India's foreign policy.

With China the aim of Indian foreign policy has been of developing a relationship of friendship, cooperation and good neighborliness, exploiting the potential for favourable growth wherever it exists, even as we seek to find a fair, reasonable and mutually acceptable solution to the outstanding border issue. Towards this aim, a series of high level visits have been exchanged, bilateral trade and economic cooperation is growing, and an Agreement on Confidence Building Measures, as part of a wider dialogue on security, has been signed.

India & the US-A Dialogue between Two Great Democracies

India values its bilateral relations with the US. As democracies, both countries have many shared ideals. Relations have also continued to grow with the 15 countries of the European Union, and with Japan. These countries are important economic partners of India, especially in the wake of our economic reforms. However, in pursuing bilateral relations, we have sought to preserve the independence of our viewpoint and protect our national interests from the pressures of conformity.

Our relations with Russia have grown over the years to constitute an important foreign policy priority for both countries. There is a recognition in both counties to the strategic dimension of our multifaceted ties. The considerable goodwill for India in Russia has been further cemented in recent years.

Economic diplomacy has been a key component of India's foreign policy. Apart from long established Divisions in the Ministry to deal with economic issues, an Investment Publicity Unit (IPU) was specifically set up in 1990 with a view to disseminating economic information and coordinating the economic and commercial activities of Indian Missions abroad in the light of the recent economic reforms underway in the country. One aspect of economic diplomacy has been the promotion of South-South Cooperation. The Indian Economic and Technical Cooperation (ITEC) Program was established in 1964. Today it extends to 110 countries in Asia, East Europe, Africa and Latin America and facilitates the training of as many as 1000 foreign candidates in Indian institutions each year.

As many as 20 million people of Indian origin live and work abroad and constitute an important link with the mother country. An important role of India's foreign policy has been to ensure their welfare and well being within the framework of the laws of the country where they live.

The strength of any foreign policy depends also on the professional abilities of those who implement it, both at Headquarters and in the field. With a view to ensuring this, the Foreign Service Institute was established to undertake specialist training for entrants into the Indian Foreign Service, and conduct several other specialist courses for Indian and foreign diplomats.

It is difficult to enumerate the achievements of a country's foreign policy in exactly quantifiable terms. With this as a qualification, it would be a fair assessment to make that Indian foreign policy has sought to preserve, with conviction and consistency, the principles that were enunciated by the founding fathers of the Republic, both in the development of bilateral relations, and in international forums, where our views have won recognition and respect. A significant factor underlying this achievement has been the consensus, cutting across political divides, within the country, on what the basic aims and objectives of Indian foreign policy should be.

Non-Aligned Movement

The Non-Aligned Movement (NAM) is an international organisation of states considering themselves not formally aligned with or against any major power bloc. The movement is largely the brainchild of India's first Prime Minister Jawaharlal Nehru, president of Egypt Gamal Abdul Nasser and Yugoslav president Josip Broz Tito. It was founded in Belgrade (1961); as of 2009, it has 118 members and 17 observer countries. The purpose of the organisation as stated in the *Havana Declaration of 1979* is to ensure "the national independence, sovereignty, territorial integrity and security of non-aligned countries" in their "struggle against imperialism, colonialism, neo-colonialism, racism, and all forms of foreign aggression, occupation, domination, interference or hegemony as well as against great power and bloc politics." They represent nearly two-thirds of the United Nations's members and comprise 55% of the world population, particularly countries considered to be developing or part of the third world.

Members have, at various times, included: Yugoslavia, Argentina, SWAPO, Cyprus and Malta. Brazil has never been a formal member of the movement, but shares many of the aims of NAM and frequently sends observers to the Non-Aligned Movement's summits. While the organisation was intended to be as close an alliance as NATO (1949) or the Warsaw Pact (1955), it has little cohesion and many of its members were actually quite closely aligned with one or another of the great powers. Additionally, some members were involved in serious conflicts with other members (e.g. India and Pakistan, Iran and Iraq). The movement fractured from its own internal contradictions when the Soviet Union invaded Afghanistan in 1979. While the Soviet allies supported the invasion, other members (particularly Islamic nations) of the movement did not.

Because the Non-Aligned Movement was formed as an attempt to thwart the Cold War, it has struggled to find relevance since the Cold War ended. After the breakup of Yugoslavia, a founding member, its membership was suspended in 1992 at the regular Ministerial Meeting of the Movement, held in New York during the regular yearly session of the General Assembly of the United Nations. At the Summit of the Movement in Jakarta, Indonesia (September 1, 1992 – September 6, 1992) Yugoslavia was suspended or expelled from the Movement. The successor states of the SFR Yugoslavia have expressed little interest in membership, though some have observer status. In 2004, Malta and Cyprus ceased to be members and joined the European Union. Belarus remains the sole member of the Movement in Europe. Turkmenistan, Belarus and Dominican Republic are the most recent entrants. The application of Bosnia-Herzegovina and Costa Rica were rejected in 1995 and 1998.

Member states of the Non-Aligned Movement (2009). Light blue states have observer status.

Origins

Independent countries, who chose not to join any of the Cold War blocs, were also known as non aligned nations.

The term "non-alignment" itself was coined by Indian Prime Minister Nehru during his speech in 1954 in Colombo, Sri Lanka. In this speech, Nehru described the five pillars to be used as a guide for Sino-Indian relations, which were first put forth by Chinese Premier Zhou Enlai. Called Panchsheel (five restraints), these principles would later serve as the basis of the Non-Aligned Movement.

The five principles were:

- Mutual respect for each other's territorial integrity and sovereignty
- Mutual non-aggression
- Mutual non-interference in domestic affairs
- Equality and mutual benefit
- Peaceful coexistence.

A significant milestone in the development of the Non-aligned movement was the 1955 Bandung Conference, a conference of Asian and African states hosted by Indonesian president Sukarno. The attending nations declared their desire not to become involved in the Cold War and adopted a "declaration on promotion of world peace and cooperation", which included Nehru's five principles. Six years after Bandung, an initiative of Yugoslav president Tito led to the first official Non-Aligned Movement Summit, which was held in September 1961 in Belgrade.

At the Lusaka Conference in September 1970, the member nations added as aims of the movement the peaceful resolution of disputes and the abstention from the big power military alliances and pacts. Another added aim was opposition to stationing of military bases in foreign countries.

The founding fathers of the Non-aligned movement were: Nehru of India, Sukarno of Indonesia and Josip Broz Tito of Yugoslavia, Gamal Abdul Nasser of Egypt and Kwame Nkrumah of Ghana. Their actions were known as 'The Initiative of Five'.

Organisational Structure and Membership

Requirements of the NAM with the key beliefs of the United Nations. The latest requirements are now that the candidate country has displayed practices in accordance with:

- Respect for fundamental human rights and for the purposes and principles of the Charter of the United Nations.

- Respect for the sovereignty and territorial integrity of all nations.
- Recognition of the equality of all races and of the equality of all nations, large and small.
- Abstention from intervention or interference in the internal affairs of another country.
- Respect for the right of each nation to defend itself singly or collectively, in conformity with the Charter of the United Nations.
- Refraining from acts or threats of aggression or the use of force against the territorial integrity or political independence of any country.
- Settlement of all international disputes by peaceful means, in conformity with the Charter of the United Nations.
- Promotion of mutual interests and cooperation.
- Respect for justice and international obligations.

Policies and Ideology

Secretaries General of the NAM had included such diversified figures as Suharto, an authoritarian anti-communist, and Nelson Mandela, a democratic socialist and famous anti-apartheid activist. Consisting of many governments with vastly different ideologies, the NAM is unified by its commitment in world peace and security. At the seventh summit held in New Delhi in March 1983, the movement described itself as the "history's biggest peace movement". The movement places equal emphasis on disarmament. NAM's commitment to peace pre-dates its formal institutionalisation in 1961. The Brioni meeting between heads of governments of India, Egypt and Yugoslavia in 1956 recognised that there exists a vital link between struggle for peace and endeavours for disarmament.

The Non-aligned movement believes in policies and practices of cooperation, especially those that are multilateral and provide mutual benefit to all those involved. Many of the members of the NAM are also members of the United Nations and both organisations have a stated policy of peaceful cooperation, yet successes that the NAM has had in multilateral agreements tends to be ignored by the larger, western and developed nation dominated UN. African concerns about apartheid were linked with Arab-Asian concerns about Palestine and success of multilateral cooperation in these areas has been a stamp of moderate success for the NAM. The NAM has played a major role in various ideological conflicts throughout its existence, including extreme opposition to apartheid regimes and support of liberation movements in various locations including Zimbabwe and South Africa. The support of these sorts of movements stems from a belief that every state has the right to base policies and practices with national interests in mind and not as a result of relations to a particular power bloc. The Non-aligned movement has become a voice of support for issues facing developing nations and is still contains ideals that are legitimate within this context.

Contemporary Relevance

Since the end of the Cold War and the formal end of colonialism, the Non-aligned movement has been forced to redefine itself and reinvent its purpose in the current world system. A major question has been whether many of its foundational ideologies, principally national independence, territorial integrity, and the struggle against colonialism and imperialism, can be applied to contemporary issues. The movement has emphasised its principles of multilateralism, equality, and mutual non-aggression in attempting to become a stronger voice for the global South, and an instrument that can be utilised to promote the needs of member nations at the international level and strengthen their political leverage when negotiating with developed nations.

In its efforts to advance Southern interests, the movement has stressed the importance of cooperation and unity amongst member states, but as in the past, cohesion remains a problem since the size of the organisation and the divergence of agendas and allegiances present the ongoing potential for fragmentation. While agreement on basic principles has been smooth, taking definitive action vis-à-vis particular international issues has been rare, with the movement preferring to assert its criticism or support rather than pass hard-line resolutions.

The movement continues to see a role for itself, as in its view, the world's poorest nations remain exploited and marginalised, no longer by opposing superpowers, but rather in a uni-polar world, and it is Western hegemony and neo-colonialism that, that the movement has really re-aligned itself against. It opposes foreign occupation, interference in internal affairs, and aggressive unilateral measures, but it has also shifted to focus on the socioeconomic challenges facing member states, especially the inequalities manifested by globalisation and the implications of neo-liberal policies. The non-aligned movement has identified economic underdevelopment, poverty, and social injustices as growing threats to peace and security

The Non-Aligned Movement: Description and History

The Non-Aligned Movement is a Movement of 115 members representing the interests and priorities of developing countries. The Movement has its origin in the Asia-Africa Conference held in Bandung, Indonesia in 1955. The meeting was convened upon the invitation of the Prime Ministers of Burma, Ceylon, India, Indonesia and Pakistan and brought together leaders of 29 states, mostly former colonies, from the two continents of Africa and Asia, to discuss common concerns and to develop joint policies in international relations. Prime Minister Nehru, the acknowledged senior statesman, along with Prime Ministers Soekarno and Nasser, led the conference. At the meeting Third World leaders shared their similar problems of resisting the pressures of the major powers, maintaining their independence and opposing colonialism and neo-colonialism, specially western domination.

Following this meeting a preparatory meeting for the First NAM Summit Conference was held in Cairo, from 5-12 June 1961. Where the invitations for Bandung were on a regional basis, the invitations for the first Summit were based on each invited country's commitment to a set of shared principles.

At the Cairo preparatory meeting the participants discussed in detail the principal aims and objectives of a policy of non-alignment. These were adopted as criteria for membership as well as for the invitations to the First Summit Conference.

The criteria are the following:

1. The country should have adopted an independent policy based on the coexistence of States with different political and social systems and on non-alignment or should be showing a trend in favour of such a policy.
2. The country concerned should be consistently supporting the Movements for National Independence.

3. The country should not be a member of a multilateral military alliance concluded in the context of Great Power conflicts.
4. If a country has a bilateral military agreement with a Great Power, or is a member of a regional defence pact, the agreement or pact should not be one deliberately concluded in the context of Great Power conflicts.
5. If it has conceded military bases to a Foreign Power the concession should not have been made in the context of Great Power conflicts.

The above criteria and principles of NAM, adopted at the Cairo preparatory meeting, have been reaffirmed by the Heads of State or Government during the XI Summit in Cartagena.

The first Conference of Non-Aligned Heads of State or Government, at which 25 countries were represented, was convened at Belgrade in September 1961, largely through the initiative of Yugoslavian President Tito. At that stage his biggest concern was that an accelerating arms race might result in war between the Soviet Union and the USA.

Political Issues

Since its inception the Movement therefore attempted to create an independent path in world politics that would not result in Member States becoming pawns in the struggles between the major powers. This resulted in a large part of its history being influenced by the global tension of the Cold War between the two super powers.

The Movement therefore this issue as a priority item on its agenda and its work. However, the Cold War was not the sole or only critical issue on the agenda of the Non-Aligned Movement. A cursory glance at the history of the Movement reveals three basic elements which influenced the approaches of the Movement to international issues.

These are the right of independent judgement, the struggle against imperialism and neo-colonialism, and the use of moderation in relations with all big powers.

In the present day context the Movement not only remains focused on the above areas but also works towards the restructuring of the international economic order.

Economic Issues

Because of great power rivalry during the Cold War Era many economic projects were set up in developing countries as part of the rivalry but suffered as a result of the quest for influence. During the years the focus of Non-Aligned Summits therefore shifted away from essentially politically issues, to the advocacy of solutions to global economic and other problems. The Jakarta Summit in 1992 was a turning point in Non-Aligned history since this was the first Summit after the end of the Cold War. It allowed the Movement to shift its focus in a direction that also enabled It to work across to groupings such as the G-7 and the EU. South Africa assumed the position as the Chair at a time when this transitional phase was still ongoing.

Responsibilities of the Nam Chair

The Chair is at the same time delegated certain responsibilities for promoting the principles and activities of the Movement. To facilitate the Chairs' responsibilities a number of structures aimed at improving the coordination and functioning of the existing mechanisms of the Movement were created. Of these mechanisms the most important is the Co-ordinating Bureau (CoB) at the United Nations in New York, which forms the focal point for coordination. Since the Non-Aligned countries meet regularly at the UN and conduct much of their work there, the Chairs' Permanent Representative to the United Nations in New York functions as the Chair of the CoB. The Bureau reviews and facilitates the harmonisation of the work of the NAM Working Groups, Contact Groups, Task Forces and Committees. The Heads of State or Government entrusted the Co-ordinating Bureau with the task of intensifying its action to further strengthen coordination and mutual cooperation among Non-Aligned countries, including unified action in the United Nations and other international fora, on issues of common concern.

Another important mechanism is the Troika of past, serving and future Chairs. This concept is operationalised at the discretion of the incumbent Chair and can act as a clearinghouse for solutions of problems and issues confronting developing countries on which the Movement must take a position.

The Methodology of the Movement was reviewed at a Meeting of the Ministerial Committee on Methodology in Cartagena,

Colombia in 1996 and the decisions taken there is reflected in the Cartagena document on Methodology.

Five Principles of Peaceful Coexistence

The Five Principles of Peaceful Coexistence or Panchsheel are a series of agreements between the People's Republic of China and India. It was formed in 1954, within the context of decolonization, to ensure that newly independent nations would not have the same aggressive relationship they once had with colonizers. The 5 principles called the panchsheel, which form the basis of the Non-Aligned movement, were laid down by Jawaharlal Nehru. This narrow agreement between India, PRC spurred the Asian-African Conference, whose ten principles expanded on the Five Principles below:

1. Mutual respect for each other's territorial integrity and sovereignty
2. Mutual non-aggression
3. Mutual non-interference in each other's internal affairs
4. Equality and mutual benefit
5. Peaceful coexistence.

The Five Principles of Peaceful Coexistence were first put forth by India at the start of negotiations that took place in Delhi from December 1953 to April 1954 between the Delegation of the PRC Government and the Delegation of the Indian Government on the relations between the three countries with respect to disputed territory. Later, the Five Principles were formally written into the preface to the "Agreement Between the People's Republic of China and the Republic of India on Trade and cooperation Between the PRC and India" concluded between the two sides. Since June 1954, the Five Principles have been adopted in many other international documents. As norms of relations between nations, they have become widely recognized and accepted throughout the region.

Backgrounder: Five Principles of Peaceful Coexistence

BEIJING, June 14, 2004 (Xinhuanet) – June 28 this year will mark the 50th anniversary of the introduction of the Five Principles of Peaceful Coexistence, which are mutual respect for sovereignty andterritorial integrity, mutual non-aggression, non-interference in each other's internal affairs, equality and mutual benefit, and peaceful coexistence. With the end of the Second World War, movements of national independence and liberation flourished in Asia, Africa and Latin America. Newly independent nations demanded the establishment of new patterns of international relations based on equality to maintain their national sovereignty and develop their economies.

The Five Principles of Peaceful Coexistence were produced precisely in response to this strong and common demand of newly independent nations. After their rebirths, China and India, two giants in Asia, established diplomatic relations on April 1, 1950. On April 29, 1954, the two countries signed an agreement on trade and communications between the Chinese region of Tibet and India, introducing for the first time the Five Principles of Peaceful Coexistence into the preface of the agreement. In June 1954, former Chinese Premier Zhou Enlai visited India and Myanmar at the invitation of the two countries and held talks with his then Indian and Myanmese counterparts, Jawaharlal Nehru and U Nu.

Consequently, in the "Joint Declaration of Chinese and Indian Premiers" issued on June 28 and the "Joint Declaration of Chinese and Myanmese Premiers" issued on the following day, the Five Principles of Peaceful Coexistence were officially announced as the basic norms guiding the Sino-Indian and Sino-Myanmese relations.

The Sino-Indian joint declaration proposed that "these principles not only be applicable to relations between nations, but also to the general international relationship," while the Sino-Myanmese joint declaration expressed the hope that "these principles will be observed by all nations."

In April 1955 — one year after China, India and Myanmar initiated the Five Principles of Peaceful Coexistence, a total of 29 newly independent nations from Asia and Africa held the historic "Asian-African Conference" in Bandung, Indonesia. As a result of the common efforts of the participants, the conference adopted the "Declaration on Promotion of World Peace and Cooperation" and formulated the 10 principles of the Bandung conference.

These 10 principles, which contained all points in the five principles of peaceful coexistence, represented an extension and development of the latter. Since then, the Five Principles of Peaceful Coexistence have been recognized and accepted by more and more nations, international organizations and international meetings, and have been incorporated into a series of major international documents, including declarations adopted by the United Nations General Assembly.

The five principles were also reaffirmed in the documents on China's establishment of diplomatic relations with more than 160 nations, and in treaties as well as communiques China has signed with other countries. Earlier this month, the Indian government greenlighted a British film project, *Indian Summer*, based on Alex von Tunzelmann's brilliant book of the same name about the events leading up to Britain's bloody withdrawal from India in 1947 and India's partition. India has an odd tradition – generally ignored – of vetting all foreign film projects before granting permission to shoot inside the country. But the focus of *Indian Summer* – the alleged love affair between Jawaharlal Nehru, India's first prime minister, and Edwina, the wife of Britain's last viceroy to India, Lord Louis Mountbatten – elicited extraordinary responses from a Congress Party-led government that is hyperanxious about the reputation of its founding figures.

The film's international cast of superstars – Academy Award-winner Cate Blanchett playing Edwina, and Hugh Grant tipped to portray her husband, Louis – did nothing to deter New Delhi from issuing a series of silly cuts. Among them: no kissing, no scenes of physical intimacy between Nehru and Edwina, and no use of the word "love." The director, Joe Wright, whose previous films include the hugely successful *Atonement* and *Pride and Prejudice*, has no choice but to comply if he wants to shoot the film in India. And that's not all: Should Wright go ahead, the completed film will have to be shown to a government "expert" who will judge whether it depicts "a correct and balanced perspective on the topic covered."

Strictly speaking, the Indian government was merely following procedure in vetting the film project. Yet it is also true that New Delhi would not have gone to this length to protect the reputation of any other Indian leader of that time. More than 60 years after independence, Nehru's life is jealously guarded by the Congress Party, which is controlled by the Nehru-Gandhi dynasty. Nehru was not a saint, but his canonization is crucial to those who invoke his legacy to perpetuate their own hold on his party. As one historian damningly noted, the party "which was once the vehicle of a great, countrywide freedom struggle...is now merely a vehicle for the ambitions of a single family.." The rush to sanitize *Indian*

Summer highlights one of the more destructive ways in which the Congress Party maintains its grip on history, particularly when that history deals with the lives of the revered Nehru-Gandhi family: censorship.

Nehru was one of the 20th century's most phenomenal leaders, but even his most ardent admirers will admit that he was not nearly as compelling a figure as his mentor, Mohandas K. Gandhi. Yet while Gandhi's life, including the details of his controversial sex experiments, remains open to the public, Nehru's descendents—his child, Prime Minister Indira Gandhi; grandchild, Prime Minister, Rajiv Gandhi; and Rajiv's wife, Congress Party leader Sonia Gandhi— have kept his private life locked up. Scholars attempting to access Nehru's letters have been repeatedly rebuffed— with some unexpected consequences. In 1994, American historian Stanley Wolpert, who has written some of the most scintillating biographies of major South Asian leaders, flew to New Delhi to persuade Sonia Gandhi, the reigning head of the Nehru family and India's most powerful person, to give him access to Nehru's letters. He left empty-handed. The subsequent biography he published, *Nehru: A Tryst with Destiny*, made the extraordinary claim that Nehru was partly homosexual. It was based on nothing more than speculation, but was proof, if any was required, that suppressing facts has the unintended consequence of legitimizing fiction.

Censorship, however, is only one of the methods used by the Congress Party to distort history. Where it has been unable to pre-empt scholarly inquiries or predetermine their outcomes by constricting research, India's Grand Old Party has actively turned to propaganda to burnish the image of its leaders. And perhaps no other leader in the democratic world has been a greater posthumous beneficiary of propaganda than Nehru's daughter, Indira Gandhi.

Elevated to the prime ministership as a compromise candidate in 1966, Gandhi took slightly less than a decade to consign Indian democracy to the trash can. She turned the Congress Party into a family enterprise, rigged elections, sowed the seeds of violence in Kashmir and Punjab, suspended the Constitution, locked up her political opponents, and imposed an emergency rule that lasted nearly two years. During this time, thousands of people across the country were forcefully vasectomized in a population-control drive; prisons proliferated with inmates, some of whom vanished without a trace, never to return; and Indira's younger son, Sanjay, ruled the country like a thug, demolishing settlements and displacing thousands of people. So thoroughly had she demoralized the party and corrupted its machinery that when she was assassinated in 1984 her cabinet felt no qualms about electing her politically inexperienced elder son, Rajiv, as prime minister.

Indira's reign was the darkest period in free India's history. But the narrative of Indira that has been propagated since casts her as a doughty defender of India, a progressive socialist who did near-mythical things for the welfare of the poor. The Congress Party has managed to engineer her legacy by all but excising her excesses from history, using the state machinery to give her image a complete makeover.

This year, in a scathing study of the Congress Party's attempts to make India's national progress indistinguishable from the party, titled "All in the Name of the Nehru-Gandhi Family," journalist A. Surya Prakash identified 450 government projects, schemes, and institutions worth hundreds of billions of rupees that have been named after members of the Nehru-Gandhi family. From breakfast programs for the poor to the national nursery scheme for children, from drinking water projects in rural India to food security missions, from housing schemes to roads, buildings, universities, airports, national parks, sanctuaries, sports stadiums, sporting championships, museums, and even neighborhoods — almost everything that matters in India bears the name of one family, including Mumbai's "Sanjay Gandhi National Park" And the "Indira Gandhi Calf-Rearing Scheme."

Meanwhile, despite all the largesse with its family names, the Congress Party continues to inflict its corrupt ways on India. The fact that the party's principal opponent is a far-right political party, the Hindu nationalist BJP, has served it well. While attention in recent years has been focused on the kind of harm the BJP *could* do to India's independent institutions, the Congress Party has gotten away with inflicting real damage. In 2007, Italian businessman Ottavio Quattrocchi, long wanted in relation to a corruption scandal dating back to the Rajiv Gandhi years, was allowed to escape extradition from Argentina by India's federal investigation agency, the CBI (which recently dropped the case). But the most egregious assault on democratic institutions came earlier this year when, disregarding all objections, the commissionership of the Election Commission of India (ECI) was handed over to Navin Chawla, an old friend of the Nehru-Gandhi family. The ECI has an impeccable record of conducting free and fair elections across India since 1952, and the outgoing commissioner, N. Gopalaswami, repeatedly raised questions about Chawla's independence. Chawla had a long-standing relationship with the Nehru-Gandhi family: He had officiated at a wedding in the family; his wife had been a close friend of Sonia Gandhi; and, according to a biographer of Sanjay Gandhi, he was one of the men entrusted with the job of carrying out forced vasectomies in New Delhi during the emergency years. The elections that returned the Congress Party to power this year were conducted under his supervision. Since July of this year, questions about the safety of the electronic voting machines have been raised, and all the opposition parties have called for the reintroduction of paper ballots. The government dismissed them as sore losers, but there is no doubt that the reputation of the Election Commission has been profoundly undermined. Keenly aware of the totalitarian possibilities in a post-colonial democratic setup, Mahatma Gandhi had advised the Congress Party to disband itself after independence. But Asia's oldest political party, once an engine of extraordinary social change, is today a veritable fiefdom. Internal democracy is unheard of in a party that is in charge of the world's largest democracy. You can go to the Kaaba and criticize Allah, but you cannot be a congressman and question the omnipotence of the Nehru-Gandhi family. In gagging a British film to preserve its own image, the Congress Party undermines India's democracy. Most appallingly of all, it does it in the name of a man who dedicated his life to transforming India into a free and open society. This site provides comprehensive information on India Foreign Policy. The site also focuses on India's contributions and achievements as a result of its well crafted foreign policies, voicing issues of global concerns.

India foreign policies were formulated by our national leaders ever since India's independence. The principles of India's foreign policies are-

- Fostering cordial relations with other countries
- Solving conflicts by peaceful means
- Sovereignty and equality of all nations

- Independence of thought and action as per the principles of Non-align Movement or NAM
- Equality in conducting international relations.

India-the founder member of the Non-aligned Movement (NAM), raised its voice representing collective aspirations and interests of all the developing nations of the world. India Foreign Policy covers vital issues of development, peace and stability. India was the first country to raise the question of racial discrimination in South Africa in 1946 and also aims at eradicating colonialism. Indian foreign policy has been voicing the need for complete disarmament of nuclear weapons. India has taken several initiatives within the United Nations and outside, like Disarmament-an action plan for ushering in a nuclear weapons free and nonviolent world. Indian foreign policy has opposed discriminatory treaties such as the Nuclear Non-Proliferation Treaty (NPT) and Comprehensive Nuclear Test Ban Treaty (CTBT) and has refused to give up its nuclear program until all nations of the world including nuclear weapon states accepts and respects the idea of total nuclear disarmament in a phased manner.

India foreign policy has been firmly committed to the purposes and principles of the United Nations and has made significant contributions like participating in all peace-keeping operations like those in Korea, Egypt, and Congo in earlier years of its operation and then in Somalia, Angola, and Rwanda in recent years. India foreign policy focuses on active participation in the creation of a more balanced international economies. India has been an active member of the Group of 77, and later the core group of the G-15 nations. India foreign policy constantly addresses other important issues of international importance, such as environmentally sustainable development and the promotion and protection of human rights.

India Foreign Policy is well aligned with its national interests and security. A well crafted India Foreign Policy has succeeded in establishing a network of mutually beneficial relations with all countries of the world, particularly in the improving relations with its neighbours.

6

Relation with Neighbours

Foreign Relations of India

The Republic of India is the world's most-populous electoral democracy and has one of the fastest economic growth rates in the world. With the world's second largest armed forces, and fourth largest economy by purchasing power parity, India is considered to be a global power, and an emerging superpower. It is India's growing international influence that increasingly gives it a more prominent voice in global affairs.

India has a long history of collaboration with several countries and is considered a leader of the developing world. India was one of the founding members of several international organizations, most notably the United Nations, the Non-Aligned Movement, the Asian Development Bank and the G20 industrial nations. India has also played an important and influential role in other international organizations like East Asia Summit, World Trade Organization, International Monetary Fund (IMF), G8+5 and IBSA Dialogue Forum. Regional organizations India is a part of include SAARC and BIMSTEC. India has taken part in several UN peacekeeping missions and in 2007, it was the second-largest troop contributor to the United Nations. India is currently seeking a permanent seat in the UN Security Council, along with the G4 nations.

Pakistan

Despite historical and cultural links, relations between India and Pakistan have been plagued by years of mistrust and suspicion ever since the partition of India in 1947. The principal source of contention between India and its western neighbour has been the Kashmir conflict. After an invasion by Pashtun tribesmen and Pakistani paramilitary forces, the Hindu Maharaja of the Dogra Kingdom of Jammu and Kashmir, Hari Singh, and its Muslim Prime Minister, Sheikh Abdullah, signed an Instrument of Accession with New Delhi making the state an integral part of the Union of India. The First Kashmir War started after the Indian Army entered Srinagar, the capital of the state, to secure the area from the invading forces.

The war ended in December 1948 with the Line of Control dividing the erstwhile princely state into territories administered by Pakistan (northern and western areas) and India (southern, central and northeastern areas). Pakistan contested the legality of the Instrument of Accession since the Dogra Kingdom has signed a standstill agreement with it.

The Indo-Pakistani War of 1965 started following the failure of Pakistan's Operation Gibraltar, which was designed to infiltrate forces into Jammu and Kashmir to precipitate an insurgency against rule by India.

The five-week war caused thousands of casualties on both sides. It ended in a United Nations (UN) mandated ceasefire and the subsequent issuance of the Tashkent Declaration. India and Pakistan went to war again in 1971, however this time the conflict was over East Pakistan rather than Kashmir. Due to the large-scale atrocities committed by the Pakistan army, millions of Bengali refugees poured over into India. India, along with Mukti Bahini, defeated Pakistan and the Pakistani forces surrendered on the eastern front. The war resulted in the creation of Bangladesh.

Kashmir Conflict

The Kashmir conflict refers to the territorial dispute over Kashmir, the northwesternmost region of South Asia. The parties to the dispute are India, Pakistan, China and the people of Kashmir.

India claims the entire former princely state of Jammu and Kashmir and presently administers approximately 43% of the region including most of Jammu, Kashmir Valley, Laddakh and the Siachen Glacier. India's claim is contested by Pakistan which controls approximately 37% of Kashmir, mainly Azad Kashmir and the northern areas of Gilgit and Baltistan. In addition, China controls 20% of Kashmir including Aksai Chin which it occupied following the brief Sino-Indian War of 1962 and the Trans-Karakoram Tract, also known as the Shaksam Valley, that was ceded to it by Pakistan in 1963.

India's official position is that Kashmir is an integral part of India. Pakistan's official position is that Kashmir is a disputed territory whose final status must be determined by the people of Kashmir. China's official position is that Aksai Chin is a part of Tibet, which is a part of China. Certain Kashmiri independence groups believe that Kashmir should be independent of both India and Pakistan.

India and Pakistan have fought three wars over Kashmir: in 1947, 1965, and 1999. India and China have clashed once, in 1962 over Aksai Chin as well as the northeastern Indian state of Arunachal Pradesh. India and Pakistan have also been involved in several skirmishes over the Siachen Glacier.

Since after 1987 disputed rigged State elections resulted in some of the 'states legislative assembly' 'formed militant wings' later on after the election forming and creating the catalyst for the insurgency,; the Indian-administered Jammu and Kashmir has been in stife from the confrontation between the Indian Armed Forces, militants and separatists. Furthermore, India alleges these militants are supported by Pakistan. This turmoil in Jammu and Kashmir has resulted in thousands of deaths., however the insurgency over the past two decades has died down according to the Indian government.

On the other hand, there has been protest movements in Indian Administered Kashmir since 1989. The movement was created for the same reason as the insurgency; the disputed rigged elections in 1987, Kashmir dispute and grievances with the Indian government specifically the Indian Military. A 2001 report 'Pakistan's Role in the Kashmir Insurgency' of US Think tank RAND corporation noted that 'More intrinsically, the nature of the Kashmir conflict has been transformed from what was originally a secular, locally-based struggle (conducted via the Jammu Kashmir Liberation Front-JKLF) to one that is now largely carried out by foreign militants and rationalized in pan-Islamic religious terms.' Most of the militant organizations are composed of foreign mercenaries mostly from Punjab.

Indo-Pakistani War of 1947

The Indo-Pakistani War of 1947, sometimes known as the First Kashmir War, was fought between India and Pakistan over the region of Kashmir from 1947 to 1948. It was the first of four wars fought between the two newly independent nations. The result of the war still affects the geopolitics of both the countries.

Background

Prior to 1815 the area now known as "Kashmir" was referred to as the "Panjab Hill States" and comprised 22 small independent states carved out of Afghanistan Amir (King) controlled territories combined with local small rulers, from 900 AD, in Sultan Mehmood Ghaznavi time, to Afghan Amir Ahmed Shah Abdali time, born in southern Punjab Multan. Since 1757 it was ruled by the Muslim Mughal Empire, until 1857, when the British East India Company arrived to India.

These small states were ruled by Rajput kings who had sworn allegiance to the Mughal empire. In fact the Rajput of the Punjab Hill States were a major strength of the Mughal empire and had fought many battles in support of the Mughals especially against the Sikhs.

Following the rise of the British East India Company and the subsequent decline of the Mughal empire, the power of the Panjab Hill States also began to decline. They therefore became easy targets for the Sikh leader Ranjit Singh who proceeded to conquer these small states one by one. Eventually all the Panjab Hill States were conquered by Ranjit Singh and merged into one state to be called the State of Jammu.

History of Panjab castes by J. Hutchinson and J.P.Vogel lists a total of 22 states 16 Hindu and 6 Muhammadan that formed the State of Jammu following the conquest of Raja Ranjit Singh in 1820. Of these 6 Muhammadan States two (Kotli and Punch) were ruled by Mangrals, two (Bhimber and Khari-Khariyala) by Chibs, one (Rajouri) by the Jarrals and one (Khashtwar) by the Khashtwaria.

The First Anglo-Sikh War was fought between the Sikh Empire, which asserted sovereignty over Kashmir, and the East India Company between 1845 and 1846. In the Treaty of Lahore in 1846, the Sikhs were made to surrender the valuable region (the Jullundur

Doab) between the Beas River and Sutlej River and required to pay an indemnity of 1.2 million rupees.

Because they could not readily raise this sum, the East India Company allowed the Dogra ruler Gulab Singh to acquire Kashmir from the Sikh kingdom in exchange for making a payment of 750,000 rupees to the East India Company. Gulab Singh became the first Maharaja of the newly formed princely state of Jammu and Kashmir, founding a dynasty, The Royal House of Jammu and Kashmir, that was to rule the state, the second-largest principality during the British Raj, until India gained its independence in 1947.

Partition of India

Before and after the withdrawal of the British from India in 1947, the princely state of Kashmir and Jammu came under pressure from both India and Pakistan to agree to become part of one of the newly independent countries. According to the instruments of accession relating to the Partition of India, the rulers of princely states were to be given the choice of either acceding to India or Pakistan, or remaining independent. The Maharaja of Kashmir, Hari Singh chose the latter and tried to avoid accession to either country. When British forces withdrew there was a Muslim revolution in western Kashmir and the region was invaded by Pashtun tribals from the North West Frontier Province (NWFP).

Fearing that his forces would be unable to withstand the assault, the Maharaja asked for Indian military assistance. India set a condition that Kashmir must accede to India for it to receive assistance. Whereupon the Government of India recognized the accession of the erstwhile princely state to India, and was considered the new Indian state of Jammu and Kashmir, Indian troops were sent to the state to defend it against the Pakistani forces. The legitimacy of this accession is still disputed. Due to a lack of demographic data concerning religious affiliations, it is difficult to determine whether public opinion was a factor in Hari Singh's decision.

Pakistan was of the view that the Maharaja of Kashmir had no right to call in the Indian Army, because it held that the Maharaja of Kashmir was not a heredity ruler, that he was merely a British appointee. There had been no such position as the "Maharaja of Kashmir" prior to British rule. Hence Pakistan decided to take action, but British-appointed Army Chief of Pakistan Douglas

Gracey did not send troops to the Kashmir front and refused to obey the order to do so given by Mohammad Ali Jinnah, Governor-General of Pakistan. Gracey's argument was that Indian forces occupying Kashmir represented the British Crown and hence he could not engage in a military encounter with Indian forces. Pakistan finally did manage to send troops to Kashmir but by then the Indian forces had taken control of approximately two thirds of the former principality.

Summary of War

The war was fought within the borders of the former princely state of Kashmir and Jammu by Indian Army, paramilitary and the erstwhile princely state forces opposed by Pakistan Army, paramilitary and local militias from the NWFP (the Pakistani forces referred to themselves as the Azad Kashmir forces (*Azad* in Urdu means liberated or free)). The princely state forces were unprepared for the initial assault of AZK forces, having been deployed thinly on the borders of the princely state for purposes of maintaining border security and deterring militant activity. The princely state defenses quickly collapsed in the face of the assault, some individuals and units joining the AZK forces.

The initial successes by AZK forces were not vigorously pressed, giving an opportunity for India to airlift its forces into Kashmir after the state had acceded to India.. With Indian reinforcements opposing AZK forces, the offensive ran out of steam towards the end of 1947, except in the High Himalayas sector where AZK forces made substantial progress until they were turned back at the outskirts of Leh in late June 1948. Throughout 1948 many small-scale battles were fought, but none gave a strategic advantage to either side and the fronts gradually solidified along what would became known as the Line of Control. A formal cease-fire was declared on 31 December 1948.

Stages of the War

This war has been split into ten stages by time. The individual stages are detailed below.

Initial Invasion (Operation Gulmarg)

The objective of the initial invasion was to capture control of the Kashmir valley including its principal city, Srinagar, the summer capital of the state (Jammu being the winter capital). The state forces stationed in the border regions around Muzaffarabad and Domel were quickly defeated by AZK forces (some state forces mutinied and joined the AZK) and the way to the capital was open. Rather than advancing toward Srinagar before state forces could regroup or be reinforced, the invading forces remained in the captured cities in the border region engaging in looting and other crimes against their inhabitants. In the Punch valley, the state forces retreated into towns where they were besieged.

Indian Defence of the Kashmir Valley

After the accession, India airlifted troops and equipment to Srinagar, where they reinforced the princely state forces, established a defence perimeter and defeated the AZK forces on the outskirts of the city. The successful defence included an outflanking manoeuvre by Indian armoured cars. The defeated AZK forces were pursued as far as Baramula and Uri and these towns were recaptured.

In the Punch valley, AZK forces continued to besiege state forces.

In Gilgit, the state paramilitary forces (the Gilgit Scouts) joined the invading AZK forces, who thereby obtained control of this northern region of the state. The AZK forces were also joined by troops from Chitral, whose ruler, the Mehtar of Chitral, had acceded to Pakistan.

Attempted Link-up at Punch and Fall of Mirpur

Indian forces ceased pursuit of AZK forces after recapturing Uri and Baramula, and sent a relief column southwards, in an attempt to relieve Punch. Although the relief column eventually reached Punch, the siege could not be lifted. A second relief column reached Kotli, but was forced to evacuate its garrison.

Meanwhile, Mirpur was captured by AZK forces on the 25th of November 1947. Then there was a massacre of Hindus and Sikhs and loot, and more later in Alibeg camp. Around 20 thousand people reported killed, also atrocities on women were reported.

Fall of Jhanger and Attacks on Naoshera and Uri

The Pakistani/AZK forces attacked and captured Jhanger. They then attacked Naoshera unsuccessfully. Other Pakistani/AZK forces made a series of unsuccessful attacks on Uri. In the south a minor

Indian attack secured Chamb. By this stage of the war the front line began to stabilise as more Indian troops became available.

Operation Vijay: Counterattack to Jhanger

The Indian forces launched a counterattack in the south recapturing Jhanger and Rajauri. In the Kashmir Valley the Pakistani/AZK forces continued attacking the Uri garrison. In the north Skardu was brought under siege by Pakistani/AZK forces.

Indian Spring Offensive

The Indians held onto Jhanger against numerous counterattacks from the AZK, who were increasingly supported by regular Pakistani Forces. In the Kashmir Valley the Indians attacked, recapturing Tithwail. The AZK made good progress in the High Himalayas sector, infiltrating troops to bring Leh under siege, capturing Kargil and defeating a relief column heading for Skardu.

Operations Gulab and Erase

The Indians continued to attack in the Kashmir Valley sector driving north to capture Keran and Gurais. They also repelled a counterattack aimed at Tithwail. In the Punch Valley the forces besieged in Punch broke out and temporarily linked up with the outside world again. The Kashmir State army was able to defend Skardu from the Gilgit Scouts and thus they were not able to proceed down the Indus valley towards Leh. In August the Chitral Forces under Mata-ul-Mulk besieged Skardu and with the help of artillery were able to take Skardu. This freed the Gilgit Scouts to push further into Laddakh.

Operation Duck

During this time the front began to settle down with less activity by either side, the only major event was an unsuccessful attack by the Indians towards Dras (Operation Duck). The siege of Punch continued.

Operation Easy; Punch link-up

The Indians now started to get the upper hand in all sectors. Punch was finally relieved after a siege of over a year. The Gilgit forces in the High Himalayas, who had previously made good progress, were finally defeated. The Indians pursued as far as Kargil before being forced to halt due to supply problems. The

Zoji-La pass was forced by using tanks (which had not been thought possible at that altitude) and Dras was recaptured. The use of tanks was based on experience gained in Burma in 1945.

Moves up to Cease-fire

At this stage Indian Prime Minister Jawahar Lal Nehru decided to ask UN to intervene. A UN cease-fire was arranged for the 31 December 1948. A few days before the cease-fire the Pakistanis launched a counter attack, which cut the road between Uri and Punch. After protracted negotiations a cease-fire was agreed to by both countries, which came into effect. The terms of the cease-fire as laid out in the UNCIP resolution. of August 13, 1948 were adopted by the UN on January 5, 1949.

This required Pakistan to withdraw its forces, both regular and irregular, while allowing India to maintain minimum strength of its forces in the state to preserve law and order. On compliance of these conditions a plebiscite was to be held to determine the future of the territory. In all, 1,500 soldiers died on each side during the war and Pakistan was able to acquire roughly two-fifths of Kashmir, including five of the fourteen eight thousanders plus peaks of the world, while India maintained the remaining three fifths of Kashmir, including the most populous and fertile regions.

Military Insights Gained from the War

On the use of Armour

The use of light tanks and armoured cars was important at two stages of the war. Both of these Indian victories involved very small numbers of AFVs. These were:-

- The defeat of the initial thrust at Srinagar, which was aided by the arrival of 2 armoured cars in the rear of the irregular forces.
- The forcing of the Zoji-La pass with 11 Stuart M5 light tanks.

This may show that armour can have a significant psychological impact if it turns up at places thought of as impossible. It is also likely that the invaders did not deploy anti-tank weapons to counter these threats. Even the lightest weapons will significantly encumber leg infantry units, so they may well have been perceived as not worth the effort of carrying about, and left in rear areas. This will greatly enhance the psychological impact of the armour when it does appear. The successful use of armour in this campaign strongly influenced Indian tactics in the 1962 war where great efforts were made to deploy armour to inhospitable regions (although with much less success in that case).

Progression of Front Lines:

- It is interesting to chart the progress of the front lines. After a certain troop density is reached progress was very slow with victories being counted in the capture of individual villages or peaks. Where troop density was lower (as it was in the High Himalayas sector and at the start of the war) rates of advance can be very high

Indo-Pakistani War of 1965

The Indo-Pakistani War of 1965 was a culmination of skirmishes that took place between April 1965 and September 1965 between India and Pakistan. This conflict became known as the Second Kashmir War fought by India and Pakistan over the disputed region of Kashmir, the first having been fought in 1947. The war began following Pakistan's Operation Gibraltar, which was designed to infiltrate forces into Jammu and Kashmir to precipitate an insurgency against rule by India. The five-week war caused thousands of casualties on both sides. It ended in a United Nations (UN) mandated ceasefire and the subsequent issuance of the Tashkent Declaration.

Much of the war was fought by the countries' land forces in Kashmir and along the International Border between India and Pakistan. This war saw the largest amassing of troops in Kashmir since the Partition of British India in 1947, a number that was overshadowed only during the 2001–2002 military standoff between India and Pakistan. Most of the battles were fought by opposing infantry and armoured units, with substantial backing from air forces, and naval operations. Many details of this war, like those of other Indo-Pakistani Wars, remain unclear.

Pre-war Escalation

Since Partition of British India in 1947, Pakistan and India remained in contention over several issues. Although the Kashmir conflict was the predominant issue dividing the nations, other border disputes existed, most notably over the Rann of Kutch, a barren region in the Indian state of Gujarat. When Junagadh, a former princely state, had been integrated into India, whose Muslim prince wanted to join Pakistan.

On March 20, 1965, and later in April 1965, fighting broke out between India and Pakistan in the Rann of Kutch due to intentional provocation by the latter. Initially involving border police from both nations, the disputed area soon witnessed intermittent skirmishes between the countries' armed forces. In June 1965, British Prime Minister Harold Wilson successfully persuaded both countries to end hostilities and set up a tribunal to resolve the dispute. The verdict, which came later in 1968, saw Pakistan awarded 350 square miles (900 km^2) of the Rann of Kutch, as against its original claim of 3500 square miles.

After its success in the Rann of Kutch, Pakistan, under the leadership of General Ayub Khan, believed the Indian Army would be unable to defend itself against a quick military campaign in the disputed territory of Kashmir as the Indian military had suffered a loss to China in 1962. Pakistan believed that the population of Kashmir was generally discontented with Indian rule and that a resistance movement could be ignited by a few infiltrating saboteurs. Pakistan attempted to ignite the resistance movement by means of a covert infiltration, codenamed Operation Gibraltar The Pakistani infiltrators were soon discovered, however, their presence reported by local Kashmiris, and the operation ended in a complete failure.

Pakistan claimed to have been concerned by attempts of India to absorb Kashmir – a state claimed by Pakistan as "disputed", into the Indian Union. The basis for this claim was the application of Articles 356 and 357 of the Indian Constitution that allow the President of India to declare President's Rule in the State.

The War

On August 15, 1965, Indian forces crossed the border and launched an attack on the territory of Kashmir administered by Pakistan. Pakistani reports cite this attack as unprovoked while assessments from India and neutral sources cite this as a response to Pakistan's infiltration into Jammu and Kashmir as part of Operation Gibraltar. Initially, the Indian Army met with considerable success, capturing three important mountain positions after a prolonged artillery barrage. By the end of August, however, both sides had relative progress; Pakistan had made progress in areas such as Tithwal, Uri and Punch and India had captured the Haji Pir Pass, eight kilometers into Pakistan-occupied Kashmir.

On September 1, 1965, Pakistan launched a counterattack, called Operation Grand Slam, with the objective to capture the vital town of Akhnoor in Jammu, which would sever communications and cut off supply routes to Indian troops. Attacking with an overwhelming ratio of troops and technically superior tanks, Pakistan made gains against Indian forces, who were caught unprepared and suffered heavy losses. India responded by calling in its air force to blunt the Pakistani attack. The next day, Pakistan retaliated, its air force attacked Indian forces and air bases in both Kashmir and Punjab. India's decision to open up the theatre of attack into Pakistani Punjab forced the Pakistani army to relocate troops engaged in the operation to defend Punjab. Operation Grand Slam therefore failed, as the Pakistan Army was unable to capture Akhnoor; it became one of the turning points in the war when India decided to relieve pressure on its troops in Kashmir by attacking Pakistan further south.

India crossed the International Border on the Western front on September 6, marking an official beginning of the war. On September 6, the 15th Infantry Division of the Indian Army, under World War II veteran Major General Prasad, battled a massive counterattack by Pakistan near the west bank of the Ichogil Canal (BRB Canal), which was a *de facto* border of India and Pakistan. The General's entourage itself was ambushed and he was forced to flee his vehicle. A second, this time successful, attempt to cross the Ichhogil Canal was made over the bridge in the village of Barki, just east of Lahore. These developments brought the Indian Army within the range of Lahore International Airport. As a result, the United States requested a temporary ceasefire to allow it to evacuate its citizens in Lahore. However, the Pakistani counter attack took Khem Karan from Indian forces which tried to divert the attention of Pakistanis from Khem Karan by an attack on Bedian and the adjacent villages.

The thrust against Lahore consisted of the 1st Infantry Division supported by the three tank regiments of the 2nd Independent Armoured Brigade; they quickly advanced across the border, reaching the Ichhogil (BRB) Canal by 6 September. The Pakistani

Army held the bridges over the canal or blew up those it could not hold, effectively stalling any further advance by the Indians on Lahore. One unit of the Indian Jat Regiment, 3 Jat, had also crossed the Ichogil canal and captured the town of Batapore (Jallo Mur to Pakistan) on the west side of the canal. The same day, a counter offensive consisting of an armoured division and infantry division supported by Pakistan Air Force Sabres forced the Indian 15th Division to withdraw to its starting point. Although 3 Jat suffered minimal casualties, the bulk of the damage being taken by ammunition and stores vehicles, the higher commanders had no information of 3 Jat's capture of Batapore and misleading information led to the command to withdraw from Batapore and Dograi to Ghosal-Dial. This move brought extreme disappointment to Lt-Col Desmond Hayde, CO of 3 Jat. Dograi was eventually recaptured by 3 Jat on 21 September, for the second time but after a much harder battle due to Pakistani reinforcements.

On the days following September 9, both nations' premiere formations were routed in unequal battles. India's 1st Armoured Division, labelled the "pride of the Indian Army", launched an offensive towards Sialkot. The Division divided itself into two prongs, was forced back by the Pakistani 6th armoured division at Chawinda and was forced to withdraw after suffering heavy losses of nearly 100 tanks. The Pakistanis followed up their success by launching Operation Windup, which forced the Indians back farther. Similarly, Pakistan's pride, the 1st Armoured Division, pushed an offensive towards Khem Karan, with the intent to capture Amritsar (a major city in Punjab, India) and the bridge on River Beas to Jalandhar.

The Pakistani 1st Armoured Division never made it past Khem Karan, however, and by the end of September 10 lay disintegrated by the defences of the Indian 4th Mountain Division at what is now known as the Battle of *Asal Uttar* (lit. meaning – "Real Answer", or more appropriate English equivalent – "Fitting Response"). The area became known as 'Patton Nagar' (Patton Town), because of the large number of US-made Pakistani Patton tanks. Approximately 97 Pakistani tanks were destroyed or abandoned, with only 32 Indian tanks destroyed or damaged. The Pakistani 1st Armoured Division less 5th Armoured Brigade was next sent to Sialkot sector behind Pakistani 6th Armoured Division where it didn't see action as 6th Armoured Division was already in process of routing Indian 1st Armoured Division which was superior to it in strength.

The war was heading for a stalemate, with both nations holding territory of the other. The Indian army suffered 3,000 battlefield deaths, while Pakistan suffered 3,800. The Indian army was in possession of 710 mile^2 (1,840 km^2) of Pakistani territory and the Pakistan army held 210 mile^2 (545 km^2) of Indian territory. The territory occupied by India was mainly in the fertile Sialkot, Lahore and Kashmir sectors, while Pakistani land gains were primarily south in deserts opposite to Sindh and in Chumb sector near Kashmir in north.

Aerial Warfare

The war saw aircraft of the Indian Air Force (IAF) and the Pakistan Air Force (PAF) engaging in combat for the first time since independence. Though the two forces had previously faced off in the First Kashmir War during the late 1940s, that engagement was very limited in scale compared to the 1965 conflict.

The IAF was flying large numbers of Hawker Hunter, Indian-manufactured Folland Gnats, de Havilland Vampires, EE Canberra bombers and a squadron of MiG-21s. The PAF's fighter force comprised 102 F-86F Sabres and 12 F-104 Starfighters, along with 24 B-57 Canberra bombers. During the conflict the PAF was out-numbered by around 5:1.

The PAF's aircraft were largely of American origin, whereas the IAF flew an assortment of Soviet and European aeroplanes. It has been widely reported that the PAF's American aircraft were superior to those of the InAF, but according to some experts this is untrue because the InAF's MiG-21, Hawker Hunter and Folland Gnat fighters actually had higher performance than their PAF counter-part, the F-86 Sabre. Although the InAF's de Havilland Vampire fighter-bombers were outdated in comparison to the F-86 Sabre, the Hawker Hunter fighters were superior in both power and speed to the F-86 according to Air Cdre (retired) Sajjad Haider, who lead the PAF's No.19 Squadron in combat during the war.

According to the Indians, the F-86 was vulnerable to the diminutive Folland Gnat, nicknamed "Sabre Slayer". The PAF's F-104 Starfighter of the PAF was the fastest fighter operating in the subcontinent at that time and was often referred to as "the pride of the PAF". However, according to Air Cdre (retired) Sajjad

Haider who flew with the PAF's No.19 Squadron, the F-104 did not deserve this reputation. Being "a high level interceptor designed to neutralise Soviet strategic bombers in altitudes above 40,000 feet," rather than engage in dogfights with agile fighters at low altitudes, it was "unsuited to the tactical environment of the region." It can be argued that, although the IAF is believed to have feared the Starfighter, in combat it was not as effective as the IAF's far more agile, albeit much slower, Folland Gnat fighter.

The two countries have made contradictory claims of combat losses during the war and few neutral sources have verified the claims of either country. The PAF claimed it shot down 104 IAF planes and lost 19 of its own, while the IAF claimed it shot down 73 PAF planes and lost 35. According to one independent source, the PAF flew 86 F-86 Sabres, 10 F-104 Starfighters and 20 B-57 Canberras in a parade soon after the war was over. Thus disproving the IAF's claim of downing 73 PAF fighters, which at the time constituted nearly the entire Pakistani front-line fighter force.

Indian sources have pointed out that, despite PAF claims of losing only a squadron of combat craft, Pakistan sought to acquire additional aircraft from Indonesia, Iraq, Iran, Turkey and China within 10 days of the beginning war. But this could be explained by the 5:1 disparity in numbers faced by the PAF.

Tank Battles

The 1965 war witnessed some of the largest tank battles since World War II. At the beginning of the war, the Pakistani Army had both a numerical advantage in tanks, as well as better equipment overall. Pakistani armour was largely American-made; it consisted mainly of Patton M-47 and M-48 tanks, but also included many M4 Sherman tanks, some M24 Chaffee light tanks and M36 Jackson tank destroyers, equipped with 90 mm guns. The bulk of India's tank fleet were older M4 Sherman tanks; some were up-gunned with the French high velocity CN 75 50 guns and could hold their own, whilst some older models were still equipped with the inferior 75 mm M3 L/40 gun. Besides the M4 tanks, India fielded the British-made Centurion Tank Mk 7, with the 105 mm Royal Ordnance L7 gun, and the AMX-13, PT-76, and M3 Stuart light tanks. Pakistan fielded a greater number and more modern artillery; its guns out-ranged those of the Indian artillery, according to Pakistan's Major General T.H. Malik.

At the outbreak of war in 1965, Pakistan had about 15 armoured cavalry regiments, each with about 45 tanks in three squadrons. Besides the Pattons, there were about 200 M4 Shermans re-armed with 76 mm guns, 150 M24 Chaffee light tank and a few independent squadrons of M36B1 tank destroyers. Most of these regiments served in Pakistan's two armoured divisions, the 1st and 6th Armoured divisions – the latter being in the process of formation.

The Indian Army of the time possessed 17 cavalry regiments, and in the 1950s had begun modernizing them by the acquisition of 164 AMX-13 light tanks and 188 Centurions. The remainder of the cavalry units were equipped with M4 Shermans and a small number of M3A3 Stuart light tanks. India had only a single armoured division, the 1st 'Black Elephant' Armoured Division, also called 'Fakhr I Hind' ('Pride of India'), which consisted of the 17th cavalry Poona Horse, the 4th Hodson's Horse, the 16th 'Black Elephant' Cavalry, the 7th Light Cavalry, the 2nd Royal Lancers, the 18th Cavalry and the 62nd Cavalry, the two first named being equipped with Centurions,. There was also the 2nd Independent Armoured Brigade, one of whose three regiments, the 3rd Cavalry, was also equipped with Centurions.

Despite the qualitative and numerical superiority of Pakistani armour, Pakistan was outfought on the battlefield by India, which made progress into the Lahore-Sialkot sector, whilst halting Pakistan's counteroffensive on Amritsar.; they were sometimes employed in a faulty manner, such as charging prepared defenses during the defeat of Pakistan's 1st Armoured Division at Assal Uttar.

Although India's tank formations experienced same results, India's attack at the Battle of Chawinda, led by its 1st Armoured Division and supporting units, was brought to a grinding halt by newly raised 6th Armoured Division(ex-100th independent brigade group) in the Chawinda sector.

The Indians lost 12 tanks at Chawinda. One true winner to emerge was India's Centurion battle tank, with its 105 mm gun and heavy armor, which proved superior to the overly complex Pattons and their exaggerated reputations..However, in the Sialkot sector outnumbered Pattons performed exceedingly well in the hands of the 25th Cavalry and other regiments of the 6th Armoured

Division, which exacted a disproportionately heavy toll of Centurions from the Poona Horse and Hodson's Horse.

The Indian Army has made much of the fact that some of its Centurions survived repeated hits; yet have failed to point out that the majority of tanks in the Sialkot sector were Shermans whose guns were inadequate even in 1944. Neither the Indian nor Pakistani Army showed any great facility in the use of armoured formations in offensive operations, whether the Pakistani 1st Armoured Division at Asal Uttar or the Indian 1st Armoured Division at Chawinda. In contrast, both proved adept with smaller forces in a defensive role such a the 2nd Armoured Brigade at Asal Uttar and the 25th Cavalry at Chawinda, where they defeated their better equipped but clumsier foes

Naval Hostilities

The navies of India and Pakistan did not play a prominent role in the war of 1965, although Pakistani accounts dispute this. On September 7, a flotilla of the Pakistani Navy carried out a small scale bombardment of the Indian coastal town and radar station of Dwarka, which was 200 miles (300 km) south of the Pakistani port of Karachi. Codenamed Operation Dwarka, it did not fulfil its primary objective of disabling the radar station and there was no immediate retaliatory response from India. Later, some of the Indian fleet sailed from Bombay to Dwarka to patrol the area and deter further bombardment. Foreign authors have noted that the "insignificant bombardment" of the town was a "limited engagement, with no strategic value."

According to some Pakistani sources, one submarine, PNS Ghazi, kept the Indian Navy's aircraft carrier INS Vikrant besieged in Bombay throughout the war. Indian sources claim that it was not their intention to get into a naval conflict with Pakistan, and wished to restrict the war to a land-based conflict. Moreover, they note that the Vikrant was in dry dock in the process of refitting. Some Pakistani defence writers have also discounted claims that the Indian Navy was bottled up in Bombay by a single submarine, instead stating that 75% of the Indian Navy was under maintenance in harbour.

Covert Operations

The Pakistan Army launched a number of covert operations

to infiltrate and sabotage Indian airbases. On September 7, 1965, the Special Services Group (SSG) commandos were parachuted into enemy territory. According to Chief of Army Staff General Musa Khan, about 135 commandos were airdropped at three Indian airfields(Halwara, Pathankot and Adampur). The daring attempt proved to be an "unmitigated disaster". Only 22 commandos returned to Pakistan as planned, 93 were taken prisoner (including one of the Commanders of the operations, Major Khalid Butt), and 20 were killed in encounters with the army, police or civilians The reason for the failure of the commando mission is attributed to the failure to provide maps, proper briefings and adequate planning or preparation

Despite failing to sabotage the airfields, Pakistan sources claim that the commando mission affected some planned Indian operations. As the Indian 14th Division was diverted to hunt for paratroopers, the Pakistan Air Force found the road filled with transport, and destroyed many vehicles.

India responded to the covert activity by announcing rewards for captured Pakistani spies or paratroopers. Meanwhile, in Pakistan, rumors spread that India had retaliated with its own covert operations, sending commandos deep into Pakistan territory, but these rumors were later determined to be unfounded.

Neutral Assessments

There have been several neutral assessments of the losses incurred by both India and Pakistan during the war. Most of these assessments agree that India had a upper hand over Pakistan when ceasefire was declared. Some of the neutral assessments are mentioned below –

- According to the United States Library of Congress Country Studies: The war was militarily inconclusive; each side held prisoners and some territory belonging to the other. Losses were relatively heavy—on the Pakistani side, twenty aircraft, 200 tanks, and 3,800 troops. Pakistan's army had been able to withstand Indian pressure, but a continuation of the fighting would only have led to further losses and ultimate defeat for Pakistan. Most Pakistanis, schooled in the belief of their own martial prowess, refused to accept the possibility of their country's military defeat by "Hindu India" and were, instead, quick to blame their failure to attain their military aims on what they considered to be the ineptitude of Ayub Khan and his government.

- TIME magazine reported that India held 690 mi^2 of Pakistan territory while Pakistan held 250 mi^2 of Indian territory in Kashmir and Rajasthan. Additionally, Pakistan had lost almost half its armour temporarily. The same article stated that-Severely mauled by the larger Indian armed forces, Pakistan could continue the fight only by teaming up with Red China and turning its back on the U.N.
- Devin T. Hagerty wrote in his book *"South Asia in world politics"* – The invading Indian forces outfought their Pakistani counterparts and halted their attack on the outskirts of Lahore, Pakistan's second-largest city. By the time United Nations intervened on September 22, Pakistan had suffered a clear defeat.
- In his book *"National identity and geopolitical visions"*, Gertjan Dijkink writes – The superior Indian forces, however, won a decisive victory and the army could have even marched on into Pakistani territory had external pressure not forced both combatants to cease their war efforts.
- An excerpt from Stanley Wolpert's *India*, summarizing the Indo-Pakistani War of 1965, is as follows: In three weeks the second Indo-Pak War ended in what appeared to be a draw when the embargo placed by Washington on U.S. ammunition and replacements for both armies forced cessation of conflict before either side won a clear victory. India, however, was in a position to inflict grave damage to, if not capture, Pakistan's capital of the Punjab when the cease-fire was called, and controlled Kashmir's strategic Uri-Poonch bulge, much to Ayub's chagrin.
- In his book titled *The greater game: India's race with destiny and China*, David Van Praagh wrote – India won the war. It gained 1,840 square kilometers of Pakistani territory: 640 square kilometers in Azad Kashmir, Pakistan's portion of the state; 460 square kilometers of the Sailkot sector; 380 square kilometers far to the south of Sindh; and most critical, 360 square kilometers on the Lahore front. Pakistan took 540 square kilometers of Indian territory: 490 square kilometers in the Chhamb sector and 50 square kilometers around Khem Karan.

- Dennis Kux's *"India and the United States estranged democracies"* also provides a summary of the war. Although both sides lost heavily in men and materiel, and neither gained a decisive military advantage, India had the better of the war. New Delhi achieved its basic goal of thwarting Pakistan's attempt to seize Kashmir by force. Pakistan gained nothing from a conflict which it had instigated.
- *"A region in turmoil: South Asian conflicts since 1947"* by Robert Johnson mentions – India's strategic aims were modest – it aimed to deny Pakistani Army victory, although it ended up in possession of 720 square miles of Pakistani territory for the loss of just 220 of its own.
- An excerpt from William M. Carpenter and David G. Wiencek's *"Asian security handbook: terrorism and the new security environment"* – A brief but furious 1965 war with India began with a covert Pakistani thrust across the Kashmiri cease-fire line and ended up with the city of Lahore threatened with encirclement by Indian Army. Another UN-sponsored cease-fire left borders unchanged, but Pakistan's vulnerability had again been exposed.
- English historian John Keay's *"India: A History"* provides a summary of the 1965 war – The 1965 Indo-Pak war lasted barely a month. Pakistan made gains in the Rajasthan desert but its main push against India's Jammu-Srinagar road link was repulsed and Indian tanks advanced to within a sight of Lahore. Both sides claimed victory but India had most to celebrate.
- Uk Heo and Shale Asher Horowitz write in their book *"Conflict in Asia: Korea, China-Taiwan, and India-Pakistan"* – Again India appeared, logistically at least, to be in a superior position but neither side was able to mobilize enough strength to gain a decisive victory.
- Newsweek magazine, however, praised the Pakistani military's ability to hold of the much larger Indian Army. "By just the end of the week, in fact, it was clear that the Pakistanis were more than holding their own."

Ceasefire

The United States and the Soviet Union used significant diplomatic tools to prevent any further escalation in the conflict between the two South Asian nations. The Soviet Union, led by Premier Alexey Kosygin, hosted ceasefire negotiations in Tashkent (now in Uzbekistan), where Indian Prime Minister Lal Bahadur Shastri and Pakistani President Ayub Khan signed the Tashkent Agreement, agreeing to withdraw to pre-August lines no later than February 25, 1966.

With declining stockpiles of ammunition, Pakistani leaders feared the war tilting in India's favour. Therefore, they quickly accepted the ceasefire in Tashkent. Despite strong opposition from Indian military leaders, India budged to growing international diplomatic pressure and accepted the ceasefire. On September 22, the United Nations Security Council unanimously passed a resolution that called for an unconditional ceasefire from both nations. The war ended the following day.

India's Prime Minister, Shastri, suffered a fatal heart attack soon after the declaration of the ceasefire. As a consequence, the public outcry in India against the ceasefire declaration transformed into a wave of sympathy for the ruling Indian National Congress. The ceasefire was criticized by many Pakistanis who, relying on fabricated official reports and the controlled Pakistani press, believed that the leadership had surrendered military gains. The protests led to student riots. Pakistan State's reports had suggested that their military was performing admirably in the war – which they incorrectly blamed as being initiated by India – and thus the Tashkent Declaration was seen as having forfeited the gains. Some recent books written by Pakistani authors, including one by ex-ISI chief titled "The Myth of 1965 Victory", allegedly exposed Pakistani fabrications about the war, but all copies of the book were bought by Pakistan Army to prevent publication because the topic was "too sensitive".

India and Pakistan accused each other of ceasefire violations; India charged Pakistan with 585 violations in 34 days, while Pakistan countered with accusations of 450 incidents by India. In addition to the expected exchange of small arms and artillery fire, India reported that Pakistan utilized the ceasefire to capture the Indian village of Chananwalla in the Fazilka sector. This village was recaptured by Indian troops on 25 December. On October 10, a B-57 Canberra on loan to the PAF was damaged by 3 SA-2 missiles fired from the IAF base at Ambala A Pakistani Army Auster was shot down on 16 December, killing one Pakistani army captain and on 2 February 1967, an AOP was shot down by IAF Hunters.

The ceasefire remained in effect until the start of the Indo-Pakistani War of 1971.

Intelligence Failures

Strategic miscalculations by both India and Pakistan ensured that the war ended in a stalemate –

Indian Miscalculations

Indian military intelligence gave no warning of the impending Pakistan invasion. The Indian Army failed to recognize the presence of heavy Pakistani artillery and armaments in Chumb and suffered significant losses as a result.

The "Official History of the 1965 War", drafted by the Ministry of Defence of India in 1992, was a long suppressed document that revealed other miscalculations. According to the document, on September 22 when the Security Council was pressing for a ceasefire, the Indian Prime Minister asked commanding Gen. Chaudhuri if India could possibly win the war, were he to delay accepting the ceasefire. The general replied that most of India's frontline ammunition had been used up and the Indian Army had suffered considerable tank losses. It was determined later that only 14% of India's frontline ammunition had been fired and India held twice the number of tanks as Pakistan. By this time, the Pakistani Army had used close to 80% of its ammunition.

Air Chief Marshal (retd) P.C. Lal, who was the Vice Chief of Air Staff during the conflict, points to the lack of coordination between the IAF and the Indian army. Neither side revealed its battle plans to the other. The battle plans drafted by the Ministry of Defence and General Chaudhari, did not specify a role for the Indian Air Force in the order of battle. This attitude of Gen. Chaudhari was referred to by ACM Lal as the "Supremo Syndrome", a patronizing attitude sometimes held by the Indian army towards the other branches of the Indian Military.

Pakistani Miscalculations

The Pakistani Army's failures started with the supposition that a generally discontented Kashmiri people, given the opportunity provided by the Pakistani advance, would revolt against their Indian rulers, bringing about a swift and decisive surrender of Kashmir. The Kashmiri people, however, did not revolt. Instead, the Indian Army was provided with enough information to learn of Operation Gibraltar and the fact that the Army was battling not insurgents, as they had initially supposed, but Pakistani Army regulars.

The Pakistani Army also failed to recognize that the Indian policy makers would order an attack on the southern sector in order to open a second theatre of conflict. Pakistan was forced to dedicate troops to the southern sector to protect Sialkot and Lahore instead using them to support penetrating into Kashmir.

"Operation Grand Slam", which was launched by Pakistan to capture Akhnoor, a town northeast of Jammu and a key region for communications between Kashmir and the rest of India, was also a failure. Many Pakistani commentators criticized the Ayub Khan administration for being indecisive during Operation Grand Slam.

These critics claim that the operation failed because Ayub Khan knew the importance of Akhnur to India (having called it India's "jugular vein") and did not want to capture it and drive the two nations into an all-out war. Despite progress being made in Akhnur, General Ayub Khan relieved the commanding Major General Akhtar Hussain Malik and replaced him with Gen. Yahya Khan. A 24-hour lull ensued the replacement, which allowed the Indian army to regroup in Akhnur and successfully oppose a lackluster attack headed by General Yahya Khan. "The enemy came to our rescue", asserted the Indian Chief of Staff of the Western Command. Later, Akhtar Hussain Malik criticized Ayub Khan for planning Operation Gibraltar, which was doomed to fail, and for relieving him of his command at a crucial moment in the war. Malik threatened to expose the truth about the war and the army's failure, but later dropped the idea for fear of being banned.

Some authors have noted that Pakistan might have been emboldened by a war game – conducted in March 1965, at the Institute of Defence Analysis, USA. The exercise concluded that, in the event of a war with India, Pakistan would win. Other authors like Stephen Philip Cohen, have consistently commented that the Pakistan Army had "acquired an exaggerated view of the weakness of both India and the Indian military... the 1965 war was a shock".

Pakistani Air Marshal and Commander-in-Chief of PAF during the war, Nur Khan, later said that the Pakistan Army, and not India, should be blamed for starting the war. However propaganda in Pakistan about the war continued; the war was not rationally analysed in Pakistan, with most of the blame being heaped on the leadership and little importance given to intelligence failures that persisted until the debacle of the 1971 war, when then East Pakistan was invaded by India and seceded from West Pakistan, leading to the creation of Bangladesh.

Involvement of other Nations

The United States of America, which had previously supplied military equipment to India and Pakistan, imposed an embargo against further supplies to both countries once the war had started. The US was apprehensive that military equipment that it had provided to be used in a battle against communism, would instead be used by the countries to fight one another. The American embargo especially affected Pakistan since the majority of its equipment was provided by America. This would cause Pakistan to believe that it could not continue the war beyond September.

Following imposition of the American embargo, other NATO allies (including the UK) discontinued providing military equipment to the nations.

Both before and during the war, China had been a major military associate of Pakistan and had invariably admonished India, with whom it had fought a war in 1962. There were also reports of Chinese troop movements on the Indian border to support Pakistan. As such, India agreed to the UN mandate in order to avoid a war on both borders.

India's participation in the Non-Aligned Movement yielded little support from its members. Pakistan, however, gained assistance from countries of Asia with large Islamic populations, including Turkey, Iran and Indonesia. The USSR was more neutral than most other nations during the war and even invited both nations to talks that it would host in Tashkent.

Tashkent Declaration

The Tashkent Declaration of January 10, 1966 was a peace agreement between India and Pakistan. In September of 1965 before the two had engaged in the short run Indo-Pakistani War of 1965. Peace had been achieved on September 23 by the intervention of the great powers who pushed the two nations to a cease fire for fears the conflict could escalate and draw in other powers.

A meeting was held in Tashkent in the Uzbek SSR, USSR (now in Uzbekistan) beginning on January 4, 1966 to try to create a more permanent settlement. The Soviets, represented by Premier Kosygin moderated between Indian Prime Minister Lal Bahadur Shastri and Pakistani President Muhammad Ayub Khan.

The conference was viewed as a great success and the declaration that was released was hoped to be a framework for lasting peace. The declaration stated that

- Indian and Pakistani forces would pull back to their pre-conflict positions
- The nations would not interfere in each other's internal affairs
- Economic and diplomatic relations would be restored
- The two leaders would work towards building good relations between the two countries.

The day after the declaration Indian Prime Minister Shastri died of a sudden heart attack. There are many conspiracy theories regarding the death of Lal Bahadur Shashtri with the major one accusing the next PM of India Mrs. Indira Gandhi as the main conspirator. The agreement was criticized in India because it did not contain a no-war pact or any renunciation of guerrilla warfare in Kashmir. The two countries would again be at war in 1971, leading to division of Pakistan.

Indo-Pakistani Relations

Indo-Pakistani relations are grounded in the political, geographic, cultural, and economic links between the Republic of India and the Islamic Republic of Pakistan the two largest countries of South Asia. The two countries share much of their common geographic location, but differ starkly in religious demographics. India is a secular country with Hindu majority at about 80% of the total population and Muslims being the largest religious minority with about 13% of the population. Pakistan, on the other hand, is an Islamic country with 97% population being Muslim, and only about 1.8% Hindus. Diplomatic relations between the two are defined by the history of the violent partition of British India into these two states, and numerous military conflicts and territorial disputes thereafter.

Much of South Asia came under direct control of Great Britain in the late 18th century. The British Raj over the Indian subcontinent lasted for almost 150 years. 95% of the people living in South Asia practised either Hinduism and Islam. The Muslim League, headed by Quaid e Azam Mohammad Ali Jinnah, proposed the Two Nation Theory in the early 20th century. According to the theory, Muslims and others shared little in common, and British India should be divided into two separate countries, one for the Muslims and the other for the Hindu majority, which he feared would suppress the Muslim minority. The campaign gained momentum in early 1940s and by the end of World War II, British India's partition looked inevitable. The Partition of India in 1947 created two large countries independent from Britain: Pakistan as two wings in the East and West, separated by India in the middle. Soon after Independence, India and Pakistan established diplomatic relations. Subsequent years were marked by bitter periodic conflict, and the nations went to war four times. The war in 1971 ended in defeat and another partition of Pakistan. The eastern wing split off as a new country named Bangladesh, while the western wing continued as Pakistan.

There have been some improvements in relations since the mid-2000s. Most notably, Pakistan released an Indian man accused of being a spy in 2008: he had been detained since 1975. But relations soured slightly after the 2008 Mumbai Terrorist Attacks by an alleged group partially consisting of Pakistani based militants.

Seeds of Conflict

About half a million Muslims and Hindus were killed in communal riots following the partition of the British Empire. Millions of Muslims living in India and Hindus and Sikhs living in Pakistan emigrated in one of the most colossal transfers of population in the modern era. Both countries accused each other of not providing adequate security to the minorities emigrating through their territory. This served to increase tensions between the newly-born countries.

According to the British plan for the partition of British India, all the 680 princely states were allowed to decide which of the two countries to join. With the exception of a few, most of the Muslim-majority princely-states acceded to Pakistan while most of the Hindu-majority princely states joined India. However, the decisions of some of the princely-states would shape the Pakistan-India relationship considerably, in the years to come.

Junagadh Dispute

Junagadh is one of the modern districts of Saurastra, Gujarat

Junagadh was a state on the southwestern end of Gujarat, with the principalities of Manavadar, Mangrol and Babriawad. The Arabian Sea stood between it and Pakistan. The state had an overwhelming Hindu population which constituted more than 80% of its citizens, while the ruler of the state was a Muslim. On August 15 1947, the ruler of the state, Nawab of Junagadh Mahabat Khan acceded to Pakistan. Pakistan confirmed the acceptance of the accession in September 1947. India did not accept the accession as legitimate.

The Indian point of view was that since Junagadh was a state with a predominantly Hindu population it should be a part of India. Additionally, since the state was encircled by Indian territory it should have been a part of India. Indian politicians also stated that by giving Pakistan a predominantly Hindu region to govern, the basis of the two nation theory was contradicted.

The Pakistani point of view was that since Junagadh had a ruler and governing body who chose to accede to Pakistan, they should be allowed to do so. Junagadh, having a coastline, could have maintained maritime links with Pakistan. Additionally, Pakistani politicians stated that the two nation theory did not necessarily mean a clear division of land and absolute transfer of populations as the sheer magnitude of such a proceeding would wreak havoc upon millions.

Neither of the ten states were able to resolve this issue amicably and it only added fuel to an already charged environment.

Sardar Patel, India's then Home Minister, felt that if Junagadh was permitted to go to Pakistan, it would create communal unrest across Gujarat. The government of India gave Pakistan time to void the accession and hold a plebiscite in Junagadh to pre empt any violence in Gujarat. Samaldas Gandhi formed a government-in-exile, the *Arzi Hukumat* (in Urdu: *Arzi*: Transitional, *Hukumat*:

Government) of the people of Junagadh. Patel ordered the annexation of Junagadh's three principalities.

Kashmir Dispute

Kashmir was a princely state, ruled by a Sikh, Maharaja Hari Singh. The Maharaja of Kashmir was equally hesitant to join either India–, because he knew his Muslim subjects would not like to join a Hindu-based and Hindu-majority nation–, or Pakistan– which as a Sikh he was personally averse to. Pakistan coveted the Himalayan kingdom, while Indian leader Mahatma Gandhi and Indian PM Jawaharlal Nehru hoped that the kingdom would join India. Hari Singh signed a *Standstill Agreement* (preserving status quo) with Pakistan, but did not make his decision by August 15, 1947.

Rumours spread in Pakistan that Hari Singh was trying to accede Kashmir to India. Alarmed by this threat, a team of Pakistani forces were dispatched into Kashmir, fearing an Indian invasion of the region. Backed by Pakistani paramilitary forces, Pashtuns invaded Kashmir in September 1947. Kashmir's security forces were too weak and ill-equipped to fight against Pakistan. Troubled by the deteriorating political pressure that was being applied to Hari Singh and his governance, the Maharaja asked for India's help. However, the Constitution of India barred the Indian Armed Forces' intervention since Kashmir did not come under India's jurisdiction.

Desperate to get India's help and get Kashmir back in his own control, the Maharaja acceded Kashmir to India (which was against the will of the majority of Kashmiris), and signed the Instrument of Accession. By this time the raiders were close to the capital, Srinagar. On October 27, 1947, the Indian Air Force airlifted Indian troops into Srinagar and made an intervention. The Indian troops managed to seize parts of Kashmir which included Jammu, Srinagar and the Kashmir valley itself, but the strong and intense fighting, flagged with the onset of winter, made much of the state impassable. After weeks of intense fighting between Pakistan and India, Pakistani leaders and the Indian Prime Minister Nehru declared a ceasefire and sought U.N. arbitration with the promise of a plebiscite.

Sardar Patel had argued against both, describing Kashmir as a bilateral dispute and its accession as justified by international law. In 1957, north-western Kashmir was fully integrated into Pakistan, becoming Azad Kashmir (Pakistan-administered Kashmir), while the other portion was acceded to Indian control, and the state of Jammu and Kashmir (Indian-administered Kashmir) was created. In 1962, China occupied Aksai Chin, the northeastern region bordering Laddakh. In 1984, India launched Operation Meghdoot and captured more than 80% of the Siachen Glacier.

Pakistan maintains Kashmiris' rights to self-determination through a plebiscite in accordance with an earlier Indian statement and a UN resolution. Pakistan also points to India's failure of not understanding its own political logic and applying it to Kashmir, by taking their opinion on the case of the accession of Junagadh as an example (that the Hindu majority state should have gone to India even though it had a Muslim ruler), that Kashmir should also rightfully and legally have become a part of Pakistan since majority of the people were Muslim, even though they had a Hindu ruler. Pakistan also states that at the very least, the promised plebiscite should be allowed to decide the fate of the Kashmiri people.

India on the other hand asserts that the Maharaja's decision, which was the norm for every other princely state at the time of independence, and subsequent elections, for over 40 years, on Kashmir has made it an integral part of India. This opinion has often become controversial, as Pakistan asserts that the decision of the ruler of Junagadh also adhered to Pakistan. Due to all such political differences, this dispute has also been the subject of wars between the two countries in 1947 and 1965, and a limited conflict in 1999. The state/province remains divided between the two countries by the Line of Control (LoC), which demarcates the ceasefire line agreed upon in the 1947 conflict.

Other Territorial Disputes

Pakistan is locked in other territorial disputes with India such as the Siachen Glacier and Kori Creek. Pakistan is also currently having dialogue with India regarding the Baglihar Dam being built over the River Chenab in Jammu and Kashmir.

Bengal Refugee Crisis

In 1949, India recorded close to 1 million Hindu refugees, who flooded into West Bengal and other states from East Pakistan (Now Bangladesh), owing to communal violence, intimidation and repression from authorities.

The plight of the refugees outraged Hindus and Indian nationalists, and the refugee population drained the resources of Indian states, which were unable to absorb them. While not ruling out war, Prime Minister Nehru and Sardar Patel invited Liaquat Ali Khan for talks in Delhi. Although many Indians termed this appeasement, Nehru signed a pact with Liaquat Ali Khan that pledged both nations to the protection of minorities and creation of minority commissions. Although opposed to the principle, Patel decided to back this Pact for the sake of peace, and played a critical role in garnering support from West Bengal and across India, and enforcing the provisions of the Pact. Khan and Nehru also signed a trade agreement, and committed to resolving bilateral disputes through peaceful means. Steadily, hundreds of thousands of Hindus returned to East Pakistan, but the thaw in relations did not last long, primarily owing to the Kashmir dispute.

India – Sri Lanka Relations

Bilateral relations between the Democratic Socialist Republic of Sri Lanka and the Republic of India have been generally friendly, but were controversially affected by the Sri Lankan civil war and by the failure of Indian intervention during the war. India is the only neighbour of Sri Lanka, separated by the Palk Strait; both nations occupy a strategic position in South Asia and have sought to build a common security umbrella in the Indian Ocean. The two largest ethnic groups of Sri Lanka are Sinhala and Tamil.

Development of Bilateral Relations

India and Sri Lanka established diplomatic relations when the latter gained its independence in 1948. Both nations proceeded to establish extensive cultural, commercial, strategic and defence ties to establish a common sphere of influence in the region, adopting non-alignment to control Western and Soviet influence. The close relationship between the then-Indian Prime Minister Indira Gandhi and then-Sri Lankan Prime Minister Sirimavo Bandaranaike led to the development of strong bilateral relations. In 1971, Indian armed forces helped squash a Communist rebellion against the Sri Lankan government.

Bhutan

Historically, ties with India have been close. Both countries signed a Friendship treaty in 1949, where India would assist Bhutan in foreign relations. On February 8, 2007, the Indo-Bhutan Friendship Treaty was substantially revised under the Bhutanese King, Jigme Khesar Namgyel Wangchuck. Whereas in the Treaty of 1949 Article 2 read as "The Government of India undertakes to exercise no interference in the internal administration of Bhutan. On its part the Government of Bhutan agrees to be guided by the advice of the Government of India in regard to its external relations."

In the revised treaty it now reads as, "In keeping with the abiding ties of close friendship and cooperation between Bhutan and India, the Government of the Kingdom of Bhutan and the Government of the Republic of India shall cooperate closely with each other on issues relating to their national interests. Neither government shall allow the use of its territory for activities harmful to the national security and interest of the other." The revised treaty also includes in it the preamble "Reaffirming their respect for each other's independence, sovereignty and territorial integrity", an element that was absent in the earlier version. The Indo-Bhutan Friendship Treaty of 2007 strengthens Bhutan's status as an independent and sovereign nation.

Tata Power, is building a hydro-electric dam. This dam, will greatly develop the Bhutanese economy, by providing employment, and by selling electricity, to India, to fulfil India's burgeoning energy needs. Due to this dam, Bhutan, grew at 20+%, the second highest growth rate in the world.

Bhutan–India Relations

The bilateral relations between the Himalayan Kingdom of Bhutan and the Republic of India have been traditionally close. With independence in 1947, India inherited the suzerainty over Bhutan enjoyed by the British Raj. Although modified and modernised since, India remains influential over Bhutan's foreign policy, defence and commerce.

Background

For much of its history, Bhutan has preserved its isolation from the outside world, staying out of international organisations and maintaining few bilateral relations. Bhutan became a protectorate of British India after signing a treaty in 1910 allowing the British to "guide" its foreign affairs and defence. Bhutan was one of the first to recognize India's independence in 1947 and both nations fostered close relations, their importance augmented by the annexation of Tibet in 1950 by the People's Republic of China and its border disputes with both Bhutan and India, which saw close ties with Nepal and Bhutan to be central to its "Himalayan frontier" security policy. India shares a 605 kilometres (376 miles) border with Bhutan and is its largest trading partner, accounting for 98 percent of its exports and 90 percent of its imports.

1949 Treaty

On August 8, 1949 Bhutan and India signed the Treaty of Friendship, calling for peace between the two nations and non-interference in each other's internal affairs. However, Bhutan agreed to let India "guide" its foreign policy and both nations would consult each other closely on foreign and defence affairs. The treaty also established free trade and extradition protocols.

The occupation of Tibet by Communist China brought both nations even closer. In 1958, the then-Indian Prime Minister Jawaharlal Nehru visited Bhutan and reiterated India's support for Bhutan's independence and later declared in the Indian Parliament that any aggression against Bhutan would be seen as aggression against India. The period saw a major increase in India's economic, military and development aid to Bhutan, which had also embarked on a programme of modernisation to bolster its security. While India repeatedly reiterated its military support to Bhutan, the latter expressed concerns about India's ability to protect Bhutan against China while fighting a two-front war involving Pakistan. Despite good relations, India and Bhutan did not complete a detailed demarcation of their borders until the period between 1973 and 1984. Border demarcation talks with India generally resolved disagreements except for several small sectors, including the middle zone between Sarpang and Geylegphug and the eastern frontier with the Indian state of Arunachal Pradesh.

Burma

India was one of the leading supporters of Burmese independence and established diplomatic relations after Burma's independence from Great Britain in 1948. For many years, Indo-Burmese relations were strong due to cultural links, flourishing commerce, common interests in regional affairs and the presence of a significant Indian community in Burma. India provided considerable support when Burma struggled with regional insurgencies. However, the overthrow of the democratic government by the Military of Burma led to strains in ties. Along with much of the world, India condemned the suppression of democracy and Burma ordered the expulsion of the Burmese Indian community, increasing its own isolation from the world. Only China maintained close links with Burma while India supported the pro-democracy movement.

However, due to geo-political concerns, India revived its relations and recognised the new name of Myanmar in 1993 overcoming strains over drug trafficking, the suppression of democracy and the rule of the military junta in Burma. Burma is situated to the south of the states of Mizoram, Manipur, Nagaland and Arunachal Pradesh in Northeast India and the proximity of the People's Republic of China gives strategic importance to Indo-Burmese relations. The Indo-Burmese border stretches over 1,600 miles and some insurgents in Northeast India seek refuge in Myanmar. Consequently, India has been keen on increasing military cooperation with Myanmar in its counter-insurgency activities. In 2001, the Indian Army completed the construction of a major road along its border with Myanmar. India has also been building major roads, highways, ports and pipelines within Myanmar in an attempt to increase its strategic influence in the region and also to counter China's growing strides in the Indochina peninsula. Indian companies have also sought active participation in oil and natural gas exploration in Myanmar. In February 2007, India announced a plan to develop the Sittwe port, which would enable ocean access from Indian Northeastern states like Mizoram, via the Kaladan River.

India is a major customer of Myanmarese oil and gas. In 2007, Indian exports to Myanmar totalled US$185 million, while its imports from Myanmar were valued at around US$810 million, comprising mostly of oil and gas. India has granted US$100 million credit to fund highway infrastructure projects in Myanmar, while US$ 57 million has been offered to upgrade Myanmarese railways. A further US$27 million in grants has been pledged for road and rail projects. India is one of the few countries that has provided military assistance to the Myanmarese junta. However, there has been increasing pressure on India to cut some of its military supplies to Myanmar. Relations between the two remain close which was evident in the aftermath of Cyclone Nargis, when India was one of the few countries whose relief and rescue aid proposals were accepted by Myanmar's ruling junta.

Burma–India Relations

Bilateral relations between Burma (officially the Union of Myanmar) and the Republic of India have improved considerably since 1993, overcoming strains over drug trafficking, the suppression of democracy and the rule of the military junta in Burma. Burma is situated to the south of the states of Mizoram, Manipur, Nagaland and Arunachal Pradesh in Northeast India. The proximity of the People's Republic of China give strategic importance to Indo-Burmese relations. The Indo-Burmese border stretches over 1,600 miles.

Background

India was one of the leading supporters of Burmese independence and established diplomatic relations after Burma's independence from Great Britain in 1948. For many years, Indo-Burmese relations were strong due Burma previously having been a province of India, due to cultural links, flourishing commerce, common interests in regional affairs and the presence of a significant Indian community in Burma. India provided considerable support when Burma struggled with regional insurgencies. However, the overthrow of the democratic government by the Military of Burma led to strains in ties. Along with much of the world, India condemned the suppression of democracy and Burma ordered the expulsion of the Burmese Indian community, increasing its own isolation from the world. Only China maintained close links with Burma while India supported the pro-democracy movement.

A major breakthrough occurred in 1987 when the then-Indian Prime Minister Rajiv Gandhi visited Burma, but relations worsened after the military junta's bloody repression of pro-democracy agitations in 1988, which led to an influx of Burmese refugees into India. However, since 1993 the governments of the Indian Prime Ministers P.V. Narasimha Rao and Atal Bihari Vajpayee changed course and began cultivating ties with Myanmar, as part of a wider foreign policy approach aimed to increase India's participation and influence in Southeast Asia and to counteract the growing influence of the People's Republic of China..

Sino-Indian Relations

Sino-Indian relations, also called India-China relations, refer to the ties and relations between the People's Republic of China and the Republic of India. The economic and diplomatic importance of China and India, which are the two most populous states and the world's fastest growing major economies, has in recent years increased the significance of their bilateral relationship.

Relations between China and India date back to ancient times. China and India are two of the world's oldest civilizations and have coexisted in peace for millennia. Trade relations via the Silk Road acted as economic contact between the two regions. However, since the early 1950s, their relationship has been characterized by border disputes, resulting in military conflict (the Sino-Indian War of 1962

Sino-Indian War

The Sino-Indian War, was a war between China and India that occurred in 1962. A disputed Himalayan border was the main pretext for war, but other issues played a role. There had been a series of violent border incidents after the 1959 Tibetan uprising, when India had granted asylum to the Dalai Lama. India initiated a Forward Policy in which it placed outposts along the border, including several north of the McMahon Line, the eastern portion of a Line of Actual Control proclaimed by Chinese Premier Zhou Enlai in 1959.

The Chinese launched simultaneous offensives in Laddakh and across the McMahon Line on 20 October 1962, coinciding with the Cuban Missile Crisis. Chinese troops advanced over Indian forces in both theatres, capturing Rezang la in Chushul in the western theatre, as well as Tawang in the eastern theatre. The war ended when the Chinese declared a ceasefire on 20 November 1962, and later withdrew from the disputed area.

The Sino-Indian War is notable for the harsh conditions under which much of the fighting took place, entailling large-scale combat at altitudes of over 4,250 metres (14,000 feet). This presented enormous logistics problems for both sides. The Sino-Indian War was also noted for the non-deployment of the navy or air force by either the Chinese and Indian sides.

Location

China and India share a long border, sectioned into three stretches by Nepal and Bhutan, which follows the Himalayan mountains between Burma and what was then West Pakistan. A number of disputed regions lie along this border. At its western end is the Aksai Chin region, an area the size of Switzerland, that sits between the Chinese autonomous region of Xinjiang, and Tibet (which China declared as autonomous regions in 1965). The eastern border, between Burma and Bhutan, comprises the present Indian state of Arunachal Pradesh (formerly the North East Frontier Agency). Both of these regions were overrun by China in the 1962 conflict.

Most combat took place at high altitudes. The Aksai Chin region is a vast desert of salt flats around 5,000 metres above sea level, and Arunachal Pradesh is extremely mountainous with a number of peaks exceeding 7000 metres. According to military doctrine, to be successful an attacker generally requires a 3:1 ratio of numerical superiority over the defender; in mountain warfare this ratio should be considerably higher as the terrain favours defence. China was able to take advantage of this: the Chinese Army had possession of the highest ridges in the regions. The high altitude and freezing conditions also cause logistical and welfare difficulties; in past similar conflicts (such as the Italian Campaign of World War I) more casualties have been caused by the harsh conditions than enemy action. The Sino-Indian War was no different, with many troops on both sides dying in the freezing cold.

Background

The cause of the war was a dispute over the sovereignty of the widely-separated Aksai Chin and Arunachal Pradesh border regions. Aksai Chin, claimed by India to belong to Kashmir and by China to be part of Xinjiang, contains an important road link that connects the Chinese regions of Tibet and Xinjiang. China's construction of this road was one of the triggers of the conflict. Arunachal Pradesh (called South Tibet by China) is also claimed by both nations—although it is roughly the size of Austria, it is sparsely inhabited (by numerous local tribes) due to its mountainous terrain. The Indian state Arunachal Pradesh has a population of over one million as of today.

The Johnson Line

The western portion of the Sino-Indian boundary originates in 1834, with the Sikh Confederation's conquest of Laddakh. In 1842 the Sikh Confederacy, which at the time ruled over much of Northern India (including the frontier regions of Jammu and Kashmir), signed a treaty which guaranteed the integrity of its existing borders with its neighbours. The British defeat of the Sikhs in 1846 resulted in transfer of sovereignty over Laddakh, part of the Jammu and Kashmir region, to the British, and British commissioners contacted Chinese officials to negotiate the border. The boundaries at its two extremities, Pangong Lake and Karakoram Pass, were well-defined, but the Aksai Chin area in between lay undefined.

In 1865, British surveyor W H Johnson came to an agreement with the Maharaja of Kashmir, in whose service he was employed, on a proposed "Johnson Line" which placed Aksai Chin in Kashmir. China rejected the arrangement, and the British government also harboured doubts, so decided to take up the issue in an attempt to reach a settlement. However in 1892, before the issue had been resolved, China erected boundary markers at Karakoram Pass on the ancient caravan route between Xinjiang and Laddakh (which were disputed by the British Indian Government).

Throughout most of the 19th century Great Britain and the expanding Russian Empire were jockeying for influence in Central Asia, and Britain decided to hand over Aksai Chin to Chinese administration as a buffer against Russian invasion. The newly-created border was known as the MacCartney-MacDonald Line, and both British-controlled India and China now began to show Aksai Chin as Chinese. In 1911 the Xinhai Revolution resulted in power shifts in China, and by 1918 (in the wake of the Russian Bolshevik Revolution) the British no longer saw merit in China's continuing possession of the region.

On British maps the border was redrawn as the original Johnson Line, but despite this reversion the new border was left unmanned and undemarcated. According to Neville Maxwell, the British had used as many as 11 different boundary lines in the region, as their claims shifted with the political situation. By the time of Indian independence in 1947, the Johnson Line had become India's official western boundary. On 1 July 1954, Indian Prime Minister Jawaharlal Nehru definitively stated the Indian position. He claimed that Aksai Chin had been part of the Indian Laddakh region for centuries, and that the border (as defined by the Johnson Line) was non-negotiable. According to George N. Patterson, when the Indian government finally produced a report detailing the alleged proof of India's claims to the disputed area, "the quality of the Indian evidence was very poor, including some very dubious sources indeed".

During the 1950s, China constructed a road through Aksai Chin, connecting Xinjiang and Tibet, which ran south of the Johnson Line in many places. Aksai Chin was easily accessible to the Chinese, but access from India, which meant negotiating the Karakoram mountains, was more problematic. Consequently India did not even learn of the existence of the road until 1957 – finally confirmed when the road was shown in Chinese maps published the following year.

The McMahon Line

In 1826 India and China gained a common border, including the area of what is now called Myanmar, following British annexations in the Anglo-Burmese Wars. In 1847, Major J. Jenkins, Agent for the North East Frontier, reported that the Tawang was part of Tibet. In 1872, four monastic officials from Tibet arrived in Tawang and supervised a boundary settlement with Major R. Graham, NEFA official, which included the Tawang Tract as part of Tibet. Thus, in the last half of the 19th century, it was clear that the British treated the Tawang Tract as part of Tibet. This boundary was confirmed in a June 1, 1912 note from the British General Staff in India, stating that the "present boundary (demarcated) is south of Tawang, running westwards along the foothills from near Ugalguri to the southern Bhutanese border."

A 1908 map of The Province of Eastern Bengal and Assam (32 miles to the inch), prepared for the Foreign Department of the Government of India, showed the international boundary from Bhutan continuing to the Baroi River, following the Himalayas foothill alignment. In 1913, representatives of Great Britain, China and Tibet attended a conference in Simla regarding the borders between Tibet, China and British India. Whilst all three representatives initialed the agreement, Beijing later objected to the proposed boundary between the regions of *Outer Tibet* and *Inner Tibet* and did not ratify it. The details of the Indo-Tibetan boundary was not revealed to China at the time. The foreign secretary of the British Indian government, Henry McMahon, who drew up the proposal, decided to bypass the Chinese (although instructed not to by his superiors) and settle the border bilaterally by negotiating directly with Tibet.

According to later Indian claims, this border was intended to run through the highest ridges of the Himalayas, as the areas south of the Himalayas were traditionally Indian. However, the McMahon Line lay south of the boundary India claims. India's government held the view that the Himalayas were the ancient boundaries of the Indian subcontinent, and thus should be the modern boundaries of India while it is the position of the Chinese government that the disputed area in the Himalayas have been geographically and culturally part of Tibet since ancient times.

Months after the Simla agreement, China set up boundary markers south of the McMahon Line. T O'Callaghan, an official in the Eastern Sector of the North East Frontier, relocated all these markers to a location slightly south of the McMahon Line, and then visited Rima to confirm with Tibetan officials that there was no Chinese influence in the area. The British-run Government of India initially rejected the Simla Agreement as incompatible with the Anglo-Russian Convention of 1907, which stipulated that neither party was to negotiate with Tibet "except through the intermediary of the Chinese government". The British and Russians cancelled the 1907 agreement by joint consent in 1921. It was not until the late 1930s that the British started to use the McMahon Line on official maps of the region.

China took the position that the Tibetan government should not have been allowed to make a such a treaty, rejecting Tibet's claims of independent rule. For its part, Tibet did not object to any section of the McMahon Line excepting the demarcation of the trading town of Tawang, which the Line placed under British-Indian jurisdiction. However, up until World War II, Tibetan officials were allowed to administer Tawang with complete authority. Due to the increased threat of Japanese and Chinese expansion during this period, British Indian troops secured the town as part of the defence of India's eastern border. In the 1950s India began actively patrolling the region. It found that, at multiple locations, the highest ridges actually fell north of the McMahon Line. Given India's historic position that the original intent of the Line was to separate the two nations by the highest mountains in the world, in these locations India extended its forward posts northward to the ridges, regarding this move as compliant with the original border proposal, although the Simla Convention did not explicitly state this intention.

Events Leading up to War

Tibet Controversy

The 1940s saw huge change in South Asia with the Partition of India in 1947 (resulting in the establishment of the two new states of India and Pakistan), and the establishment of the People's Republic of China in 1949. One of the most basic policies for the new Indian government was that of maintaining cordial relations with China, reviving its ancient friendly ties. India was among the first nations to grant diplomatic recognition to the newly-created PRC.

At the time, Chinese officials issued no condemnation of Nehru's claims or made any opposition to Nehru's open declarations of control over Aksai Chin. In 1956, Chinese Premier Zhou Enlai stated that he had no claims over Indian controlled territory. He later argued that Aksai Chin was already under Chinese jurisdiction, implying that there was therefore no contradiction with his earlier statement since China did not regard the region as "Indian controlled", and that since the British hand-over China had regarded the McCartney MacDonald Line as the relevant border. Zhou later argued that as the boundary was undemarcated and had never been defined by treaty between any Chinese or Indian government, the Indian government could not unilaterally define Aksai Chin's borders.

However, within a short time the PRC announced its intention to reclaim Tibet, and later extended its influence by placing border posts within the Indian-claimed territory of Aksai Chin. India protested against these moves and decided to look for a diplomatic solution to ensure a stable Sino-Indian border. To resolve any doubts about the Indian position, Prime Minister Jawaharlal Nehru declared in parliament that India regarded the McMahon Line as its official border. The Chinese expressed no concern at this statement, and in 1951 and 52, the government of China asserted that there were no frontier issues to be taken up with India.

In 1954, Prime Minister Nehru wrote a memo calling for India's borders to be clearly defined and demarcated: in line with previous Indian philosophy, Indian maps showed a border that, in some places, lay north of the McMahon Line. Chinese Premier Zhou Enlai, in November 1956, again repeated Chinese assurances that the People's Republic had no claims on Indian territory, although official Chinese maps showed 120,000 square kilometres of territory claimed by India as Chinese. CIA documents created at the time revealed that Nehru had ignored Burmese premier Ba Swe when he warned Nehru to be cautious when dealing with Zhou. They also allege that Zhou purposefully told Nehru that there were no border issues with India.

In 1950 the Chinese People's Liberation Army invaded Tibet. Four years later, in 1954, China and India negotiated the Five Principles of Peaceful Coexistence by which the two nations agreed to abide in settling their disputes. India presented a frontier map which was accepted by China, and the Indian government under Prime Minister Nehru promoted the slogan *Hindi-Chini bhai-bhai* (Indians and Chinese are brothers). According to Georgia Tech political analyst John W Garver, Nehru's policy on Tibet was to create a strong Sino-Indian partnership which would be catalyzed through agreement and compromise on Tibet. Garver believes that Nehru's previous actions had given him confidence that China would be ready to form an "Asian Axis" with India.

This apparent progress in relations suffered a major setback when, in 1959, Nehru accommodated the Tibetan religious leader, the Dalai Lama, who was fleeing Lhasa after a failed Tibetan uprising against Chinese rule. The Chairman of the Chinese Communist Party, Mao Zedong, was enraged and asked the Xinhua News Agency to produce reports on Indian expansionists operating in Tibet.

Border incidents continued through this period. In August 1959, the PLA took an Indian prisoner at Longju, which had an ambiguous position in the McMahon Line, and two months later in Aksai Chin a clash led to the death of nine Indian frontier policemen. On 2 October, Soviet Premier Nikita Khrushchev defended Nehru in a meeting with Mao. This action reinforced China's impression that the Soviet Union, the United States and India all had expansionist designs over China. The PLA (People's Liberation Army) went so far as to prepare a self-defensive counterattack plan. Negotiations were restarted between the nations, but no progress was made.

As a consequence of their non-recognition of the McMahon Line, China's maps showed both the North East Frontier Area (NEFA) and Aksai Chin to be Chinese territory. In 1960, Zhou Enlai unofficially suggested that India drop its claims to Aksai Chin in return for a Chinese withdrawal of claims over NEFA. Adhering to his stated position, Nehru believed that China did not have a legitimate claim over either of these territories, and thus was not ready to concede them. This adamance was perceived in China as Indian opposition to Chinese rule in Tibet. Nehru declined to conduct any negotiations on the boundary until Chinese troops withdrew from Aksai Chin; a position supported by the international community. India produced numerous reports on the negotiations, and translated Chinese reports into English to help inform the international debate. China believed that India was simply securing its claim lines in order to continue its "grand plans in Tibet". India's stance that China withdraw from Aksai Chin caused continual deterioration of the diplomatic situation to the point at which internal forces were pressurizing Nehru to take a military stance against China.

The Forward Policy

At the beginning of 1961, Nehru appointed General B M Kaul as army Chief of General Staff, but he refused to increase military spending and prepare for a possible war. That summer, China's continuing patrols south of the McMahon Line provoked an Indian response known as the "Forward Policy". According to James Barnard Calvin of the U.S. Navy, in 1959, India started sending Indian troops and border patrols into disputed areas. This program created both skirmishes and deteriorating relations between India and China. The aim of this policy was to create outposts behind advancing Chinese troops to interdict their supplies, forcing them north of the disputed line (McMahon). There were eventually 60 such outposts, including 43 north of the McMahon Line, to which

India claimed sovereignty. China viewed this as further confirmation of Indian expansionist plans directed towards Tibet. According to the Indian official history, implementation of the Forward Policy was intended to provide evidence of Indian occupation in the previously unoccupied region through which Chinese troops had been patrolling. Kaul was confident, through contact with Indian Intelligence and CIA information, that China would not react with force. Indeed at first the PLA simply withdrew, but eventually Chinese forces began to counter-encircle the Indian positions which clearly encroached into the north of McMahon Line. This led to a tit-for-tat Indian reaction, with both forces attempting to outmanoeuver each other. However, despite the escalating nature of the dispute, the two forces withheld from engaging each other directly.

Chinese attention was diverted for a time by the military activity of the Nationalists on Taiwan, but on 23 June the U.S. assured China that a Nationalist invasion would not be permitted. China's heavy artillery facing Taiwan could then be moved to Tibet. It took China six to eight months to gather the resources needed for the war, according to Anil Athale, author of the official Indian history. The Chinese sent a large quantity of non-military supplies to Tibet through the Indian port of Calcutta.

Early Incidents

Various border conflicts and "military incidents" between India and China flared up throughout the summer and autumn of 1962. In May, the Indian Air Force was told not to plan for close air support, although it was assessed as being a feasible way to repel the unbalanced ratio of Chinese to Indian troops. In June, a skirmish caused the deaths of dozens of Chinese troops. The Indian Intelligence Bureau received information about a Chinese buildup along the border which could be a precursor to war.

During the period of June–July 1962, the Indian military planners began advocating "probing actions" against the Chinese, and accordingly, moved mountain troops forward to cut off Chinese supply lines. According to Patterson, the Indian motives were threefold:

1. Test Chinese resolve and intentions regarding India.
2. Test whether India would enjoy Soviet backing in the event of a Sino-Indian war.

3. Create sympathy for India within the US, with whom relations had deteriorated after the Indian annexation of Goa.

On 10 July 1962, 350 Chinese troops surrounded an Indian occupied post in Chushul (north of the McMahon Line) but withdrew after a heated argument via loudspeaker. On 22 July, the Forward Policy was extended to allow Indian troops to push back Chinese troops already established in disputed territory. Whereas Indian troops were previously ordered to fire only in self-defence, all post commanders were now given discretion to open fire upon Chinese forces if threatened. In August, the Chinese military improved its combat readiness along the McMahon Line and began stockpiling ammunition, weapons and gasoline.

Confrontation at Thag La

In June 1962, Indian forces established an outpost at Dhola, on the southern slopes of the Thag La Ridge. Dhola lay north of the McMahon Line but south of the ridges which India interpreted that the McMahon Line was supposed to represent. In August, China issued diplomatic protests and began occupying positions at the top of Thag La. On 8 September, a 60-strong PLA unit descended to the south side of the ridge and occupied positions that dominated one of the Indian posts at Dhola. Fire was not exchanged but Nehru said to the media that the Indian Army had instructions to "free our territory" and the troops had been given discretion to use force. On 11 September, it was decided that "all forward posts and patrols were given permission to fire on any armed Chinese who entered Indian territory".

However, the operation to occupy Thagla was flawed in that Nehru's directives were unclear and it got underway very slowly because of this. In addition to this, each man had to carry 35 kg of luggage over the long trek and this severely slowed down the reaction. By the time the Indian battalion reached the point of conflict, Chinese units controlled both banks of the Namka Chu River. On 20 September, Chinese troops threw grenades at Indian troops and a firefight developed, triggering a long series of skirmishes for the rest of September.

Some Indian troops, including Brigadier Dalvi who commanded the forces at Thag La, were also concerned that the territory they were fighting for was not strictly territory that "we should have been convinced was ours". According to Neville Maxwell, even members of the Indian defence ministry were categorically concerned with the validity of the fighting in Thag La.

On 3 October, a week before the triggering of the war, Zhou Enlai visited Nehru in New Delhi promising there would be no war. On 4 October, Kaul assigned some troops with securing regions south of the Thagla Ridge. Kaul decided to first secure Yumtso La, a strategically important position, before re-entering the lost Dhola post. Kaul had then realised that the attack would be desperate and the Indian government tried to stop escalation into an all-out war. Indian troops travelling to Thagla had suffered in the previously unexperienced conditions, two Gurkha troops died of pulmonary edema.

On 10 October, an Indian Punjabi patrol of 50 troops to Yumtso La were met by an emplaced Chinese position of some 1,000 soldiers. Indian troops were in no position for battle, as Yumtso La was 16,000 feet (4,900 m) above sea level and Kaul did not plan on having artillery support for the troops. The Chinese troops opened fire on the Indians under their belief that they were north of the McMahon Line. The Indians were surrounded by Chinese positions which used mortar fire. However, they managed to hold off the first Chinese assault, inflicting heavy casualties.

At this point, the Indian troops were in a position to push the Chinese back with mortar and machine gun fire. However, Brigadier Dalvi opted not to fire, as it would mean decimating the Rajput who were still in the area of the Chinese regrouping. They helplessly watched the Chinese ready themselves for a second assault. In the second Chinese assault, the Indians began their retreat, realising the situation was hopeless. The Indian patrol suffered 25 casualties, with the Chinese suffering 33. The Chinese troops held their fire as the Indians retreated, and then buried the Indian dead with military honours, as witnessed by the retreating soldiers. This was the first occurrence of heavy fighting in the war.

This attack had grave implications for India and Nehru tried to solve the issue, but by 18 October it was clear that the Chinese were preparing for an attack on India, with massive troop buildups on the border. A long line of mules and porters had also been observed supporting the buildup and reinforcement of positions south of the Thagla ridge.

Chinese and Indian Preparations

Motives: Two of the major factors leading up to China's eventual conflicts with Indian troops were India's stance on the disputed borders and perceived Indian subversion in Tibet. There was "a perceived need to punish and end perceived Indian efforts to undermine Chinese control of Tibet, Indian efforts which were perceived as having the objective of restoring the pre-1949 status quo ante of Tibet". The other was "a perceived need to punish and end perceived Indian aggression against Chinese territory along the border". John W. Garver argues that the first perception was incorrect based on the state of the Indian military and polity in the 1960s, it was, nevertheless a major reason for China's going to war. However, he argues the Chinese perception of Indian aggression to be "substantially accurate".

The CIA's recently declassified POLO documents reveal contemporary American analysis of Chinese motives during the war. According to this document, "Chinese apparently were motivated to attack by one primary consideration—their determination to retain the ground on which PLA forces stood in 1962 and to punish the Indians for trying to take that ground".

Another factor which affected China's decision for war with India was a perceived need to stop a Soviet-US-India encirclement and isolation of China. India's relations with the Soviet Union and United States were both strong at this time, but the Soviets were preoccupied by the Cuban Missile Crisis and would not interfere with the Sino-Indian War. P.B. Sinha suggests that China timed the war exactly in parallel with American actions so as to avoid any chance of American or Soviet involvement. American buildup of forces around Cuba occurred on the same day as the first major clash at Dhola while China's buildup between the 10th and 20th of October coincided exactly with the United States establishment of a blockade against Cuba which began on the 20th of October.

Garver argues that the Chinese correctly assessed Indian border policies, particularly the Forward Policy, as attempts for incremental seizure of Chinese-controlled territory. On Tibet, Garver argues that one of the major factors leading to China's decision for war with India was a common tendency of humans "to attribute others behaviour to interior motivations, while attributing their own behaviour to situational factors". Studies from China published in the 1990s confirmed that the root cause for China going to war with India was the perceived aggression in Tibet, with the forward policy simply catalyzing the Chinese reaction.

Neville Maxwell and Allen Whiting argue that the Chinese leadership believed they were defending territory they believed to be legitimately Chinese, and which was already under de facto Chinese occupation prior to Indian advances, and regarded the Forward Policy as an Indian attempt at creeping annexation. Mao Zedong himself compared the Forward Policy to a strategic advance in Chinese chess:

Their [India's] continually pushing forward is like crossing the Chu Han boundary. What should we do? We can also set out a few pawns, on our side of the river. If they don't then cross over, that's great. If they do cross, we'll eat them up [chess metaphor meaning to take the opponent's pieces]. Of course, we cannot blindly eat them. Lack of forbearance in small matters upsets great plans. We must pay attention to the situation.

The motive for the Forward Policy was to cut off the supply routes for Chinese troops posted in NEFA and Aksai Chin. According to the official Indian history, the forward policy was continued because of its initial success, as it claimed that Chinese troops withdrew when they encountered areas already occupied by Indian troops. It also claimed that the Forward Policy was having success in cutting out supply lines of Chinese troops who had advanced South of the McMahon Line, though there was no evidence of such advance before the 1962 war. However, the Forward Policy rested on the assumption that Chinese forces "were not likely to use force against any of our posts, even if they were in a position to do so". No serious reappraisal of this policy took place even when Chinese forces ceased withdrawing. Nehru's confidence was probably justified given the difficulty for China to supply the area over the high altitude terrain over 5000 km from the more populated areas of China.

By early 1962, the Chinese leadership began to fear that India's intentions were to launch a massive attack against Chinese troops, and that the Indian leadership wanted a war. In 1961, the Indian army had been sent into Goa, a small region without any other international borders apart from the Indian one, after Portugal refused to surrender the exclave colony to the Indian Union.

Although this action met little to no international protest or opposition, China saw it as an example of India's expansionist nature, especially in light of heated rhetoric from Indian politicians. India's Home Minister declared, "If the Chinese will not vacate the areas occupied by it, India will have to repeat what she did in Goa. India will certainly drive out the Chinese forces", while another member of the Indian Congress Party pronounced, "India will take steps to end [Chinese] aggression on Indian soil just as she ended Portuguese aggression in Goa". By mid-1962, it was apparent to the Chinese leadership that negotiations had failed to make any progress, and the Forward Policy was increasingly perceived as a grave threat as Delhi increasingly sent probes deeper into border areas and cut off Chinese supply lines. Foreign Minister Marshal Chen Yi commented at one high-level meeting, "Nehru's forward policy is a knife. He wants to put it in our heart. We cannot close our eyes and await death." The Chinese leadership believed that their restraint on the issue was being perceived by India as weakness, leading to continued provocations, and that a major counterblow was needed to stop perceived Indian aggression.

Xu Yan, prominent Chinese military historian and professor at the PLA's National Defence University, gives an account of the Chinese leadership's decision to go to war. By late September 1962, the Chinese leadership had begun to reconsider their policy of "armed coexistence", which had failed to address their concerns with the forward policy and Tibet, and consider a large, decisive strike.

The Chinese leadership initially held a sympathetic view towards India as the latter had been ruled by British colonial masters for centuries. However, Nehru's forward policy convinced PRC leadership that the independent Indian leadership was a reincarnation of British imperialism. Thus, the Indian government must be taught an unforgettable lesson. Mao Zedong stated: "Rather than being constantly accused of aggression, it's better to show the world what really happens when China indeed moves its muscles."

Military Planning

The Indian side was confident war would not be triggered and made little preparations. India had only two divisions of troops in the region of the conflict. In August 1962, Brigadier D.K. Palit claimed that a war with China in the near future could be ruled out. Even in September 1962, when Indian troops were ordered to "expel the Chinese" from Thag La, Maj. General J.S. Dhillon expressed the opinion that ""experience in Laddakh had shown that a few rounds fired at the Chinese would cause them to run away." Because of this, the Indian army was completely unprepared when the attack at Yumtso La occurred.

Recently declassified CIA documents which were compiled at the time reveal that India's estimates of Chinese capabilities made them neglect their military in favour of economic growth. It is claimed that if a more military-minded man had been in place instead of Nehru, India would have been more likely to have been ready for the threat of a counter-attack from China.

On 6 October 1962, the Chinese leadership convened. Lin Biao reported that PLA intelligence units had determined that Indian units might assault Chinese positions at Thag La on 10 October (Operation Leghorn). The Chinese leadership and the Central Military Council decided upon war to launch a large-scale attack to punish perceived military aggression from India. In Beijing, a larger meeting of Chinese military was convened in order to plan for the coming conflict.

The Mao and the Chinese leadership issued a directive laying out the objectives for the war. A main assault would be launched in the eastern sector, which would be coordinated with a smaller assault in the western sector. All Indian troops within China's claimed territories in the eastern sector would be expelled, and the war would be ended with a unilateral Chinese ceasefire and withdrawal to prewar positions, followed by a return to the negotiating table. India led the Non-Aligned Movement, Nehru enjoyed international prestige, and China, with a larger military would be portrayed as an aggressor. However, he said that a well-fought war "will guarantee at least thirty years of peace" with India, and determined the benefits to offset the costs.

On 8 October, additional veteran and elite divisions were ordered to prepare to move into Tibet from the Chengdu and Lanzhou military regions.

On October 12, Nehru declared that he had ordered the Indian army to "clear Indian territory in the NEFA of Chinese invaders" and personally met with Kaul, issuing instructions to him.

On October 14, an editorial on People's Daily issued China's final warning to India: "So it seems that Mr. Nehru has made up his mind to attack the Chinese frontier guards on an even bigger scale....It is high time to shout to Mr. Nehru that the heroic Chinese troops, with the glorious tradition of resisting foreign aggression, can never be cleared by anyone from their own territory... If there are still some maniacs who are reckless enough to ignore our well-intentioned advice and insist on having another try, well, let them do so. History will pronounce its inexorable verdict... At this critical moment...we still want to appeal once more to Mr. Nehru: better rein in at the edge of the precipice and do not use the lives of Indian troops as stakes in your gamble." [5]

Marshal Liu Bocheng headed a group to determine the strategy for the war. He concluded that the opposing Indian troops were among India's best, and to achieve victory would require deploying crack troops and relying on force concentration to achieve decisive victory. On 16 October, this war plan was approved, and on the 18th, the final approval was given by the Politburo for a "self defensive counter-attack", scheduled for 20 October.

Chinese Offensive

On 20 October 1962, the Chinese People's Liberation Army launched two attacks, 1000 kilometers apart. In the western theatre, the PLA sought to expel Indian forces from the Chip Chap valley in Aksai Chin while in the eastern theatre, the PLA sought to capture both banks of the Namka Chu river. Some skirmishes also took place at the Nathula Pass, which is in the Indian state of Sikkim (an Indian protectorate at that time). Gurkha rifles travelling north were targeted by Chinese artillery fire. After four days of fierce fighting, the three regiments of Chinese troops succeeded in securing a substantial portion of the disputed territory.

Eastern Theatre

Chinese troops launched an attack on the southern banks of the Namka Chu River on 20 October. The Indian forces were undermanned, with only an understrength battalion to support them, while the Chinese troops had three regiments positioned on the north side of the river. The Indians expected Chinese forces to cross via one of five bridges over the river and defended those crossings. However their strategy was wrong. As the Indian troops settled for the night on the banks of the river, the PLA crossed over the shallow October river and made their way to the other side. They gathered themselves up into battalions on the Indian-held south side of the river in the camouflage of the night, with each battalion assigned against a separate group of Rajputs.

At 5:14 am, Chinese mortar fire began attacking the Indian positions. Simultaneously, the Chinese cut the Indian telephone lines so that the Indians could not make contact with CHQ. At about 6:30 am, the Chinese infantry, who had been positioned behind the Indians in the night, made their surprise attack and forced the Indians to leave their trench positions.

The Chinese troops overwhelmed the Indians. Proceeding attacks from flanking positions south of the McMahon Line overwhelmed the Indian troops and caused withdrawal from Namka Chu. Fearful of continued losses, Indian troops escaped into Bhutan. However, Chinese forces respected the border and ignored Tsang Le. Now the Chinese troops had occupied the area which was under dispute in the confrontations at Thag La, but they continued to advance into the rest of NEFA.

On 22 October, at 12:15 am, the PLA launched a mortar attack on Walong, on the McMahon line. 400 troops proceeded to launch fire on the Indians posted there. Lights fired by Indian troops on 23 October showed the presence of numerous Chinese milling around the valley. The Indians tried to use their mortars against the Chinese but the PLA then lit a bushfire to create great confusion amongst the enemy troops. The Chinese eventually captured Walong at the cost of more than 200 dead or wounded, while Indian casualties were also heavy.

On 23 October, Chinese troops launched a three-pronged attack on Tawang, which the Indians evacuated without any resistance.

Western Theatre

On the Aksai Chin front, China already controlled most of the disputed territory. China quickly and efficiently got rid of remnants of Indian troops. On 20 October, operations in the Chip Chap Valley, Galwan Valley, and Pangong Lake were successful for the PLA. Many outposts and garrisons comprised were unable to defend against the surrounding Chinese troops. Most Indian troops positioned in these posts fought and were either killed or taken prisoner. India did not support its troops, as the Galwan post had been surrounded by China in August and had received no land support from India since then. After the 20 October attack, this post was not heard from again.

Late on 19 October, Chinese troops launched various attacks throughout the western theatre. By 22 October, all posts north of Chushul had been cleared.

Later on 24 October, there was a battle on the Rezang La Ridge to defend an air strip from impending Chinese takeover. The Chinese suffered 1,000 casualties, while the Indians lost 109 killed,. among them Major Shaitan Singh.

After realizing the magnitude of the attack, Indian Western Command withdrew many of the isolated outposts to the south-east. Daulet Beg Oldi was also evacuated, but it was south of the Chinese claim line and was not approached by Chinese forces. Indian troops were withdrawn so that they could regroup and be ready if China probed south of their claim line.

Indian forces were hampered by their significant inferiority in numbers and lack of combat readiness. The Indian deployment was sparsely put and needed new commanders in the second phase of the war.

Lull in the Fighting

By 24 October, the PLA had entered territory previously administered by India to give the PRC a diplomatically strong position over India. The majority of Chinese forces had advanced sixteen kilometres south of the border. Four days of fighting were followed by a three-week lull. Zhou ordered the troops to stop advancing as he attempted to negotiate with Nehru. The Indian forces had retreated into more heavily fortified positions around Se La and Bombdi La which would be difficult to assault. Zhou sent Nehru a letter, proposing

1. A negotiated settlement of the boundary
2. That both sides disengage and withdraw twenty kilometers from present lines of actual control
3. A Chinese withdrawal north in NEFA
4. That China and India not cross lines of present control in Aksai Chin.

Nehru's 27 October reply expressed interest in the restoration of peace and friendly relations and suggested a return to the "boundary prior to 8 September 1962". He was categorically concerned about a mutual twenty kilometer withdrawal after "40 or 60 kilometers of blatant military aggression". He wanted the creation of a larger immediate buffer zone and thus resist the possibility of a repeat offensive. Zhou's 4 November reply repeated his 1959 offer to return to the McMahon Line in NEFA and the Chinese traditionally claimed MacDonald Line in Aksai Chin.

Facing Chinese forces maintaining themselves on Indian soil and trying to avoid political pressure, the Indian parliament announced a national emergency and passed a resolution which stated their intent to "drive out the aggressors from the sacred soil of India". The United States and the United Kingdom supported India's response, however the Soviet Union was preoccupied with the Cuban Missile Crisis and did not offer the support it had provided in previous years. With the backing of other great powers, a 14 November letter by Nehru to Zhou once again rejected his proposal.

Neither side declared war, used their air force, or fully broke off diplomatic relations; however, the conflict is commonly referred to as a war. This war coincided with the Cuban Missile Crisis and was viewed by the western nations at the time as another act of aggression by the Communist bloc. According to Calvin, the Chinese side evidently wanted a diplomatic resolution and discontinuation of the conflict.

Continuation of War

After Zhou received Nehru's letter, the fighting resumed on the eastern theatre on 14 November (Nehru's birthday), with an Indian attack on Walong, claimed by China, launched from the defensive position of Se La and inflicting heavy casualties on the Chinese. The Chinese resumed military activity on Aksai Chin and NEFA hours after the Walong battle.

Eastern Theatre

On the eastern theatre, the PLA attacked Indian forces near Se La and Bomdi La on 17 November. These positions were defended by the Indian 4th Division. Instead of attacking by road as expected, PLA forces approached via a mountain trail, and their attack cut off a main road and isolated 10,000 Indian troops. Se La was very high, and faced with this strategic problem, the Chinese captured Thembang, which was a supply route to Se La.

Western Theatre

On the western theatre, PLA forces launched a heavy infantry attack on 18 November near Chushul. Their attack started at 4:35 am, despite a mist surrounding most of the areas in the region. At 5:45 the Chinese troops advanced to attack 2 platoons of Indian troops at Gurung Hill.

The Indians did not know what was happening, as communications were dead. As a patrol was sent, China attacked with greater numbers. Indian artillery could not hold off against superior Chinese forces. By 9:00 am, Chinese forces attacked Gurung Hill directly and Indian commanders withdrew from the area.

The Chinese had been simultaneously attacking Rezang La which was held by 118 Indian troops. At 5:05 am, Chinese troops launched their attack audaciously. Chinese medium machine gun fire pierced through the Indian tactical defences.

At 6:55 am the sun rose and the Chinese attack on the 8th platoon began in waves. Fighting continued for the next hour, until the Chinese signalled that they had destroyed the 7th platoon. Indians tried to use light machine guns on the medium machine guns from the Chinese but after 10 minutes the battle was over. Logistical inadequacy once again hurt the Indian troops. The Chinese gave the Indian troops a respectful military funeral. The battles also saw the death of Major Shaitan Singh of the Kumaon Regiment, who had been instrumental in the first battle of Rezang La. The Indian troops were forced to withdraw to high mountain positions. Indian sources believed that their troops were just coming to grips with the mountain combat and finally called troops. However, the Chinese declared a ceasefire, ending the bloodshed.

Indians suffered heavy casualties, with dead Indian troops' bodies being found in the ice, frozen with weapons in hand. Chinese forces also suffered heavy casualties, especially at Rezang La. This signalled the end of the war in Aksai Chin as China had reached their claim line-many Indian troops were ordered to withdraw from the area. China claimed that the Indian troops wanted to fight on until the bitter end. However, the war ended with their withdrawal, so as to limit the amount of casualties.

The PLA penetrated close to the outskirts of Tezpur, Assam, a major frontier town nearly fifty kilometers from the Assam-

North-East Frontier Agency border. The local government ordered the evacuation of the civilians in Tezpur to the south of the Brahmaputra River, all prisons were thrown open, and government officials who stayed behind destroyed Tezpur's currency reserves in anticipation of a Chinese advance.

Ceasefire

China had reached its claim lines so the PLA did not advance farther, and on 19 November it declared a unilateral cease-fire. Zhou Enlai declared a unilateral ceasefire to start on midnight, 21 November. Zhou's ceasefire declaration stated,

Beginning from 21 November 1962, the Chinese frontier guards will cease fire along the entire Sino-Indian border. Beginning from 1 December 1962, the Chinese frontier guards will withdraw to positions 20 kilometers behind the line of actual control which existed between China and India on 7 November 1959. In the eastern sector, although the Chinese frontier guards have so far been fighting on Chinese territory north of the traditional customary line, they are prepared to withdraw from their present positions to the north of the illegal McMahon Line, and to withdraw twenty kilometers back from that line. In the middle and western sectors, the Chinese frontier guards will withdraw twenty kilometers from the line of actual control.

Zhou had first given the ceasefire announcement to Indian charge d'affaires on 19 November, (before India's request for United States air support) but New Delhi did not receive it until 24 hours later. The aircraft carrier was ordered back after the ceasefire and thus American intervention on India's side in the war was avoided. Retreating Indian troops, who hadn't come into contact with anyone knowing of the ceasefire, and Chinese troops in NEFA and Aksai Chin, were involved in some minor battles but for the most part the ceasefire signalled an end to the fighting. The United States Air Force flew in supplies to India in November 1962, but neither side wished to continue hostilities. Toward the end of the war India increased her support for Tibetan refugees and revolutionaries, some of them having settled in India, as they were fighting the same common enemy in the region. The Nehru administration ordered the raising of an elite Indian-trained "Tibetan Armed Force" composed of Tibetan refugees. The CIA had already begun operations in bringing about change in Tibet.

World Opinion

The Chinese military action has been viewed by the United States as part of the PRC's policy of making use of aggressive wars to settle its border disputes and to distract from its internal issues. According to James Calvin from the United States Marine Corps, western nations at the time viewed China as an aggressor during the China-India border war, and the war was part of a monolithic communist objective for a world dictatorship of the proletariat. This was further triggered by Mao Zedong's views that: "The way to world conquest lies through Havana, Accra, and Calcutta". Calvin believes that Chinese actions show a "pattern of conservative aims and limited objectives, rather than expansionism" and blames this particular conflict on India's provocations towards China.

However, Calvin also expresses that China, in the past, has been adamant to gain control over regions to which it has a "traditional claim", which triggered the dispute over NEFA and Aksai Chin and indeed Tibet. Calvin's assumption, based on the history of the Cold War and the Domino Effect, assumed that China might ultimately try to regain control of everything that it considers as "traditionally Chinese" which in its view includes the entirety of South East Asia.

The Kennedy administration was disturbed by what they considered "blatant Chinese communist aggression against India". In a May 1963 National Security Council meeting, contingency planning on the part of the United States in the event of another Chinese attack on India was discussed. Defence Secretary Robert McNamara and General Maxwell Taylor advised the president to use nuclear weapons should the Americans intervene in such a situation. Kennedy insisted that Washington defend India as it would any ally, saying, "We should defend India, and therefore we will defend India". The Johnson Administration considered and then rejected giving nuclear weapons technology to the Indians.

The non-aligned nations, perhaps unsurprisingly, remained non-aligned, and only the United Arab Republic openly supported India. Of the non-aligned nations, six, Egypt, Burma, Cambodia, Sri Lanka, Ghana and Indonesia, met in Colombo on 10 December 1962. The proposals stipulated a Chinese withdrawal of 20 km from the customary lines without any reciprocal withdrawal on India's behalf. The failure of these six nations to unequivocally condemn China deeply disappointed India. In 1972, Chinese Premier Zhou explained the Chinese point of view to President Nixon of the US. As for the causes of the war, Zhou asserted that China did not try and expel Indian troops from south of the McMahon line and that three open warning telegrams were sent to Nehru before the war. However, Indian patrols south of the McMahon line were expelled and suffered casualties in the Chinese attack. Zhou also told Nixon that Chairman Mao ordered the troops to return to show good faith. The Indian government maintains that the Chinese military could not advance further south due to logistical problems and the cut-off of resource supplies.

While Western nations did not view Chinese actions favourably because of fear of the Chinese and competitiveness, Pakistan, which had had a turbulent relationship with India ever since the Indian partition, improved its relations with China after the war. Prior to the war, Pakistan also shared a disputed boundary with China, and had proposed to India that the two countries adopt a common defence against "northern" enemies (i.e China), which was rejected by India. However, China and Pakistan took steps to peacefully negotiate their shared boundaries, beginning on 13 October 1962, and concluding in December of that year.

Pakistan also expressed fear that the huge amounts of western military aid directed to India would allow it to threaten Pakistan's security in future conflicts. Mohammed Ali, External Affairs Minister of Pakistan, declared that massive Western aid to India in the Sino-Indian dispute would be considered an unfriendly act towards Pakistan. As a result Pakistan made efforts to improve its relations with China. The following year, China and Pakistan peacefully settled disputes on their shared border, and negotiated the China-Pakistan Border Treaty in 1963, as well as trade, commercial, and barter treaties.

On 2 March 1963, Pakistan conceded its northern claim line in Pakistani-controlled Kashmir to China in favour of a more southerly boundary along the Karakoram Range. The border treaty largely set the border along the MacCartney-Macdonald Line. India's military failure against China would embolden Pakistan to initiate the Second Kashmir War with India. However, it effectively ended in a stalemate as Calvin states that the Sino-Indian War had caused the previously passive government to take a stand on actively modernizing India's military.

China offered diplomatic support to Pakistan in this war but did not offer military support. In January 1966, China condemned the Tashkent Agreement between India and Pakistan as a Soviet-US plot in the region. In the Indo-Pakistani War of 1971, Pakistan expected China to provide military support, but it was left alone as India successfully helped the rebels in East Pakistan to found the new nation-state of Bangladesh.

Aftermath

China: According to the China's official (communist) military history, the war achieved China's policy objectives of securing borders in the western sector, as China retained de facto control of the Aksai Chin. After the war, India abandoned the Forward Policy, and the de facto borders stabilized along the Line of Actual Control.

However according to James Calvin even though China had won a military victory it may have lost in terms of its international image. Western nations, especially the United States, were already suspicious of Chinese attitudes, motives and actions. These nations saw China's goals as world conquest, and clearly viewed China as the aggressor in the Border War. China's first nuclear weapon test in October 1964, and her support of Pakistan in the 1965 India Pakistan War tended to confirm the American view of communist world objectives, including Chinese influence over Pakistan.

India

The aftermath of the war saw sweeping changes in the Indian military to prepare it for similar conflicts in the future, and placed pressure on Indian prime minister Jawaharlal Nehru, who was seen as responsible for failing to anticipate the Chinese attack on India. Indians reacted with a surge in patriotism and memorials were erected for many of the Indian troops who died in the war. Arguably, the main lesson India learned from the war was the need to strengthen its own defences and a shift from Nehru's foreign policy with China based on his stated concept of "brotherhood". Because of India's inability to anticipate Chinese aggression, Prime Minister Nehru faced harsh criticism from government officials, for having promoted pacifist relations with China. Indians in general became highly skeptical of China and its military. Many Indians view the war as a betrayal of India's attempts at establishing a long-standing peace with China and started to question Nehru's usage of the term "Hindi-Chini bhai-bhai" (meaning "Indians and Chinese are brothers"). The war also put an end to Nehru's earlier hopes that India and China would form a strong Asian Axis to counteract the increasing influence of the Cold War bloc superpowers.

The unpreparedness of the army was blamed on Defence Minister Menon, who resigned his government post to allow for someone who might modernize India's military further. India's policy of weaponisation via indigenous sources and self-sufficiency was thus cemented. Sensing a weakened army, Pakistan, a close ally of China, began a policy of provocation against India by infiltrating Jammu and Kashmir and ultimately triggering the Second Kashmir War with India in 1965. However, India had set up the Henderson-Brooks-Bhagat Report to determine what the reason was behind India's unpreparedness in the war, and was prepared for the Pakistani military. The result was inconclusive, since sources were divided on what decides victory. Some sources argued that since India had captured more territory than Pakistan, India had clearly won. However, others argued that India had taken significant losses considering the country's larger military and hence, the outcome of the war was inconclusive. Two years later, in 1967, there was a short border skirmish known as the Chola Incident between Chinese and Indian soldiers. In this incident 8 Chinese soldiers and 4 Indian soldiers were killed.

British journalist Neville Maxwell, controversial writer regarding India, writes that the "hopelessly ill-prepared Indian Army that provoked China on orders emanating from Delhi, and paid the price for its misadventure in men, money and national humiliation". As a result of the war, the Indian government commissioned an investigation, resulting in the classified Henderson-Brooks-Bhagat Report on the causes of the war and the reasons for failure. India's performance in high-altitude combat in 1962 led to an overhaul of the Indian Army in terms of doctrine, training, organization and equipment. Maxwell also claimed that the Indian role in international affairs after the border war was also greatly reduced after the war and India's standing in the non-aligned movement suffered.

According to James Calvin, an analyst from U.S. Navy India gained many benefits from the 1962 conflict. This war united the country as never before. India got 32,000 square miles of disputed territory even if she felt that NEFA was hers all along. The new Indian republic had avoided international alignments; by asking for help during the war, India demonstrated her willingness to accept military aid from several sectors. And, finally, India recognized the serious weaknesses in her army. She would more than double her military manpower in the next two years and she would work hard to resolve the military's training and logistic problems. India's efforts to improve her military posture significantly enhanced her army's capabilities and preparedness.

Maldives

India enjoys a considerable influence over Maldives' foreign policy and provides extensive security cooperation especially after Operation Cactus in 1988 during which India repelled Tamil mercenaries who invaded the country. As founder member in 1985 of the South Asian Association for Regional Cooperation, SAARC, which brings together Afghanistan, Bangladesh, Bhutan, India, Maldives, Nepal, Pakistan and Sri Lanka, the country plays a very active role in SAARC. The Maldives has taken the lead in calling for a South Asian Free Trade Agreement, the formulation of a Social Charter, the initiation of informal political consultations in SAARC forums, the lobbying for greater action on environmental issues, the proposal of numerous human rights measures such as the regional convention on child rights and for setting up a SAARC Human Rights Resource Centre. The Maldives is also an advocate of greater international profile for SAARC such as through formulating common positions at the UN. But the Maldives claims the Indian-administered territory of Minicoy as part of its country, that is inhabited by Muslims.

India is starting the process to bring the island country into India's security grid. The move comes after the moderate Islamic nation approached New Delhi earlier this year over fears that one of its island resorts could be taken over by terrorists given its lack of military assets and surveillance capabilities. India is also signing an agreement later this year which includes following things.

India will permanently base two helicopters in the country to enhance its surveillance capabilities and ability to respond swiftly to threats. One helicopter from the Coast Guard is likely to be handed over during Antony's visit while another from the Navy will be cleared for transfer shortly. Maldives has coastal radars on only two of its 26 atolls. India will help set up radars on all 26 for seamless coverage of approaching vessels and aircraft.

The coastal radar chain in Maldives will be networked with the Indian coastal radar system. India has already undertaken a project to install radars along its entire coastline. The radar chains of the two countries will be interlinked and a central control room in India's Coastal Command will get a seamless radar picture.

The Indian Coast Guard (ICG) will carry out regular Dornier sorties over the island nation to look out for suspicious movements or vessels. The Southern Naval Command will overlook the inclusion of Maldives into the Indian security grid.

Military teams from Maldives will visit the tri-services Andaman Nicobar Command (ANC) to observe how India manages security and surveillance of the critical island chain.

Nepal

Relations between India and Nepal are close yet fraught with difficulties stemming from geography, economics, the problems inherent in big power-small power relations, and common ethnic and linguistic identities that overlap the two countries' borders. In 1950 New Delhi and Kathmandu initiated their intertwined relationship with the Treaty of Peace and Friendship and accompanying letters that defined security relations between the two countries, and an agreement governing both bilateral trade and trade transiting Indian soil. The 1950 treaty and letters stated that "neither government shall tolerate any threat to the security of the other by a foreign aggressor" and obligated both sides "to inform each other of any serious friction or misunderstanding with any neighbouring state likely to cause any breach in the friendly relations subsisting between the two governments." These accords cemented a "special relationship" between India and Nepal that granted Nepal preferential economic treatment and provided Nepalese in India the same economic and educational opportunities as Indian citizens

Indo-Nepalese Relations

Relations between India and Nepal are close yet fraught with difficulties stemming from geography, economics, the problems inherent in big power-small power relations, and common ethnic, linguistic and cultural identities that overlap the two countries borders. New Delhi and Kathmandu initiated their intertwined relationship with the 1950 Indo-Nepal Treaty of Peace and Friendshipý and accompanying letters that defined security relations between the two countries, and an agreement governing both bilateral trade and trade transiting Indian soil. The 1950 treaty and letters stated that "neither government shall tolerate any threat to the security of the other by a foreign aggressor" and obligated both sides "to inform each other of any serious friction or misunderstanding with any neighbouring state likely to cause any breach in the friendly relations subsisting between the two governments." These accords cemented a "special relationship" between India and Nepal that granted Nepal preferential economic treatment and provided Nepalese in India the same economic and educational opportunities as Indian citizens.

Independent Political History

1950-1970

In the 1950s, Nepal welcomed close relations with India, but as the number of Nepalese living and working in India increased and the involvement of India in Nepal's economy deepened in the 1960s and after, so too did Nepalese discomfort with the special relationship. Tensions came to a head in the mid-1970s, when Nepal pressed for substantial amendments in its favour in the trade and transit treaty and openly criticized India's 1975 annexation of Sikkim which was considered as part of Greater Nepal. In 1975 King Birendra Bir Bikram Shah Dev proposed that Nepal be recognized internationally as a zone of peace; he received support from China and Pakistan. In New Delhi's view, if the king's proposal did not contradict the 1950 treaty an extension of nonalignment, it was unnecessary; if it was a repudiation of the special relationship, it represented a possible threat to India's security and could not be endorsed. In 1984 Nepal repeated the proposal, but there was no reaction from India. Nepal continually promoted the proposal in international forums, with Chinese support; by 1990 it had won the support

India Foreign Relations

India's Foreign Relations reflect a traditional policy of nonalignment, the exigencies of domestic economic reform and development, and the changing post-Cold War international environment. India's relations with the world have evolved considerably since the British colonial period (1757-1947), when a foreign power monopolized external relations and defence relations. On independence in 1947, few Indians had experience in making or conducting foreign policy. However, the country's oldest political party, the Indian National Congress, had established a small foreign department in 1925 to make overseas contacts and to publicize its freedom struggle. From the late 1920s on, Jawaharlal Nehru, who had the most long-standing interest in world affairs among independence leaders, formulated the Congress stance on international issues. As a member of the interim government in 1946, Nehru articulated India's approach to the world.

During Nehru's tenure as prime minister of India (1947-64), he achieved a domestic consensus on the definition of Indian national interests and foreign policy goals—building a unified and integrated nation-state based on secular, democratic principles; defending Indian territory and protecting its security interests; guaranteeing India's independence internationally through nonalignment; and promoting national economic development unencumbered by overreliance on any country or group of countries.

These objectives were closely related to the determinants of India's foreign relations: the historical legacy of South Asia; India's geopolitical position and security requirements; and India's economic needs as a large developing nation.

From 1947 until the late 1980s, New Delhi's foreign policy goals enabled it to achieve some successes in carving out an independent international role. Regionally, India was the predominant power because of its size, its population (the world's second-largest after China), and its growing military strength. However, relations with its neighbours, Pakistan in particular, were often tense and fraught with conflict. In addition, globally India's nonaligned stance was not a viable substitute for the political and economic role it wished to play.

India's international influence varied over the years after independence. Indian prestige and moral authority were high in the 1950s and facilitated the acquisition of developmental assistance from both East and West. Although the prestige stemmed from

India's nonaligned stance, the nation was unable to prevent Cold War politics from becoming intertwined with interstate relations in South Asia. In the 1960s and 1970s, New Delhi's international position among developed and developing countries faded in the course of wars with China and Pakistan, disputes with other countries in South Asia, and India's attempt to balance Pakistan's support from the United States and China by signing the Treaty of Peace, Friendship, and Cooperation with the Soviet Union in August 1971. Although India obtained substantial Soviet military and economic aid, which helped to strengthen the nation, India's influence was undercut regionally and internationally by the perception that its friendship with the Soviet Union prevented a more forthright condemnation of the Soviet presence in Afghanistan. In the 1980s, New Delhi improved relations with the United States, other developed countries, and China while continuing close ties with the Soviet Union. Relations with its South Asian neighbours, especially Pakistan, Sri Lanka, and Nepal, occupied much of the energies of the Ministry of External Affairs.

In the 1990s, India's economic problems and the demise of the bipolar world political system have forced New Delhi to reassess its foreign policy and to adjust its foreign relations. Previous policies proved inadequate to cope with the serious domestic and international problems facing India. The end of the Cold War gutted the core meaning of nonalignment and left Indian foreign policy without significant direction. The hard, pragmatic considerations of the early 1990s were still viewed within the nonaligned framework of the past, but the disintegration of the Soviet Union removed much of India's international leverage, for which relations with Russia and the other post-Soviet states could not compensate.

Pragmatic security, economic considerations, and domestic political influences have reinforced New Delhi's reliance on the United States and other developed countries; caused New Delhi to abandon its anti-Israeli policy in the Middle East; and resulted in the courtship of the Central Asian republics and the newly industrializing economies of East and Southeast Asia. Although India shares the concerns of Russia, China, and many members of the Nonaligned Movement about the preeminent position of the United States and other developed countries, different national interests and perceptions make it improbable that India can turn cooperation with these countries to its advantage on most international issues. Furthermore, although Cold War politics have ceased to be a factor in South Asia, the most intractable problems in India's relations with Pakistan—conflict over Kashmir, support for separatists, and nuclear and ballistic missile programs—still face the two countries. India foreign relations-1995 loc data

Jawaharlal Nehru and Institutional Legacy

Nehru helped to create a country with enduring civic institutions, a strong socially responsive judiciary, a commitment civilian oversight of the army and overall egalitarianism.

Nehru's policies are credited with setting up India's infrastructure for scientific education, the Nuclear Programme, the Space Programme, the extensive Indian Railways network, and the Pharmaceutical Industry. It is to his considerable credit that he did not abuse this power and constantly attempted to deepen the democratic nature and institutions of the newly independent India. His charisma extended to the world stage where under his leadership, India was often able to be "punching above its weight." In his later years, he has been criticised by nationalists, both past and present, for not sufficiently confronting Pakistan and China in their differences with India. India's heavy defeat in the war with China seemed to bear out his critics, dimmed his public stature slightly, affecting him greatly as a person. He died shortly thereafter, having achieved so much but being found wanting.

Foreign Policy

As prime minister, Nehru pursued a foreign policy of non-alignment and became a founder and leader of the Non-Aligned Movement. He pursued India's claim to Kashmir in the face of Pakistani opposition, resulting in the First Kashmir War (1947-49). Military defeat at the hands of the People's Republic of China in the Sino-Indian War in October 1962 brought strong criticism of military unpreparedness and Nehru's policy of friendship with India's mighty neighbour.

During the Cold War on November 27, 1946, Prime Minister Nehru appealed to the United States and the Soviet Union to end nuclear testing and to start nuclear disarmament, stating that such an action would "save humanity from the ultimate disaster."

Jawaharlal Nehru

Jawaharlal Nehru was an Indian statesman who was the first (and to date the longest-serving) prime minister of India, from 1947 until 1964. A leading figure in the Indian independence movement, Nehru was elected by the Congress Party to assume office as independent India's first Prime Minister, and re-elected when the Congress Party won India's first general election in 1952. As one of the founders of the Non-aligned Movement, he was also an important figure in the international politics of the post-war era. He is frequently referred to as Pandit Nehru ("pandit" being a Sanskrit and Hindi honorific meaning "scholar" or "teacher") and, specifically in India, as Panditji (with "-ji" being a suffix to the honorific).

The son of a wealthy Indian barrister and politician, Motilal Nehru, Nehru became a leader of the left wing of the Indian National Congress when still fairly young. Rising to become Congress President, under the mentorship of Mahatma Gandhi, Nehru was a charismatic and radical leader, advocating complete independence from the British Empire. In the long struggle for Indian independence, in which he was a key player, Nehru was eventually recognized as Gandhi's political heir. Throughout his life, Nehru was also an advocate for Fabian socialism and the public sector as the means by which long-standing challenges of economic development could be addressed by poorer nations.

Education

Nehru was educated in Britain; at the independent boy's school, Harrow School and Trinity College, Cambridge.

Life and Career

Nehru was given the singular honour of raising the flag of independent India in New Delhi on 15 August 1947, the day India gained Independence. Nehru's appreciation of the virtues of parliamentary democracy, secularism and liberalism, coupled with his concerns for the poor and underprivileged, are recognised to have guided him in formulating policies that influence India to this day. They also reflect the socialist origins of his worldview. His long tenure was instrumental in shaping the traditions and structures of independent India. He is sometimes referred to as the "Architect of Modern India". His daughter, Indira Gandhi, and grandson, Rajiv Gandhi, also served as Prime Ministers of India. Gita Sahgal – a writer and journalist who addresses issues of feminism, fundamentalism, and racism, director of prize-winning documentary films, and human rights activist – is his grand-niece.

Role in Indian Independence Movement

Jawaharlal Nehru returned to India in 1912 and started legal practice. He married Kamala Kaul through a marriage arranged by his parents in 1916. Jawaharlal Nehru joined All India Home Rule League in 1917. His real initiation into politics came two years later when he came in contact with Mahatma Gandhi in 1919. At that time, Mahatma Gandhi had launched a campaign against the Rowlatt Act. Nehru was instantly attracted to Gandhi's commitment for active but peaceful, civil disobedience. Jawaharlal Nehru was elected President of the Allahabad Municipal Corporation in 1924, and served for two years as the city's chief executive.

From 1926 to 1928, Jawaharlal served as the General Secretary of the United Provinces Congress Committee. In 1928-29, the Congress's annual session under President Motilal Nehru was held. During that session Jawaharlal Nehru and Subhas Chandra Bose backed a call for full political independence, while Motilal Nehru and others wanted dominion status within the British Empire. To resolve the point, Gandhi proposed that the British be given two years to grant India dominion status and, if they did not, the Congress would launch a national struggle for full, political independence. Nehru and Bose reduced that two-year window of opportunity to one year. The British did not respond.

In December, 1929, Congress's annual session was held in Lahore, and Jawaharlal Nehru was elected as the President of the Congress Party. During that session, a resolution demanding India's independence was passed and on 26 January 1930 in Lahore, Jawaharlal Nehru unfurled free India's flag. And Gandhiji gave the call for a Civil Disobedience Movement in 1930. The movement eventually forced the British Government to acknowledge the need for major political reforms and was ultimately a great success.

When the British promulgated the Government of India Act 1935, the Congress Party decided to contest elections. Nehru stayed out of the elections, but campaigned vigorously nationwide for the party. The Congress formed governments in almost every province, and won the largest number of seats in the Central Assembly. Nehru was elected to the Congress presidency in 1936, 1937, and 1946, and came to occupy a position in the nationalist movement second only to that of Gandhi. He was arrested in 1942 during the Quit India Movement. Released in 1945, he took a leading part in the negotiations that culminated in the emergence of the dominions of India and Pakistan in August 1947, resulting in the Partition of India.

Successor To Gandhi

On 15 January 1941 Gandhiji said, "Some say Pandit Nehru and I were estranged. It will require much more than difference of opinion to estrange us. We had differences from the time we became co-workers and yet I have said for some years and say now that not Rajaji (Chakravarti Rajagopalachari) but Nehru will be my successor."

India's First Prime Minister

Nehru and his colleagues had been released as the British Cabinet Mission arrived to propose plans for transfer of power.

Once elected, Nehru headed an interim government, which was impaired by outbreaks of communal violence and political disorder, and the opposition of the Muslim League led by Muhammad Ali Jinnah, who were demanding a separate Muslim state of Pakistan.

After failed bids to form coalitions, Nehru reluctantly supported the partition of India, according to a plan released by the British on 3 June 1947. He took office as the Prime Minister of India on 15 August, and delivered his inaugural address titled "A Tryst With Destiny"

"Long years ago we made a tryst with destiny, and now the time comes when we shall redeem our pledge, not wholly or in full measure, but very substantially. At the stroke of the midnight hour, when the world sleeps, India will awake to life and freedom. A moment comes, which comes but rarely in history, when we step out from the old to the new, when an age ends, and when the soul of a nation, long suppressed, finds utterance. It is fitting that at this solemn moment we take the pledge of dedication to the service of India and her people and to the still larger cause of humanity." However, this period was marked with intense communal violence. This violence swept across the Punjab region, Delhi, Bengal and other parts of India. Nehru conducted joint tours with Pakistani leaders to encourage peace and calm angry and disillusioned refugees. Nehru would work with Maulana Azad and other Muslim leaders to safeguard and encourage Muslims to remain in India. The violence of the time deeply affected Nehru, who called for a ceasefire and UN intervention to stop the Indo-Pakistani War of 1947. Fearing communal reprisals, Nehru also hesitated in supporting the annexation of Hyderabad State.

In the years following independence, Nehru frequently turned to his daughter Indira to look after him and manage his personal affairs. Under his leadership, the Congress won an overwhelming majority in the elections of 1952. Indira moved into Nehru's official residence to attend to him and became his constant companion in his travels across India and the world. Indira would virtually become Nehru's chief of staff.

Nehru's study in Teen Murti Bhavan.

Economic Policies

Nehru presided over the introduction of a modified, Indian version of state planning and control over the economy. Creating the Planning commission of India, Nehru drew up the first Five-Year Plan in 1951, which charted the government's investments in industries and agriculture. Increasing business and income taxes, Nehru envisaged a mixed economy in which the government would manage strategic industries such as mining, electricity and heavy industries, serving public interest and a check to private enterprise.

Nehru pursued land redistribution and launched programmes to build irrigation canals, dams and spread the use of fertilizers to increase agricultural production. He also pioneered a series of *community development programs* aimed at spreading diverse cottage industries and increasing efficiency into rural India. While encouraging the construction of large dams (which Nehru called the "new temples of India"), irrigation works and the generation of hydroelectricity, Nehru also launched India's programme to harness nuclear energy.

For most of Nehru's term as prime minister, India would continue to face serious food shortages despite progress and increases in agricultural production. Nehru's industrial policies, summarised in the Industrial Policy Resolution of 1956, encouraged the growth of diverse manufacturing and heavy industries, yet state planning, controls and regulations began to impair productivity, quality and profitability. Although the Indian economy enjoyed a steady rate of growth, chronic unemployment amidst widespread poverty continued to plague the population.

Education and Social Reform

Jawaharlal Nehru was a passionate advocate of education for India's children and youth, believing it essential for India's future progress. His government oversaw the establishment of many institutions of higher learning, including the All India Institute of Medical Sciences, the Indian Institutes of Technology and the Indian Institutes of Management. Nehru also outlined a commitment in his five-year plans to guarantee free and compulsory primary education to all of India's children. For this purpose, Nehru oversaw the creation of mass village enrolment programmes and the construction of thousands of schools. Nehru also launched initiatives such as the provision of free milk and meals to children in order to fight malnutrition. Adult education centres, vocational and technical schools were also organised for adults, especially in the rural areas.

Under Nehru, the Indian Parliament enacted many changes to Hindu law to criminalize caste discrimination and increase the legal rights and social freedoms of women. A system of reservations in government services and educational institutions was created to eradicate the social inequalities and disadvantages faced by peoples of the scheduled castes and scheduled tribes. Nehru also championed secularism and religious harmony, increasing the representation of minorities in government.

National Security and Foreign Policy

Nehru led newly independent India from 1947 to 1964, during its first years of freedom from British rule. Both the United States and the Union Soviet Socialist Republic competed to make India an ally throughout the Cold War.

On the international scene, Nehru was a champion of pacifism and a strong supporter of the United Nations. He pioneered the policy of non-alignment and co-founded the Non-Aligned Movement of nations professing neutrality between the rival blocs of nations led by the U.S. and the U.S.S.R. Recognising the People's Republic of China soon after its founding (while most of the Western bloc continued relations with the Republic of China), Nehru argued for its inclusion in the United Nations and refused to brand the Chinese as the aggressors in their conflict with Korea. He sought to establish warm and friendly relations with China despite the invasion of Tibet in 1950, and hoped to act as an intermediary to bridge the gulf and tensions between the communist states and the Western bloc.

Meanwhile, Nehru had promised in 1948 to hold a plebiscite in Kashmir under the auspices of the U.N. but, as Pakistan failed to pull back troops in accordance with the UN resolution and as Nehru grew increasingly wary of the U.N., he declined to hold a plebiscite in 1953. He ordered the arrest of the Kashmiri politician Sheikh Abdullah, whom he had previously supported but now suspected of harbouring separatist ambitions; Bakshi Ghulam Mohammad replaced him.

His policy of pacifism and appeasement with respect to China also came unraveled when China annexed Aksai Chin, the region of Kashmir adjoining Tibet in 1962 that led to the Sino-Indian war.

Nehru was hailed by many for working to defuse global tensions and the threat of nuclear weapons. He commissioned the first study of the human effects of nuclear explosions, and campaigned ceaselessly for the abolition of what he called "these frightful engines of destruction."

He also had pragmatic reasons for promoting de-nuclearisation, fearing that a nuclear arms race would lead to over-militarisation that would be unaffordable for developing countries such as his own.

In 1956 he had criticised the joint invasion of the Suez Canal by the British, French and Israelis. Suspicion and distrust cooled relations between India and the U.S., which suspected Nehru of tacitly supporting the Soviet Union. Accepting the arbitration of the UK and World Bank, Nehru signed the Indus Water Treaty in

1960 with Pakistani ruler Ayub Khan to resolve long-standing disputes about sharing the resources of the major rivers of the Punjab region.

Final Years

Nehru had led the Congress to a major victory in the 1957 elections, but his government was facing rising problems and criticism. Disillusioned by intra-party corruption and bickering, Nehru contemplated resigning but continued to serve. The election of his daughter Indira as Congress President in 1959 aroused criticism for alleged nepotism, although actually Nehru had disapproved of her election, partly because he considered it smacked of "dynastism"; he said, indeed it was "wholly undemocratic and an undesirable thing", and refused her a position in his cabinet.

Indira herself was at loggerheads with her father over policy; most notably, she used his oft-stated personal deference to the Congress Working Committee to push through the dismissal of the Communist Party of India government in the state of Kerala, over his own objections. Nehru began to be frequently embarrassed by her ruthlessness and disregard for parliamentary tradition, and was "hurt" by what he saw as an assertiveness with no purpose other than to stake out an identity independent of her father.

Although the Pancha Sila (Five Principles of Peaceful Coexistence) was the basis of the 1954 Sino-Indian treaty over Tibet, in later years, Nehru's foreign policy suffered through increasing Chinese antagonism over border disputes and Nehru's decision to grant asylum to the Dalai Lama. After years of failed negotiations, Nehru authorized the Indian Army to annex Goa from Portugal in 1961.

In the 1962 elections, Nehru led the Congress to victory yet with a diminished majority. Opposition parties ranging from the right-wing Bharatiya Jana Sangh and Swatantra Party, socialists and the Communist Party of India performed well.

In a matter of months, the border disputes with China turned into open conflict. Nehru assumed that as former victims of imperialism (India being a colony itself) they shared a sense of solidarity, as expressed in the phrase "Hindi-Chini bhai bhai" (Indians and Chinese are brothers). He was dedicated to the ideals of brotherhood and solidarity among developing nations. Nehru, credulously, did not believe that one fellow Socialist country would attack another; and in any event, he felt secure behind the impregnable wall of ice that is the Himalayas. Both proved to be severe miscalculations of China's intentions and military capabilities. Following reports of his intention to confront Chinese occupation of the disputed areas—summarised in a memorable statement that he had asked the Army to "throw them (Chinese) out"-China launched a pre-emptive attack.

In a matter of days, a Chinese invasion of northeastern India exposed the weaknesses of India's military as Chinese forces came as far as Assam. Widely criticised for his government's insufficient attention to defence, Nehru was forced to sack the defence minister Krishna Menon and seek U.S. military aid. Nehru's health began declining steadily, and he was forced to spend months recuperating in Kashmir through 1963.

Some historians attribute this dramatic decline to his surprise and chagrin over the invasion of India by the Chinese, which he perceived as a betrayal of trust. Upon his return from Kashmir in May 1964, Nehru suffered a stroke and later a heart attack. He died in the early hours of 27 May 1964. Nehru was cremated in accordance with Hindu rites at the Shantivana on the banks of the Yamuna River, witnessed by hundreds of thousands of mourners who had flocked into the streets of Delhi and the cremation grounds.

Legacy

As India's first Prime minister and external affairs minister, Jawaharlal Nehru played a major role in shaping modern India's government and political culture along with sound foreign policy. He is praised for creating a system providing universal primary education, reaching children in the farthest corners of rural India. Nehru's education policy is also credited for the development of world-class educational institutions such as the All India Institute of Medical Sciences, Indian Institutes of Technology, and the Indian Institutes of Management.

"Nehru was a great man... Nehru gave to Indians an image of themselves that I don't think others might have succeeded in doing."-Sir Isaiah Berlin

Nehru is credited for establishing a widespread system of affirmative action to provide equal opportunities and rights for India's ethnic groups, minorities, women, scheduled castes and scheduled tribes. Nehru's passion for egalitarianism meant that he put the state to work to try and end widespread practices of discrimination against women and depressed classes, though with limited success in his lifetime.

Nevertheless, Nehru's stance as a unfailing nationalist led him to also implement policies which stressed commonality among Indians while still appreciating regional diversities. This proved particularly important as post-Independence differences surfaced since British withdrawal from the subcontinent prompted regional leaders to no longer relate to one another as allies against a common adversary. While differences of culture and, especially, language threatened the unity of the new nation, Nehru established programs such as the National Book Trust and the National Literary Academy which promoted the translation of regional literatures between languages and also organized the transfer of materials between regions. In pursuit of a single, unified India, Nehru warned, "Integrate or perish."

Commemoration

In his lifetime, Jawaharlal Nehru enjoyed an iconic status in India and was widely admired across the world for his idealism and statesmanship. His birthday, 14 November, is celebrated in India as *Chacha Nehru* (*Children's Day*) in recognition of his lifelong passion and work for the welfare, education and development of children and young people. Children across India remember him as *Chacha Nehru* (Uncle Nehru). Nehru remains a popular symbol of the Congress party which frequently celebrates his memory. Congress leaders and activists often emulate his style of clothing, especially the *Gandhi cap*, and his mannerisms. Nehru's ideals and policies continue to shape the Congress party's manifesto and core political philosophy. An emotional attachment to his legacy was instrumental in the rise of his daughter Indira to leadership of the Congress party and the national government.

Many documentaries about Nehru's life have been produced. He has also been portrayed in fictionalised films. The canonical performance is probably that of Roshan Seth, who played him three times: in Richard Attenborough's 1982 film *Gandhi*, Shyam Benegal's 1988 television series *Bharat Ek Khoj*, based on Nehru's *The Discovery of India*, and in a 2007 TV film entitled *The Last Days of the Raj*. In Ketan Mehta's film *Sardar*, Nehru was portrayed by Benjamin Gilani. Nehru's personal preference for the sherwani ensured that it continues to be considered formal wear in North India today; aside from lending his name to a kind of cap, the Nehru jacket is named in his honour due to his preference for that style.

Numerous public institutions and memorials across India are dedicated to Nehru's memory. The Jawaharlal Nehru University in Delhi is among the most prestigious universities in India. The Jawaharlal Nehru Port near the city of Mumbai is a modern port and dock designed to handle a huge cargo and traffic load. Nehru's residence in Delhi is preserved as the Nehru Memorial Museum and Library. The Nehru family homes at Anand Bhavan and Swaraj Bhavan are also preserved to commemorate Nehru and his family's legacy

United States of America

Historically, relations between India and the United States were somewhat cold following Indian independence, as India took a leading position in the Non-Aligned Movement, and attempted to pursue even-handed economic and military relations with the Soviet Union, although US provided support to India in 1962 during its war with China.

For most of the Cold War, the USA tended to have warmer relations with Pakistan, primarily as a way to contain Soviet-friendly India and to use Pakistan to back the Afghan Mujahideen against the Soviet occupation of Afghanistan. An Indo-Soviet twenty year friendship treaty, signed in 1971, also positioned India against the USA.

Cold War Era

India played a key role in establishing the Non-Aligned Movement in 1961. Though India pursued close relations with both USA and USSR, it decided not to join any major power bloc and refrained from joining military alliances. India, however began establishing close military relationship with the Soviet Union.

After the Sino-Indian War and the Indo-Pakistani War of 1965, India made considerable changes to its foreign policy. It developed a close relationship with the Soviet Union and started receiving massive military equipment and financial assistance from the USSR. This had an adverse effect on the Indo-USA relationship. The United States saw Pakistan as a counter-weight to pro-Soviet India and started giving the former military assistance. This created an atmosphere of suspicion between India and USA. The USA-India relationship suffered a considerable setback during the Soviet invasion of Afghanistan when India openly supported the Soviet Union.

Relations between India and the United States came to an all-time low during the early 1970s. Despite reports of atrocities in East Pakistan, and being told, most notably in the *Blood telegram,* of genocidal activities being perpetrated by Pakistani forces, U.S. Secretary of State Henry Kissinger and U.S. President Richard Nixon did nothing to discourage then Pakistani President Yahya Khan and the Pakistan Army. Kissinger was particularly concerned about Soviet expansion into South Asia as a result of a treaty of friendship that had recently been signed between India and the Soviet Union, and sought to demonstrate to the People's Republic of China the value of a tacit alliance with the United States.

During the Indo-Pakistani War of 1971, Indian Armed Forces, along with the Mukti Bahini, succeeded in liberating East Pakistan which soon declared independence. Richard Nixon, then USA President, feared that an Indian invasion of West Pakistan would mean total Soviet domination of the region, and that it would seriously undermine the global position of the United States and the regional position of America's new tacit ally, China. In order to demonstrate to China the *bona fides* of the United States as an ally, and in direct violation of the USA Congress-imposed sanctions on Pakistan, Nixon sent military supplies to Pakistan, routing them through Jordan and Iran, while also encouraging China to increase its arms supplies to Pakistan.

When Pakistan's defeat in the eastern sector seemed certain, Nixon sent the USS *Enterprise* to the Bay of Bengal, a move deemed by the Indians as a nuclear threat. The *Enterprise* arrived on station on December 11, 1971. On 6 December and 13 December, the Soviet Navy dispatched two groups of ships, armed with nuclear missiles, from Vladivostok; they trailed U.S. Task Force 74 into the Indian Ocean from 18 December 1971 until 7 January 1972. The Soviets also sent a nuclear submarine to ward off the threat posed by USS *Enterprise* in the Indian Ocean.

Though American efforts had no effect in turning the tide of the war, the incident involving USS *Enterprise* is viewed as the trigger for India's subsequent nuclear program. American policy towards the end of the war was dictated primarily by a need to restrict the escalation of war on the western sector to prevent the 'dismemberment' of West Pakistan. Years after the war, many American writers criticized the White House policies during the war as being badly flawed and ill-serving the interests of the United States. India carried out nuclear tests a few years later resulting in sanctions being imposed by United States, further drifting the two countries apart. In recent years, Kissinger came under fire for comments made during the Indo-Pakistan War in which he described Indians as "bastards." Kissinger has since expressed his regret over the comments.

India–Russia Relations

India-Russian relations refers to the bilateral relations between the Republic of India and the Russian Federation. During the Cold War, India and the Soviet Union enjoyed a strong strategic, military, economic and diplomatic relationship. After the collapse of the USSR, India improved its relations with the West but it continued its close relations with Russia. India is the second largest market for the Russian arms industry. In 2004, more than 70% of the Indian Military's hardware came from Russia, making Russia the chief supplier of arms. India has an embassy in Moscow and 2 Consulates-General (in Saint Petersburg and Vladivostok). Russia has an embassy in New Delhi and 4 Consulates-General (in Chennai, Hyderabad, Kolkata, Mumbai). Since 2000 and the visit of Vladimir Putin in India there have been an Indo-Russian Strategic Partnership.

Soviet Union and India

A cordial relationship with India that began in the 1950s represented the most successful of the Soviet attempts to foster closer relations with Third World countries. The relationship began with a visit by Indian prime minister Jawaharlal Nehru to the Soviet Union in June 1955 and Khrushchev's return trip to India in the fall of 1955. While in India, Khrushchev announced that the Soviet Union supported Indian sovereignty over the disputed territory of the Kashmir region and over Portuguese coastal enclaves.

The Soviet relationship with India rankled the Chinese and contributed to Sino-Soviet enmity during the Khrushchev period. The Soviet Union declared its neutrality during the 1959 border dispute and the Indo-China war of 1962, although the Chinese strongly objected. The Soviet Union gave India substantial economic and military assistance during the Khrushchev period, and by 1960 India had received more Soviet assistance than China had. This disparity became another point of contention in Sino-Soviet relations. In 1962 the Soviet Union agreed to transfer technology to coproduce the MiG-21 jet fighter in India, which the Soviet Union had earlier denied to China. In 1965 the Soviet Union served successfully as peace broker between India and Pakistan after an Indian-Pakistani border war.

The Soviet chairman of the Council of Ministers, Aleksei N. Kosygin, met with representatives of India and Pakistan and helped them negotiate an end to the military conflict over Kashmir.

In 1971 the former East Pakistan region initiated an effort to secede from its politicial union with West Pakistan. India supported the secession and, as a guarantee against possible Chinese entrance into the conflict on the side of West Pakistan, signed a treaty of friendship and cooperation with the Soviet Union in August 1971. In December, India entered the conflict and ensured the victory of the secessionists and the establishment of the new state of Bangladesh.

Relations between the Soviet Union and India did not suffer much during the rightist Janata Party's coalition government in the late 1970s, although India did move to establish better economic and military relations with Western countries. To counter these efforts by India to diversify its relations, the Soviet Union proffered additional weaponry and economic assistance.

During the 1980s, despite the 1984 assassination by Sikh extremists of Prime Minister Indira Gandhi, the mainstay of cordial

Indian-Soviet relations, India maintained a close relationship with the Soviet Union. Indicating the high priority of relations with the Soviet Union in Indian foreign policy, the new Indian prime minister, Rajiv Gandhi, visited the Soviet Union on his first state visit abroad in May 1985 and signed two long-term economic agreements with the Soviet Union. In turn, Gorbachev's first visit to a Third World state was his meeting with Gandhi in New Delhi in late 1986.

Gorbachev unsuccessfully urged Gandhi to help the Soviet Union set up an Asian collective security system.

Gorbachev's advocacy of this proposal, which had also been made by Brezhnev, was an indication of continuing Soviet interest in using close relations with India as a means of containing China. With the improvement of Sino-Soviet relations in the late 1980s, containing China had less of a priority, but close relations with India remained important as an example of Gorbachev's new Third World policy.

Russia and India

Relations with India have always been and I am sure will be one of the most important foreign policy priorities of our country. Our mutual ties of friendship are filled with sympathy, and trust, and openness. And we must say frankly that they were never overshadowed by disagreements or conflict. This understanding-this is indeed the common heritage of our peoples. It is valued and cherished in our country, in Russia, and in India. And we are rightfully proud of so close, so close relations between our countries.

– Dmitry Medvedev, about relations with India

We are confident that India lives in the hearts of every Russian. In the same way, I can assure you that Russia also lives in our souls as a Homeland, as people who share our emotions, our feelings of mutual respect and constant friendship. Long live our friendship!

– Pratibha Patil, about relations with Russia

Military Relations

Defence relations between India and the Russian Federation have a historical perspective. Russia has been an important supplier of defence goods for several decades. Today, the cooperation is not limited to a buyer-seller relationship but includes joint research and development, training, service to service contacts, including joint exercises. The last joint naval exercises took place in April 2007 in the Sea of Japan and joint airborne exercises were held in September 2007 in Russia.

There is an Inter-Governmental commission on military-technical cooperation co-chaired by the two Defence Ministers. The Seventh session of this Inter-Governmental Commission was held in October 2007 in Moscow. During the visit, an Agreement on joint development and production of prospective multi role fighters was signed between the two countries.

India–Russia original cooperation agreement was signed in December 1988. It has seen the trade of a multitude of defence equipment to India and also the emergence of that country as a development partner as opposed to purely a buyer. Two programmes that evidence this approach are the projects to form Indian-Russian joint ventures to develop and produce the Fifth Generation Fighter Aircraft (FGFA) and the Multirole Transport Aircraft (MTA). Deba R Mohanty, a senior fellow in security studies at the New Delhi-based Observer Research Foundation, told Jane's on 13 October that the original cooperation agreement has laid a "very solid foundation" for India to develop further as a development partner.

He added: "The mutual benefits are clear: India can acquire modern platforms and technologies while Russia gains access to India's growing defence market."

India and Russia have several major joint military programs such as those mentioned below:

- BrahMos cruise missile program
- INS Vikramaditya aircraft carrier program
- 5th generation fighter jet program
- Sukhoi Su-30MKI program (230+ to be built by Hindustan Aeronautics)
- Ilyushin/HAL Tactical Transport Aircraft.

Additionally, India has purchased/leased several military hardware from Russia:

- T-90S Bhishma program. (1000+ to be built in India)

- Akula-II nuclear submarine (2 to be leased with an option to buy them when the lease expires)
- Tu-22M3 bombers (4 ordered)
- US$900 million upgrade of MiG-29
- Mil Mi-17 (80 ordered)
- Ilyushin Il-76 Candid (6 ordered to fit Israeli Phalcon radar).

Russia's MiG-35 is competing in the Indian MRCA Competition and is considered to be the front-runner for the winning bid, given India's already, largely Russian-built air force. The Farkhor Air Base in Tajikistan is currently jointly operated by India and Russia.

Economic Relations

Bilateral trade turnover is modest and stood at US $ 3 bn in 2006-07, out of which Indian Exports to Russia were valued at US $ 908 mn. Main Indian exports to Russia are pharmaceuticals; tea, coffee & spices; apparel & clothing; edible preparations; and engineering goods. Main Indian imports from Russia are iron and steel; fertilizers; non-ferrous metals; paper products; coal, coke & briquettes; cereals; and rubber. Indo-Russian trade is expected to reach US$10 billion by 2010.

The India-Russia Inter-Governmental Commission on Trade, Economic, Scientific, Technological and Cultural Cooperation (IRIGC) has had 13 sessions so far and is co-chaired by the External Affairs Minister from the Indian side and a Deputy Prime Minister from the Russian side. There are six Joint Working Groups [WG] under the IRIGC, namely, WG on Trade and Economy [trade and financial matters], WG on Energy [oil and gas, thermal and hydel power, non-conventional energy], WG on Metallurgy and Mining [steel, non-ferrous metal, coal], WG on Science & Technology; WG on Communication and Information Technology; and WG on Culture and Tourism. The 13th of the IRIGC was held in Moscow on 12 October 2007.

The two countries have set-up India-Russia Forum on Trade and Investment at the level of the two Commerce Ministers to promote trade, investment and economic cooperation. The first Forum was held in New Delhi on 12-13 February 2007 which was attended by the Minister of Commerce and Industry and the

Russian Minister of Economic Development and Trade, apart from a large number of business representatives from both sides. The Minister of Commerce & Industry, Shri Kamal Nath participated in the 11th Saint Petersburg International Economic Forum on 9-10 June 2007.

In February 2006, India and Russia also set-up a Joint Study Group to examine ways to increase trade to US $ 10 bn by 2010 and to study feasibility of a Comprehensive Economic Cooperation Agreement (CECA). The Group finalized its report after its fourth meeting in Moscow in July 2007. It has been agreed that a Joint Task Force would monitor the implementation of the recommendation made in the Joint Stdy Group Report, including considering CECA.

Cooperation in the Energy Sector

Energy sector is an important area in Indo-Russian bilateral relations. In 2001, ONGC-Videsh Limited acquired 20% stake in the Sakhalin-I oil and gas project in the Russian Federation, and has invested about US $ 1.7 billion in the project. The Russian company Gazprom and Gas Authority of India Ltd. have collaborated in joint development of a block in the Bay of Bengal. Kudankulam Nuclear Power Project with two units of 1000 MW each is a good example of Indo-Russian nuclear energy cooperation. Both sides have expressed interest in expanding cooperation in the energy sector.

In December 2008, Russia and India signed an agreement to build civilian nuclear reactors in India during a visit by the Russian president to New Delhi.

Space Cooperation

Space is another key sector of cooperation between the two countries. During President Vladimir Putin's visit to India in December 2004, two space-related bilateral agreements were signed viz. Inter-Governmental umbrella Agreement on cooperation in the outer space for peaceful purposes and the Inter Space Agency Agreement on cooperation in the Russian satellite navigation system "GLONASS". Subsequently a number of follow-up agreements on GLONASS have been signed. In November 2007, the two countries have signed an agreement on joint lunar exploration. These space cooperation programmes are under implementation.

Science and Technology

The ongoing cooperation in the field of science & technology, under the Integrated Long-Term Programme of cooperation (ILTP) is the largest cooperation programme in this sphere for both India and Russia. ILTP is coordinated by the Department of Science and Technology from the Indian side and by the Russian Academy of Sciences and Russian Ministry of Industry & Science and Technology from the Russian side. Development of SARAS Duet aircraft, semiconductor products, super computers, poly-vaccines, laser science and technology, seismology, high-purity materials, software & IT and Ayurveda have been some of the priority areas of cooperation under the ILTP. Under this programme, eight joint Indo-Russian centres have been established to focus on joint research and development work. Two other Joint Centres on Non-ferrous Metals and Accelerators and Lasers are being set up in India. A Joint Technology Centre based in Moscow to bring cutting edge technologies to the market is also under processing. An ILTP Joint Council met in Moscow on 11-12 October 2007 to review cooperation and give it further direction. In August 2007, an MoU was signed between Department of Science and Technology and Russian Foundation of Basic Research, Moscow to pursue scientific cooperation.

North-South Transport Corridor

The "North-South" Transport Corridor Agreement [INSTC] has been ratified by all the three original signatory states, viz. India, Iran and Russia, and has come into force since 16 May, 2002. This route is expected to reduce the cost of movement of goods between India and Russia and beyond. The 3rd Coordination Council Meeting of the INSTC was held in October 2005 in New Delhi and the 4th meeting was held in Aktau, Kazakhstan in October 2007 to discuss further streamlining the operation of the corridor.

Cooperation in the Sphere of Culture

India–Russia relations in the field of culture are historical. Five Chairs relating to Indology have been established in Moscow,

Saint Petersburg, Kazan and Vladivostok. Days of Russian Culture were held in India in November 2003, in Delhi, Kolkata and Mumbai. "Days of Indian Culture" in Russia were organized from September-October 2005 in Russia. 130th birth anniversary of Nikolai Roerich and 100th birth anniversary of Svyatoslav Roerich were celebrated in India in October 2004. Chief Minister of National Capital Territory of Delhi led a delegation for participating in the event "Days of Delhi in Moscow" from 28 May-1 June 2006. The "Year of Russia in India" is being held in 2008. It will be followed by the "Year of India in Russia" in 2009. There is a Hindi Department, in theUniversity of Moscow.

Bibliography

Adikaram, E. W.: *Early History of Buddhism in Ceylon,* D. S. Puswella, Migoda, 1946.

Agrawala, V. S.: *Shiva Mahadeva: The Great God,* Veda Academy, Varanasi, 1966.

Ahmad, Imtiaz: *State and Foreign Policy: India's Role in South Asia,* Vikas, New Delhi, 1993.

Ahmad, Jamil-ud-din: *Some Recent Speeches and Writings of Mr. Jinnah,* Lahore, Ashraf, 1952.

Aiyar, R. Krishnaswami: *Outlines of Vedaanta,* Chetana, Bombay, 1978.

Archer, W. G.: *The Kama Sutra,* Unwin Hyman, London, 1990.

Ashton, S.R. : *British Policy Towards the Indian States, 1905-1939,* London, Curzon, 1982.

Aurobindo, Sri: *Vyasa and Valmiki,* Acharya Press, Pondicherry, 1956.

Avalon, Arthur and Ellen: *Hymns to the Goddess,* Ganesh and Co., Madras, 1964.

Aziz, Ashraf: *Light of the Universe: Essays on Hindustani Film Music,* Three Essays Collective, New Delhi, 2003.

Bagchi, P. C.: *Studies in Dharmashastra,* University of Calcutta Press, Calcutta, 1939.

Bahadur, K.P.: *The Wisdom of Vedaanta,* Sterling Publishers Private Limited, New Delhi, 1996.

Banerjea, J. N.: *Pauranic and Vedanta Religion,* University of Calcutta, Calcutta, 1996.

Bankimchandra, C.: *Essentials of Dharma,* Sanskrit Book Depot, Calcutta 1979.

Basu, Manoranjan: *Dharmashastra: A General Study,* Shrimati Mira Basu, Calcutta, 1976.

Beaumont, Roger : *Sword of the Raj: The British Army in India, 1747-1947*, Indianapolis, Bobbs-Merrill, 1977.

Benjamin, Joseph : *Scheduled Castes in Indian Politics and Society*, New Delhi, Ess Ess Publications, 1989.

Bhattacharyya, B.: *Nispannayogavali of Mahapandita Abhyakara Gupta*, Oriental Institute, Baroda, 1949.

Borchert, Bruno: *Mysticism: Its History and Challenge*, Samuel Wiser, York Beach, 1994.

Bose, D. N.: *Dharmashastra: Their Philosophy and Occult Secrets*, Kali Press, Calcutta, 1965.

Bowle, John: *The Imperial Achievement: The Rise and Transformation of the British Empire*, Little, Brown, 1974.

Brockington, J. L.: *Righteous Rama: The Evolution of an Epic*, Oxford, London, 1984.

Bromley, D.: *Krishna Consciousness in the West*, Bucknell University Press, Lewisburg, 1989.

Brooks, E.: *The Original Analects: Sayings of Confucius and His Successors*. Columbia University Press, New York, 1988.

Bruhn, Klaus: *The Jina-Images of Deogarh*, MacMillan, Leiden, 1969.

Burke, Mary Louise: *Swami Vivekananda in America: New Discoveries*, Advaita Ashrama, Calcutta, 1966.

Chaudhary, M.: *Partition and the Curse of Rehabilitation*, Calcutta, Bengal Rehabilitation Organization, 1964.

Chaudhuri, Nirad: *Thy Hand, Great Anarch! India: 1921-1952*, London, Chatto & Windus, 1987.

Coomeraswamy, Ananda K.: *Buddha and the Gospel of Buddhism*, MacMillan, London, 1928.

Crawford, Cromwell S.: *Ram Mohan Roy: His Era and Ethics*, Acharya Press, New Delhi, 1984.

Dalton, Dennis : *Gandhi's Power : Nonviolence in Action*, New Delhi, OUP, 2001.

Danielou, Alain: *The Complete Kama Sutra*, Park Street Press, Rochester, 2000.

Dasgupta, Shahana: *Rani Lakshmibai: The Indian Heroine*, Rupa & Company, Calcutta, 2002.

Datta, V.N.: *Sati: Widow Burning in India*, Manohar, New Delhi, 1990.

David, M. D.: *John Wilson and his Institutions*, Mumbai, 1957.

De Bary: *Self and Society in Ming Thought*, Columbia University Press, New York, 1970.

De, Sushil Kumar: *Ancient Indian Erotics and Erotic Literature*, Firma K. L. Mukhopadhyay, Calcutta, 1959.

Deak, Istvan: *The Lawful Revolution: Louis Kossuth and the Hungarians 1848-1849*, Columbia University Press, 1979.

Dhar, Niranjan: *Vedanta and Bengal Renaissance*, Minerva Associates, Calcutta, 1977.

Dikshit, D.P. *Political History of the Chalukyas of Badami*. New Delhi: Abhinav, 1980.

Donat, K.: *Meditate the Tantric Yoga Way*, George Allen and Unwin, London, 1973.

Doniger, W.: *The Rig Veda: An Anthology*, Penguin, New York, 1981.

Duboi, Abbe: *Hindu Manners, Customs and Ceremonies*, Fifth Indian Impression, CUP, 1985.

Dwivedi, M.: *The Principal Upanishads*, Adyar Library, Madras, 1931.

Eaton, Richard M.: *Sufis of Bijapur, 1300-1700: Social Roles of Sufis in Medieval India*, Princeton University Press, Princeton, 1978.

Edwardes, Michael: *Battles of the Indian Mutiny*, London; B. T. Batsford Ltd., 1963.

Erickson, Erik H.: *Gandhi's Truth: On the Origins of Militant Nonviolence*, Norton, New York, 1970.

Farquhar, J.N.: *Modern Religious Movements in India*, Munshiram, New Delhi, 1967.

Fay, Peter Ward: *The Opium War, 1840-42*, University of North Carolina Press, 1975.

Fisher, Michael H.: *The Politics of British Annexation of India - 1757-1857*, Oxford, 1996.

Frauwallner, E..: *History of Indian Philosophy*, Motilal, Delhi, 1973.

Gambhirananda, S.: *Brahma Sutra Shamkar Bhasya*, Adavita Ashrama, Calcutta, 1977.

Gambhirananda, Swami: *Brahma Sutra Shamkar Bhasya*, Adavita Ashrama, Calcutta, 1977.

Gandhi, M. K.: *The Story of My Experiment With Trust*, Washington, Public Affairs Press, 1948.

Garbe, R.: *The Philosophy of Ancient India*, Chicago University Press, Chicago, 1899.

Goradia, Nayana: *Lord Curzon: The Last of the British Moghuls*, New Delhi, Oxford University Press, 1993.

Goudriaan, T.: *Ritual and Speculation in Early Tantrism*, State University of New York Press, New York, 1992.

Gough, A.E.: *The Philosophy of the Upanisads and Ancient Indian Metaphysics*, MacMillan, London, 1882.

Grant, G. P.: *Philosophy in the Mass Age*, Copp Clark, Toronto, 1959.

Grisenold, H.D.: *Insights into Modern Hinduism*, Oxford, New York, 1934.

Growse, F. S.: *The Ramayana of Tulasidasa*, Motilal Banarsidass, Delhi, 1995.

Gurumurthy, S. : *Hindu Heritage, Assimilative, Not Divisive*, Vigil, Madras 1993.

Haich, E.: *Sexual Energy and Yoga*, Aurora Press, New York, 1982.

Hasan, Murhirul: *Legacy of a Divided Nation: India's Muslims Since Independence*, New Delhi, Oxford, 1997.

Hasan, Mushirul: *India's Partition: Process, Strategy and Mobilization*, New Delhi, Oxford UP, 1993.

Heifetz, Hank: *The Origin of the Young God: Kalidasa's Kumara-sambhava*, University of California Press, Berkeley, 1985.

Heimann, Betty: *Facets of Indian Thought*, Geroge Allen & Unwin, London, 1964.

Heinsath, Charles: *Indian Nationalism and Hindu Social Reform*, Princeton University Press, Princeton, 1964.

Heschel, J.: *God in Search of Man: A Philosophy of Judaism*, Noonday Press, New York, 1997.

Hirschman, Edwin: *White Mutiny: The Ilbert Bill Crisis in India and the Genesis of the Indian National Congress*, New Delhi, Heritage, 1980.

Hixon, L.: *Mother of the Universe: Visions of the Goddess, Tantric Hymns of Enlightenment*, Quest Books, Wheaton, 1994.

Hopkins, J.: *Kalachakra Tantra Rite of Initiation*, Wisdom Publications, Boston, 1982.

Hopkirk, Peter: *The Great Game: The Struggle for Empire in Central Asia*, Kodansha, 1992.

Hume, R.E.: *The Thirteen Principle Upanishads*, Oxford University Press, London, 1971.

Hutchins, Francis: *Spontaneous Revolution: The Quit India Movement*, New Delhi, Manohar, 1971.

Irene, S.: *Vedic Heritage Teaching Program*. Arsha Vidya Gurukulam, Coimbatore, 1994.

Iyar, K.: *Vedanta: The Science of Reality*, Ganesh and Co., Mardas, 1930.

Iyengar, B.K.S.: *Light on the Yoga Sutras of Patanjali*, Aquarian Press, London 1993.

Jacob, K.: *Religion and Ethics in Advaita*, C.M.S. Press, Kottayam, 1982.

Jafar, Malik Muhammad: *Jinnah as a Parliamentarian*, Lahore, Afzar Publications, 1977.

Jain, Kailash Chand, *Lord Mahavira and His Times*, Saraswati Press, Delhi, 1974.

James, Lawrence: *The Rise and Fall of the British Empire*, St. Martin's, 1997.

James, Robert Rhodes: *The British Revolution, 1880-1939*, New York, Knopf, 1976.

Jean, M.: *Tantrik Yoga*, The Aquarian Press, Wellingborough, 1970.

John, B.: *Mantras: Sacred Words of Power*, George Allen and Unwin, London, 1977.

John, Elsner: *Pilgrimage: Past and Present in the World Religions*, Harvard University Press, Cambridge, 1995.

John, K.: *The Origin and Development of the State Cult of Confucius*, Paragon Book, New York, 1966.

Karmarkar, D.: *Sankara's Advaita*, Karnatak University, Dharwar, 1976.

Kaushik, Asha : *Globalization, Democracy and Culture : Situating Gandhian Alternatives*, Jaipur, Pointer, 2002.

Kaviraj, G.: *Aspects of Indian Thought*, University of Burdwan, Calcutta, 1966.

Kavlekar, K.K. : *Non-Brahmin Movement in Southern India, 1873-1949*, Kolhapur, Shivaji University, 19790

Keith, A.B. : *Rigveda Brahmanas*, Harvard University Press, Cambridge, 1920.

Keith, Arthur Berriedale: *The Religion and Philosophy of the Veda and Upanishads*, MacMillan, Delhi, 1925.

Kishwar, Madhu : *Religion at the Service of Nationalism, and Other Essays*, OUP, Delhi, 1998.

Klaus, K.: *A Survey of Hinduism*, State University of New York Press, Albany, 1989.

Knipe, M.: *Hinduism: Experiments in the Sacred*, Harper, San Francisco, 1991.

Knott, K.: *Hinduism, A Very Short Introduction*, Oxford University Press, New York, 1998.

Kosambi, D. D. : *The Culture and Civilisation of Ancient India in Historical Outline*, London, Routledge and Kegan Paul, 1956.

Kottackal, Jacob: *Religion and Ethics in Advaita*, C.M.S. Press, Kottayam, 1982.

Kuiper, F.B.J. : *Aryans in the Rigveda*, Rodopi, Amsterdam, 1991.

Kuppuswamy, Sastri S.: *Compromises in the History of Advaitic Thought*, Kalyani Press, Madras, 1940.

Louis, Fischer: *Essential Gandhi: An Anthology of His Writings*, Vintage, New York, 1983.

Low, D. A. and Brasted, Howard: *Freedom, Trauma, Continuities: Northern India and Independence*, New Delhi, Sage Publications, 1998.

Maheshwari, Shriram: *Rural Development in India: A Public Policy Approach*, New Delhi, Sage, 1995.

Makhan, L.: *The Ramayana of Valmiki*, Munshiram Manoharlal, New Delhi, 1978.

Mathew, Arnold: *Culture and Anarchy*, The University Press, Cambridge, 1935.

Mayer, A. : *Caste in an Indian Village: Change and Continuity 1954-1992*, Delhi, OUP, 1996.

Mazumder, Sukhendu : *Politico-Economic Ideas of Mahatma Gandhi: Their Relevance in the Present Day*, New Delhi, Concept Pub., 2004.

Mearns, David J.: *Shiva's Other Children: Religion and Social Identity amongst Overseas Indians*, Sage, Walnut Creek, 1995.

Mearns, J.: *Shiva's Other Children: Religion and Social Identity amongst Overseas Indians*, Sage, Walnut Creek, 1995.

Mehra, Parshotam: *A Dictionary of Modern Indian History, 1707-1947*, New Delhi, Oxford University Press, 1985.

Metcalf, Thomas R.: *The Aftermath of the Revolt: India, 1857-1870,* Princeton, Princeton University, 1964.

Mohan, K.: *The Mahabharata,* Munshiram Manoharlal, Delhi 1997.

Mookerjee, Ajit: *Kali The Feminine Force,* Thames and Hudson, London, 1988.

Mookerji, Satkari: *Modern Polity and Vedanta,* Sanskrit College, Calcutta, 1972.

Moon, Penderel: *The British Conquest and Dominion of India,* London, Duckworth, 1989.

Morris-Jones, W.H.: *The Government and Politics of India,* London, Hutchinson, 1971.

Nanda, B. R. : *Gandhi and His Critics,* Oxford University Press, Delhi, 1993.

Neale, Walter C.: *Economic Change in Rural India: Land Tenure and Reform in the United Provinces, 1800-1955,* New Haven, 1962.

Nevile, P.: *Lahore: A Sentimental Journey,* New Delhi, Penguin, 1993.

Oddie, G.A. : *Hindu and Christian in South-East India,* London, Curzon Press, 1991.

Pathak, Dr S.P.: *Jhansi during the British Rule,* Ramanand Vidya Bhawan, Delhi, 1987.

Preston, Diana: *The Boxer Rebellion,* Berkley Books, 2000.

Raimundo Panikkar: *The Vedic Experience: Mantramanjari,* Longman Todd, London, 1977.

Raja, C. Kunhan : *The Taittiriya Sarvanukramani of Yaska,* Madras, 1931.

Ramamurti, A.: *Advaitic Mysticism of Sankara,* Visvabharati, Santiniketan, 1974.

Ranajit Guha: *A Construction of Humanism in Colonial India,* CASA, Amsterdam, 1993.

Renou, Louis: *The Nature of Dharmashastra,* Walker and Co., New York, 1997.

Robson, Brian: *Sir Hugh Rose and the Central India Campaign,* Sutton Publishing Ltd for the Army Records Society, UK, 2000.

Satyapal Verma: *Role of Reason in Sankara Vedanta,* Parimal Publication, Delhi, 1992.

Savarkar, Vinayak Damodar : *The Indian War of Independence* 1857 Rajdhani Granthagar, Delhi, 1988.

Scheftelowitz, Isidor : *Die Kasmirische Rezension von Katyayanas Sarvanukramani,* Zeitschrift fur Indologie und Iranistik, 1922.

Shukla, D. N.: *Vastu-Shastra,* Motilal Banarsidass, Delhi, 1966.

Singh, Birendra Kumar: *Early Chalukyas of Vatapi, circa A.D. 500 to 757*, Delhi, Eastern Book Linkers, 1991.

Smith, Col. J. T. : *Silver and the India Exchanges,* Effingham Wilson, London, 1876.

Strauss, L.: *Political Philosophy,* The Bobbs Merrill Co., New York, 1975.

Swami Vishnu Tirtha: *Devatma Shakti,* Swami Shivom Tirth, Rishikesh, 1962.

Talageri, Shrikant : *Aryan Invasion Theory and Indian Nationalism,* Voice of India, Delhi, 1993.

Tejomayananda, Swami: *Hindu Culture: An Introduction,* Chinmaya Publications, Piercy, 1993.

Thapar, Romila : *Ashoka and the Decline of the Mauryas,* London, Oxford University Press, 1961.

Thompson, Edward: *The Making of the Indian Princes,* Oxford University Press, London, 1943.

Trautmann, Thomas R.: *Kautilya and the Arthasastra: A Statistical Study,* Leiden, Brill, 1971.

Trimingham, J.: *Sufi Orders in Islam,* Oxford University Press, New York, 1998.

Utpat, V.N.: *Riddles of Buddha and Ambedkar,* Itihas Patrika Prakashan, Thane 1988.

Vable, D.: *The Arya Samaj. Hindu without Hinduism.* Vikas Publ., Delhi, 1983.

Vedalankar, Pandit Nardev : *Basic Teachings of Hinduism,* Veda Niketan, Durban, 1978.

Visvantha, K.: *Essentials of Hinduism,* Narosa Pub. House, New Delhi, 1989.

Wendy Doniger: *Siva: The Erotic Ascetic,* Oxford University Press, Delhi, 1998.

Zaidi, A. Moin: *Evolution of Muslim Political Thought in India,* New Delhi: S. Chand, 1975.

Index

K

L

M

N

O

P

□□□